Cells and Heredity

interactive
SCIENCE

SAVVAS
LEARNING COMPANY

AUTHORS

You're an author!

As you write in this science book, your answers and personal discoveries will be recorded for you to keep, making this book unique to you. That is why you are one of the primary authors of this book.

✏️ **In the space below, print your name, school, town, and state. Then write a short autobiography that includes your interests and accomplishments.**

YOUR NAME

_____

SCHOOL

_____

TOWN, STATE

_____

AUTOBIOGRAPHY

_____

_____

_____

Your Photo

ISBN-13: 978-0-13-368489-6
ISBN-10:   0-13-368489-X
27   21

ON THE COVER
Petal Power
All living things, including this dahlia, are made of microscopic cells. Within each flower cell, chemical instructions called DNA determine the dahlia's petal color. DNA acts like a switch, "turning on" magenta in part of the flower while "turning off" magenta in other parts of the flower. When DNA switches "on" and "off" quickly, it produces color streaks on the white petals.

Program Authors

DON BUCKLEY, M.Sc.
*Information and Communications Technology Director,
The School at Columbia University, New York, New York*
Mr. Buckley has been at the forefront of K–12 educational technology for nearly two decades. A founder of New York City Independent School Technologists (NYCIST) and long-time chair of New York Association of Independent Schools' annual IT conference, he has taught students on two continents and created multimedia and Internet-based instructional systems for schools worldwide.

ZIPPORAH MILLER, M.A.Ed.
Associate Executive Director for Professional Programs and Conferences, National Science Teachers Association, Arlington, Virginia
Associate executive director for professional programs and conferences at NSTA, Ms. Zipporah Miller is a former K–12 science supervisor and STEM coordinator for the Prince George's County Public School District in Maryland. She is a science education consultant who has overseen curriculum development and staff training for more than 150 district science coordinators.

MICHAEL J. PADILLA, Ph.D.
Associate Dean and Director, Eugene P. Moore School of Education, Clemson University, Clemson, South Carolina
A former middle school teacher and a leader in middle school science education, Dr. Michael Padilla has served as president of the National Science Teachers Association and as a writer of the National Science Education Standards. He is professor of science education at Clemson University. As lead author of the *Science Explorer* series, Dr. Padilla has inspired the team in developing a program that promotes student inquiry and meets the needs of today's students.

KATHRYN THORNTON, Ph.D.
Professor and Associate Dean, School of Engineering and Applied Science, University of Virginia, Charlottesville, Virginia
Selected by NASA in May 1984, Dr. Kathryn Thornton is a veteran of four space flights. She has logged over 975 hours in space, including more than 21 hours of extravehicular activity. As an author on the *Scott Foresman Science* series, Dr. Thornton's enthusiasm for science has inspired teachers around the globe.

MICHAEL E. WYSESSION, Ph.D.
Associate Professor of Earth and Planetary Science, Washington University, St. Louis, Missouri
An author on more than 50 scientific publications, Dr. Wysession was awarded the prestigious Packard Foundation Fellowship and Presidential Faculty Fellowship for his research in geophysics. Dr. Wysession is an expert on Earth's inner structure and has mapped various regions of Earth using seismic tomography. He is known internationally for his work in geoscience education and outreach.

Instructional Design Author

GRANT WIGGINS, Ed.D.
President, Authentic Education, Hopewell, New Jersey
Dr. Wiggins is a co-author with Jay McTighe of *Understanding by Design, 2nd Edition* (ASCD 2005). His approach to instructional design provides teachers with a disciplined way of thinking about curriculum design, assessment, and instruction that moves teaching from covering content to ensuring understanding.
    UNDERSTANDING BY DESIGN® and UbD™ are trademarks of ASCD, and are used under license.

Planet Diary Author

JACK HANKIN
Science/Mathematics Teacher, The Hilldale School, Daly City, California Founder, Planet Diary Web site
Mr. Hankin is the creator and writer of Planet Diary, a science current events Web site. He is passionate about bringing science news and environmental awareness into classrooms and offers numerous Planet Diary workshops at NSTA and other events to train middle and high school teachers.

ELL Consultant

JIM CUMMINS, Ph.D.
Professor and Canada Research Chair, Curriculum, Teaching and Learning department at the University of Toronto
Dr. Cummins focuses on literacy development in multilingual schools and the role of technology in promoting student learning across the curriculum. *Interactive Science* incorporates essential research-based principles for integrating language with the teaching of academic content based on Dr. Cummins's instructional framework.

Reading Consultant

HARVEY DANIELS, Ph.D.
Professor of Secondary Education, University of New Mexico, Albuquerque, New Mexico
Dr. Daniels is an international consultant to schools, districts, and educational agencies. He has authored or coauthored 13 books on language, literacy, and education. His most recent works are *Comprehension and Collaboration: Inquiry Circles in Action* and *Subjects Matter: Every Teacher's Guide to Content-Area Reading.*

REVIEWERS

Contributing Writers

Edward Aguado, Ph.D.
Professor, Department of Geography
San Diego State University
San Diego, California

Elizabeth Coolidge-Stolz, M.D.
Medical Writer
North Reading, Massachusetts

Donald L. Cronkite, Ph.D.
Professor of Biology
Hope College
Holland, Michigan

Jan Jenner, Ph.D.
Science Writer
Talladega, Alabama

Linda Cronin Jones, Ph.D.
Associate Professor of Science and Environmental Education
University of Florida
Gainesville, Florida

T. Griffith Jones, Ph.D.
Clinical Associate Professor of Science Education
College of Education
University of Florida
Gainesville, Florida

Andrew C. Kemp, Ph.D.
Teacher
Jefferson County Public Schools
Louisville, Kentucky

Matthew Stoneking, Ph.D.
Associate Professor of Physics
Lawrence University
Appleton, Wisconsin

R. Bruce Ward, Ed.D.
Senior Research Associate
Science Education Department
Harvard-Smithsonian Center for Astrophysics
Cambridge, Massachusetts

Content Reviewers

Paul D. Beale, Ph.D.
Department of Physics
University of Colorado at Boulder
Boulder, Colorado

Jeff R. Bodart, Ph.D.
Professor of Physical Sciences
Chipola College
Marianna, Florida

Joy Branlund, Ph.D.
Department of Earth Science
Southwestern Illinois College
Granite City, Illinois

Marguerite Brickman, Ph.D.
Division of Biological Sciences
University of Georgia
Athens, Georgia

Bonnie J. Brunkhorst, Ph.D.
Science Education and Geological Sciences
California State University
San Bernardino, California

Michael Castellani, Ph.D.
Department of Chemistry
Marshall University
Huntington, West Virginia

Charles C. Curtis, Ph.D.
Research Associate Professor of Physics
University of Arizona
Tucson, Arizona

Diane I. Doser, Ph.D.
Department of Geological Sciences
University of Texas
El Paso, Texas

Rick Duhrkopf, Ph.D.
Department of Biology
Baylor University
Waco, Texas

Alice K. Hankla, Ph.D.
The Galloway School
Atlanta, Georgia

Mark Henriksen, Ph.D.
Physics Department
University of Maryland
Baltimore, Maryland

Chad Hershock, Ph.D.
Center for Research on Learning and Teaching
University of Michigan
Ann Arbor, Michigan

Jeremiah N. Jarrett, Ph.D.
Department of Biology
Central Connecticut State University
New Britain, Connecticut

Scott L. Kight, Ph.D.
Department of Biology
Montclair State University
Montclair, New Jersey

Jennifer O. Liang, Ph.D.
Department of Biology
University of Minnesota–Duluth
Duluth, Minnesota

Candace Lutzow-Felling, Ph.D.
Director of Education
The State Arboretum of Virginia
University of Virginia
Boyce, Virginia

Cortney V. Martin, Ph.D.
Virginia Polytechnic Institute
Blacksburg, Virginia

Joseph F. McCullough, Ph.D.
Physics Program Chair
Cabrillo College
Aptos, California

Heather Mernitz, Ph.D.
Department of Physical Science
Alverno College
Milwaukee, Wisconsin

Sadredin C. Moosavi, Ph.D.
Department of Earth and Environmental Sciences
Tulane University
New Orleans, Louisiana

David L. Reid, Ph.D.
Department of Biology
Blackburn College
Carlinville, Illinois

Scott M. Rochette, Ph.D.
Department of the Earth Sciences
SUNY College at Brockport
Brockport, New York

Karyn L. Rogers, Ph.D.
Department of Geological Sciences
University of Missouri
Columbia, Missouri

Laurence Rosenhein, Ph.D.
Department of Chemistry
Indiana State University
Terre Haute, Indiana

Sara Seager, Ph.D.
Department of Planetary Sciences and Physics
Massachusetts Institute of Technology
Cambridge, Massachusetts

Tom Shoberg, Ph.D.
Missouri University of Science and Technology
Rolla, Missouri

Patricia Simmons, Ph.D.
North Carolina State University
Raleigh, North Carolina

William H. Steinecker, Ph.D.
Research Scholar
Miami University
Oxford, Ohio

Paul R. Stoddard, Ph.D.
Department of Geology and Environmental Geosciences
Northern Illinois University
DeKalb, Illinois

John R. Villarreal, Ph.D.
Department of Chemistry
The University of Texas–Pan American
Edinburg, Texas

John R. Wagner, Ph.D.
Department of Geology
Clemson University
Clemson, South Carolina

Jerry Waldvogel, Ph.D.
Department of Biological Sciences
Clemson University
Clemson, South Carolina

Donna L. Witter, Ph.D.
Department of Geology
Kent State University
Kent, Ohio

Edward J. Zalisko, Ph.D.
Department of Biology
Blackburn College
Carlinville, Illinois

Museum of Science.

Special thanks to the Museum of Science, Boston, Massachusetts, and Ioannis Miaoulis, the Museum's president and director, for serving as content advisors for the technology and design strand in this program.

CONTENTS

CHAPTER 1 · Introduction to Cells

The Big Question 1
What are cells made of?

Vocabulary Skill: Prefixes 2
Reading Skills 3

LESSON 1
Discovering Cells 4
Unlock the Big Question 4
Inquiry Skill: Measure 10

LESSON 2
Looking Inside Cells 12
Unlock the Big Question 12
Explore the Big Question 16
Inquiry Skill: Make Models 18
Answer the Big Question 19

LESSON 3
Chemical Compounds in Cells 22
Unlock the Big Question 22
do the math! Read and Interpret a Bar Graph 26
Inquiry Skill: Draw Conclusions 26

LESSON 4
The Cell in Its Environment 28
Unlock the Big Question 28
Inquiry Skill: Predict 30, 31, 33

Study Guide & Review and Assessment 34
Review the Big Question 34
Apply the Big Question 36

Science Matters 38
• Electron Eyes • The Genographic Project

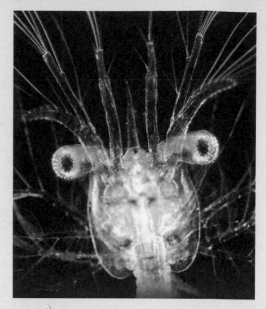

Enter the Lab zone for hands-on inquiry.

Chapter Lab Investigation:
• Directed Inquiry: Design and Build a Microscope
• Open Inquiry: Design and Build a Microscope

Inquiry Warm-Ups: • What Can You See?
• How Large Are Cells? • Detecting Starch
• Diffusion in Action

Quick Labs: • Comparing Cells • Observing Cells • Gelatin Cell Model • Tissues, Organs, Systems • What Is a Compound? • What's That Taste? • Effect of Concentration on Diffusion

my science online.com

Go to MyScienceOnline.com to interact with this chapter's content.
Keyword: Introduction to Cells

> **UNTAMED SCIENCE**
• Touring Hooke's Crib!

> **PLANET DIARY**
• Introduction to Cells

> **INTERACTIVE ART**
• Plant and Animal Cells • Specialized Cells

> **ART IN MOTION**
• Passive and Active Transport

> **VIRTUAL LAB**
• How Can You Observe Cells?

CHAPTER 2
Cell Processes and Energy

The Big Question **40**
How do living things get energy?

Vocabulary Skill: Greek Word Origins 42
Reading Skills 43

LESSON 1
Photosynthesis **44**
Unlock the Big Question 44
Inquiry Skill: Classify 46

LESSON 2
Cellular Respiration **50**
Unlock the Big Question 50
Inquiry Skill: Control Variables 54
Explore the Big Question 55
Answer the Big Question 55

LESSON 3
Cell Division **56**
Unlock the Big Question 56
do the math! Read and Interpret a Circle Graph 63
Inquiry Skill: Interpret Data 63

Study Guide & Review and Assessment **64**
Review the Big Question 64
Apply the Big Question 66

Science Matters **68**
• Athletic Trainer • Why Hearts Don't Get Cancer

Lab zone® Enter the Lab zone for hands-on inquiry.

Chapter Lab Investigation:
• Directed Inquiry: Exhaling Carbon Dioxide
• Open Inquiry: Exhaling Carbon Dioxide

Inquiry Warm-Ups: • Where Does the Energy Come From? • Cellular Respiration • What Are the Yeast Cells Doing?

Quick Labs: • Energy From the Sun • Looking at Pigments • Observing Fermentation • Observing Mitosis • Modeling Mitosis

my science online .com

Go to MyScienceOnline.com to interact with this chapter's content. Keyword: **Cell Processes and Energy**

> **UNTAMED SCIENCE**
• Yum...Eating Solar Energy

> **PLANET DIARY**
• Cell Processes and Energy

> **INTERACTIVE ART**
• Photosynthesis • Cellular Respiration • Cell Growth and Division

> **ART IN MOTION**
• Opposite Processes

> **VIRTUAL LAB** • The Inner Workings of Photosynthesis

CONTENTS

CHAPTER 3

Genetics: The Science of Heredity

The Big Question **70**
Why don't offspring always look like their parents?

Vocabulary Skill: Suffixes **72**
Reading Skills **73**

LESSON 1
What Is Heredity? **74**
Unlock the Big Question 74
Inquiry Skill: Predict 77, 79

LESSON 2
Probability and Heredity **80**
Unlock the Big Question 80
do the math! Calculate Percentage 81
Inquiry Skill: Draw Conclusions 85

LESSON 3
Patterns of Inheritance **86**
Unlock the Big Question 86
Inquiry Skill: Interpret Data 88
Explore the Big Question 90
Answer the Big Question 91

LESSON 4
Chromosomes and Inheritance **92**
Unlock the Big Question 92
Inquiry Skill: Design Experiments 93

Study Guide & Review and Assessment ... **98**
Review the Big Question 98
Apply the Big Question 100

Science Matters **102**
• Nature vs. Nurture • Seeing Spots

Lab zone® Enter the Lab zone for hands-on inquiry.

Chapter Lab Investigation:
• Directed Inquiry: Make the Right Call!
• Open Inquiry: Make the Right Call!

Inquiry Warm-Ups: • What Does the Father Look Like? • What's the Chance? • Observing Traits • Which Chromosome Is Which?

Quick Labs: • Observing Pistils and Stamens • Inferring the Parent Generation • Coin Crosses • Patterns of Inheritance • Is It All in the Genes? • Chromosomes and Inheritance • Modeling Meiosis

my science online.com

Go to MyScienceOnline.com to interact with this chapter's content. Keyword: Genetics: The Science of Heredity

UNTAMED SCIENCE
• Where'd You Get Those Genes?

PLANET DIARY
• Genetics: The Science of Heredity

INTERACTIVE ART
• Punnett Squares • Effects of Environment on Genetic Traits

ART IN MOTION
• Meiosis

CHAPTER 4

DNA: The Code of Life

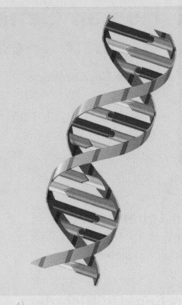

The Big Question **104**
What does DNA do?

Vocabulary Skill: Latin Word Parts 106
Reading Skills 107

LESSON 1
The Genetic Code **108**
Unlock the Big Question 108
Inquiry Skill: Infer 110

LESSON 2
How Cells Make Proteins **114**
Unlock the Big Question 114
Inquiry Skill: Design Experiments 115
Explore the Big Question 116
Answer the Big Question 117

LESSON 3
Mutations **118**
Unlock the Big Question 118
do the math! Calculate Sunscreen Strength Over Time ... 121
Inquiry Skill: Calculate 121

Study Guide & Review and Assessment **124**
Review the Big Question 124
Apply the Big Question 126

Science Matters **128**
• The Frozen Zoo • Fighting Cancer • There's Something
Fishy About This Sushi!

Lab® zone Enter the Lab zone
for hands-on inquiry.

Chapter Lab Investigation:
• Directed Inquiry: Guilty or Innocent?
• Open Inquiry: Guilty or Innocent?

Inquiry Warm-Ups: • Can You Crack the
Code? • What Is RNA? • Oops!

Quick Labs: • Modeling the Genetic Code
• Modeling Protein Synthesis • Effects of
Mutations • What Happens When There Are
Too Many Cells?

my science online.com

Go to MyScienceOnline.com to
interact with this chapter's content.
Keyword: **DNA: The Code of Life**

> **UNTAMED SCIENCE**
• Why Is This Lobster Blue?

> **PLANET DIARY**
• DNA: The Code of Life

> **INTERACTIVE ART**
• Copying DNA • Making Proteins

> **ART IN MOTION**
• Understanding DNA

> **VIRTUAL LAB**
• Track Down the Genetic Mutation

CONTENTS

CHAPTER 5

Human Genetics and Genetic Technology

The Big Question **130**
How can genetic information be used?

Vocabulary Skill: High-Use Academic Words 132
Reading Skills 133

LESSON 1
Human Inheritance **134**
Unlock the Big Question 134
Inquiry Skill: Infer 135

LESSON 2
Human Genetic Disorders **140**
Unlock the Big Question 140
Inquiry Skill: Make Models 143

LESSON 3
Advances in Genetics **146**
Unlock the Big Question 146
Inquiry Skill: Draw Conclusions 148
do the math! Plot Data and Interpret a Line Graph 149

LESSON 4
Using Genetic Information **152**
Unlock the Big Question 152
Inquiry Skill: Communicate 153
Explore the Big Question 154
Answer the Big Question 155

Study Guide & Review and Assessment **156**
Review the Big Question 156
Apply the Big Question 158

Science Matters **160**
• Mini but Mighty • CODIS: The DNA Database

Lab zone® Enter the Lab zone for hands-on inquiry.

Chapter Lab Investigation:
• Directed Inquiry: How Are Genes on the Sex Chromosomes Inherited?
• Open Inquiry: How Are Genes on the Sex Chromosomes Inherited?

Inquiry Warm-Ups: • How Tall Is Tall?
• How Many Chromosomes? • What Do Fingerprints Reveal? • Using Genetic Information

Quick Labs: • The Eyes Have It • What Went Wrong? • Family Puzzle • Selective Breeding
• Extraction in Action

my science online.com

Go to MyScienceOnline.com to interact with this chapter's content.
Keyword: Human Genetics and Genetic Technology

> UNTAMED SCIENCE
• The Case of the X-Linked Gene

> PLANET DIARY
• Human Genetics and Genetic Technology

> INTERACTIVE ART
• Pedigree • DNA Fingerprinting

> ART IN MOTION
• Understanding Genetic Engineering

> VIRTUAL LAB
• Why Does My Brother Have It and I Don't?

Change Over Time

CHAPTER 6

The Big Question 162
How do life forms change over time?

Vocabulary Skill: Identify Multiple Meanings 164
Reading Skills 165

LESSON 1
Darwin's Theory 166
Unlock the Big Question 166
Inquiry Skill: Develop Hypotheses 170, 171
Explore the Big Question 172
do the math! Calculate the Mean and Interpret Data 174
Answer the Big Question 175

LESSON 2
Evidence of Evolution 176
Unlock the Big Question 176
Inquiry Skill: Communicate 176, 179

LESSON 3
Rate of Change 180
Unlock the Big Question 180
Inquiry Skill: Make Models 183

Study Guide & Review and Assessment 184
Review the Big Question 184
Apply the Big Question 186

Science Matters 188
• The Incredible Shrinking Fish • Walking Whales

Appendices, English/Spanish Glossary, Index 190

Lab zone Enter the Lab zone for hands-on inquiry.

Chapter Lab Investigation:
• Directed Inquiry: Nature at Work
• Open Inquiry: Nature at Work

Inquiry Warm-Ups: • How Do Living Things Vary? • How Can You Classify a Species?
• Making a Timeline

Quick Labs: • Bird Beak Adaptations
• Finding Proof • Large-Scale Isolation
• Slow or Fast?

my science online.com

Go to MyScienceOnline.com to interact with this chapter's content. Keyword: Change Over Time

> **UNTAMED SCIENCE**
• Why Would a Fish Have Red Lips?

> **PLANET DIARY**
• Change Over Time

> **INTERACTIVE ART**
• What Is It Adapted To?
• Homologous Structures

> **ART IN MOTION**
• Rate of Evolution

> **REAL-WORLD INQUIRY**
• What Affects Natural Selection?

interactive SCIENCE

This is your book.
You can write in it!

Get Engaged!

At the start of each chapter, you will see two questions: an Engaging Question and the Big Question. Each chapter's Big Question will help you start thinking about the Big Ideas of Science. Look for the Big Q symbol throughout the chapter!

THE BIG ?

HOW CAN WIND KEEP YOUR LIGHTS ON?

What are some of Earth's energy sources?

This man is repairing a wind turbine at a wind farm in Texas. Most wind turbines are at least 30 meters off the ground where the winds are fast. Wind speed and blade length help determine the best way to capture the wind and turn it into power. **Develop Hypotheses** Why do you think people are working to increase the amount of power we get from wind?

Wind energy collected by the turbine does not cause air pollution

> **UNTAMED SCIENCE** Watch the **Untamed Science** video to learn more about energy resources.

174   Energy Resources

Untamed Science

Follow the Untamed Science video crew as they travel the globe exploring the Big Ideas of Science.

Interact with your textbook.   Interact with inquiry.   Interact online.

Build Reading, Inquiry, and Vocabulary Skills

In every lesson you will learn new 🔄 Reading and △ Inquiry skills. These skills will help you read and think like a scientist. Vocabulary skills will help you communicate effectively and uncover the meaning of words.

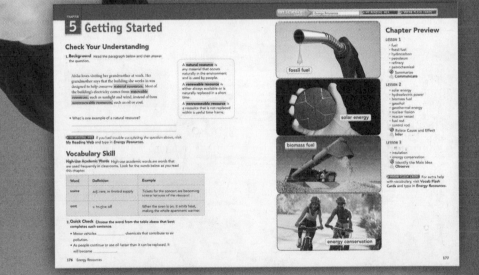

Go Online!

Look for the MyScienceOnline.com technology options. At MyScienceOnline.com you can immerse yourself in amazing virtual environments, get extra practice, and even blog about current events in science.

Explore the Key Concepts.

Each lesson begins with a series of Key Concept questions. The interactivities in each lesson will help you understand these concepts and Unlock the Big Question.

MY PLANET DIARY

At the start of each lesson, My Planet Diary will introduce you to amazing events, significant people, and important discoveries in science or help you to overcome common misconceptions about science concepts.

Desertification If the s of moisture and nutrients advance of desertlike con fertile is called **desertifica**

One cause of desertific is a period when less rain droughts, crops fail. With blows away. Overgrazing cutting down trees for fire

Desertification is a ser and graze livestock where people may face famine a central Africa. Millions of cities because they can no

apply it!

Desertification affects man areas around the world.

1 Name Which continent has the most existing dese

2 Interpret Maps Where the United States is the gre risk of desertification?

3 Infer Is desertification is existing desert? Explain. your answer.

4 CHALLENGE If an area is things people could do to

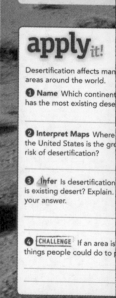

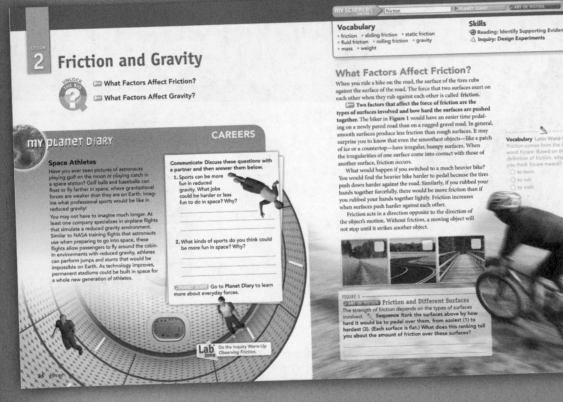

Explain what you know.

Look for the pencil. When you see it, it's time to interact with your book and demonstrate what you have learned.

apply it!

Elaborate further with the Apply It activities. This is your opportunity to take what you've learned and apply those skills to new situations.

Lab Zone

Look for the Lab zone triangle. This means it's time to do a hands-on inquiry lab. In every lesson, you'll have the opportunity to do a hands-on inquiry activity that will help reinforce your understanding of the lesson topic.

Land Reclamation Fortunately, it is possible to replace land damaged by erosion or mining. The process of restoring an area of land to a more productive state is called **land reclamation.** In addition to restoring land for agriculture, land reclamation can restore habitats for wildlife. Many different types of land reclamation projects are currently underway all over the world. But it is generally more difficult and expensive to restore damaged land and soil than it is to protect those resources in the first place. In some cases, the land may not return to its original state.

FIGURE 4 ·······························

Land Reclamation
These pictures show land before and after it was mined.

✎ **Communicate** Below the pictures, write a story about what happened to the land.

---

area becomes depleted ... a desert. The ... previously were ... KAY shun). ... example, a **drought** ... an area. During ... exposed soil easily ... and sheep and ... sertification, too. ... cannot grow crops ... occurred. As a result, ... tification is severe in ... re moving to the ... mselves on the land.

Key
- Existing desert
- High-risk area
- Moderate-risk area

...eas where there
...he map to support

...tion, what are some
...fects?

Lab Do the Quick Lab
zone Modeling S...

📖 **Assess Your Understanding**

1a. Review Subsoil has (less/more) plant and animal matter than topsoil.

b. Explain What can happen to soil if plants are removed?

c. Apply Concepts ...
that could prev... land reclam...

got it?

○ I get it! Now I know that soil management is important becau...

○ I need extra help with _____

Go to MY SCIENCE 🌐 COACH *online for help with this subject.*

---

got it?

Evaluate Your Progress.

After answering the Got It question, think about how you're doing. Did you get it or do you need a little help? Remember, MY SCIENCE 🌐 COACH is there for you if you need extra help.

INTERACT... WITH YOUR TEXTBOOK...

EXPLORE THE BIG ?

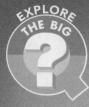

Explore the Big Question.

At one point in the chapter, you'll have the opportunity to take all that you've learned to further explore the Big Question.

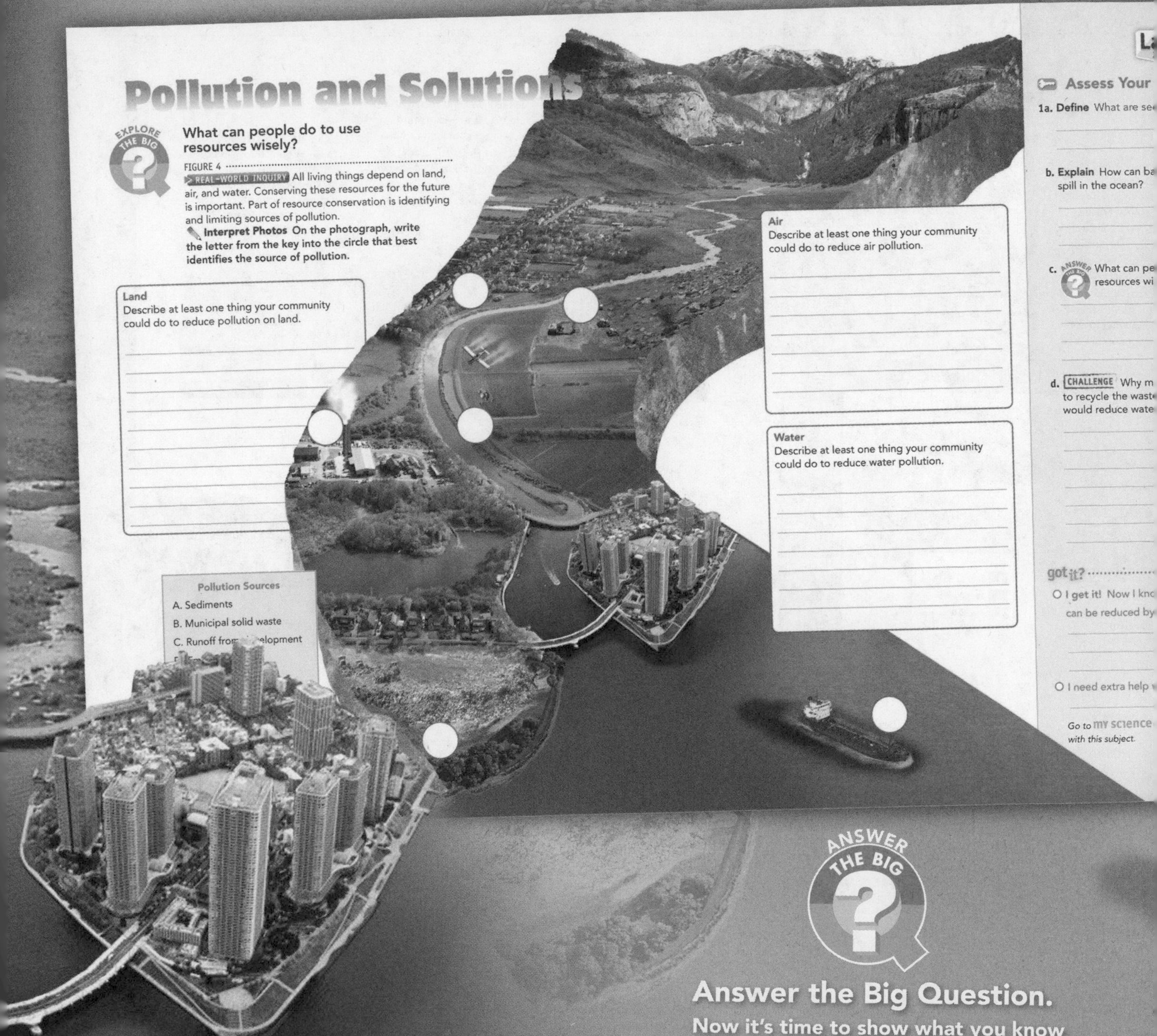

Pollution and Solutions

EXPLORE THE BIG ?

What can people do to use resources wisely?

FIGURE 4

REAL-WORLD INQUIRY All living things depend on land, air, and water. Conserving these resources for the future is important. Part of resource conservation is identifying and limiting sources of pollution.

Interpret Photos **On the photograph, write the letter from the key into the circle that best identifies the source of pollution.**

Land
Describe at least one thing your community could do to reduce pollution on land.

Air
Describe at least one thing your community could do to reduce air pollution.

Water
Describe at least one thing your community could do to reduce water pollution.

Pollution Sources
A. Sediments
B. Municipal solid waste
C. Runoff from development

La

Assess Your

1a. **Define** What are se

b. **Explain** How can ba
spill in the ocean?

c. ANSWER THE BIG ? What can pe
resources wi

d. CHALLENGE Why m
to recycle the wast
would reduce wate

got it?
O I get it! Now I kn
can be reduced by

O I need extra help

Go to MY SCIENCE
with this subject.

ANSWER THE BIG ?

Answer the Big Question.

Now it's time to show what you know and answer the Big Question.

Review What You've Learned.

Use the Chapter Study Guide to review the Big Question and prepare for the test.

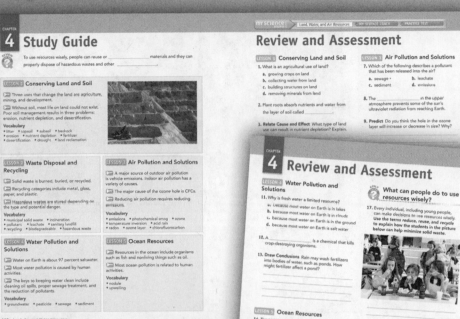

Practice Taking Tests.

Apply the Big Question and take a practice test in standardized test format.

INTERACT ... WITH YOUR TEXTBOOK...

Go to MyScienceOnline.com and immerse yourself in amazing virtual environments.

THE BIG QUESTION

Each online chapter starts with a Big Question. Your mission is to unlock the meaning of this Big Question as each science lesson unfolds.

Unit 4 > Chapter 1 > Lesson 1

<< The Big Question | Unlock the Big Question | Explore the Big Question | >>
The Big Question   Check Your Understanding   Vocabulary Skill

Populations and Communities

Tools

? The Big Question

Unit 2 > Chapter 4 > Lesson 1

Engage & Explore | Exp
Planet Diary

my planet Diary

VOCAB FLASH CARDS

Practice chapter vocabulary with interactive flash cards. Each card has an image, definitions in English and Spanish, and space for your own notes.

Unit 4 > Chapter 1 > Lesson 1   X

<< The Big Question | Unlock the Big Question | Explore the Big Question | >>
The Big Question   Untamed Science   Check Your Understanding   Vocabulary Skill   Vocabulary Flashcards

Vocabulary Flashcards   Tools

Card List   Create-a-Card 10 Cards Left   Test Me
Lesson Cards My Cards

Birth Rate
Carrying Capacity
Commensalism   Science Vocabulary
Community
Competition   ▶ Term: Community
Death Rate
Ecology   ▶ Definition: All the different populations that live
Ecosystem   together in a particular area.
Emigration
Habitat   View Spanish
Host
Immigration   Add Notes
Limiting Factor
                                                    Card 5 of

Unit 6 > Chapter 1 > Le

Engage & Explore
Apply It   Directed Virtua

Color in Light

Unit 6 > Chapter 1 > Lesson 1

Engage & Explore | Explain | Elaborate | Evaluate
Apply It   Do the Math   Art in Motion   Interactive Art   Real World Inquiry

The Nebraska Plains

▶ Bald Eagle
   Information   Media

Haliaeetus leucocephalus
Bald Eagles are 80-95 cm tall with
a wingspan of 180-230 cm. These
birds are born with all brown
feathers but grow white feathers
on their head, neck, and tail.

Layers List   ▲ Show

Next
22
of
22
Back

INTERACTIVE ART

At MyScienceOnline.com, many of the beautiful visuals in your book become interactive so you can extend your learning.

⟳ ＋ ◉ http://www.myscienceonline.com/

> PLANET DIARY

My Planet Diary online is the place to find more information and activities related to the topic in the lesson.

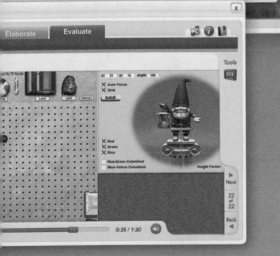

Still Growing! Mount Everest in the Himalayas is the highest mountain on Earth. Climbers who reach the peak stand 8,850 meters above sea level. You might think that mountains never change. But forces inside Earth push Mount Everest at least several millimeters higher each year. Over time, Earth's forces slowly but constantly lift, stretch, bend, and break Earth's crust in dramatic ways!

Planet Diary Go to Planet Diary to learn more about forces in the Earth's crust.

Find Your Chapter

1 Go to www.myscienceonline.com.

2 Log in with username and password.

3 Click on your program and select your chapter.

Keyword Search

1 Go to www.myscienceonline.com.

2 Log in with username and password.

3 Click on your program and select Search.

4 Enter the keyword (from your book) in the search box.

Other Content Available Online

> **UNTAMED SCIENCE** Follow these young scientists through their amazing online video blogs as they travel the globe in search of answers to the Big Questions of Science.

> **MY SCIENCE COACH** Need extra help? My Science Coach is your personal online study partner. My Science Coach is a chance for you to get more practice on key science concepts. There you can choose from a variety of tools that will help guide you through each science lesson.

> **MY READING WEB** Need extra reading help on a particular science topic? At My Reading Web you will find a choice of reading selections targeted to your specific reading level.

> VIRTUAL LAB

Get more practice with realistic virtual labs. Manipulate the variables on-screen and test your hypothesis.

BIG IDEAS OF SCIENCE

Have you ever worked on a jigsaw puzzle? Usually a puzzle has a theme that leads you to group the pieces by what they have in common. But until you put all the pieces together you can't solve the puzzle. Studying science is similar to solving a puzzle. The big ideas of science are like puzzle themes. To understand big ideas, scientists ask questions. The answers to those questions are like pieces of a puzzle. Each chapter in this book asks a big question to help you think about a big idea of science. By answering the big questions, you will get closer to understanding the big idea.

✎ **Before you read each chapter, write about what you know and what more you'd like to know.**

BIGIDEA

Living things are made of cells.

Nerve cells like this one transmit messages in your body. Other kinds of cells do different jobs.

What do you already know about what a cell does? What more would you like to know?

_____

_____

_____

Big Question:

❓ What are cells made of? Chapter 1

✎ **After reading the chapter, write what you have learned about the Big Idea.**

_____

_____

_____

BIGIDEA

Living things get and use energy.

A lion hunts and catches a zebra. The lion gets its energy from eating the zebra. The zebra got its energy from eating grass.

What do you already know about how animals and plants get food and energy? What more would you like to know?

_____

_____

_____

Big Question:

❓ How do living things get energy? Chapter 2

✎ **After reading the chapter, write what you have learned about the Big Idea.**

_____

_____

_____

BIGIDEA
Genetic information passes from parents to offspring.

Once in a while, a koala joey is born with white fur instead of the usual gray fur. Even with such a striking difference, you can tell the joey is related to its mother.

What do you already know about how offspring resemble their parents? What more would you like to know?

_____

_____

_____

Big Questions:

❓ Why don't offspring always look like their parents? Chapter 3

❓ What does DNA do? Chapter 4

❓ How can genetic information be used? Chapter 5

✏ After reading the chapters, write what you have learned about the Big Idea.

_____

_____

_____

BIGIDEA
Living things change over time.

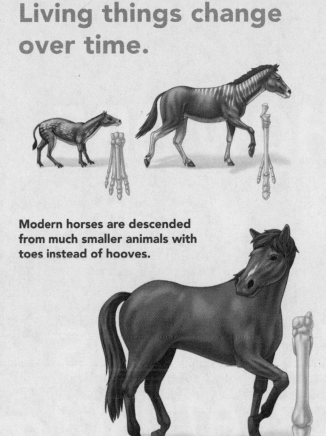

Modern horses are descended from much smaller animals with toes instead of hooves.

What do you already know about how life forms change? What more would you like to know?

_____

_____

_____

Big Question:

❓ How do life forms change over time? Chapter 6

✏ After reading the chapter, write what you have learned about the Big Idea.

_____

_____

HOW ARE YOU LIKE THIS CREATURE?

What are cells made of?

You sure don't see this sight when you look in the mirror! This deep-sea animal does not have skin, a mouth, or hair like yours. It's a young animal that lives in the Atlantic Ocean and may grow up to become a crab or shrimp. Yet you and this creature have more in common than you think.

Infer What might you have in common with this young sea animal?

_____

_____

_____

_____

_____

> **UNTAMED SCIENCE** Watch the **Untamed Science** video to learn more about cells.

Introduction to Cells

1 Getting Started

Check Your Understanding

1. **Background** Read the paragraph below and then answer the question.

You heard that a pinch of soil can contain millions of **organisms,** and you decide to check it out. Many organisms are too small to see with just your eyes, so you bring a hand **lens.** You see a few organisms, but you think you would see more with greater **magnification.**

> An **organism** is a living thing.
>
> A **lens** is a curved piece of glass or other transparent material that is used to bend light.
>
> **Magnification** is the condition of things appearing larger than they are.

- How does a hand lens help you see more objects in the soil than you can see with just your eyes?

_____

_____

> **MY READING WEB** If you had trouble answering the question above, visit **My Reading Web** and type in *Introduction to Cells.*

Vocabulary Skill

Prefixes Some words can be divided into parts. A root is the part of the word that carries the basic meaning. A prefix is a word part that is placed in front of the root to change the word's meaning. The prefixes below will help you understand some of the vocabulary in this chapter.

Prefix	Meaning	Example
chroma-	color	chromatin, *n.* the genetic material in the nucleus of a cell, that can be colored with dyes
multi-	many	multicellular, *adj.* having many cells

2. **Quick Check** Circle the prefix in the boldface word below. What does the word tell you about the organisms?

- Fishes, insects, grasses, and trees are examples of **multicellular** organisms.

_____

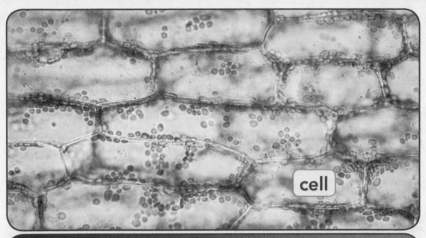

cell

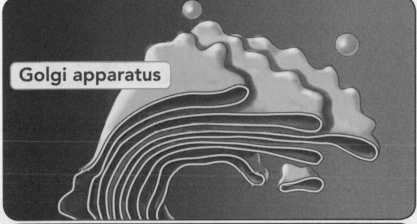

Golgi apparatus

carbohydrate

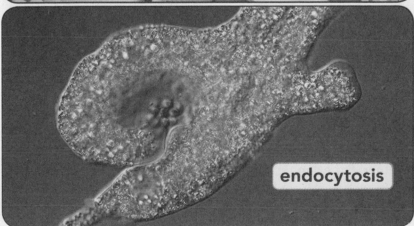

endocytosis

Chapter Preview

LESSON 1
- cell
- microscope
- cell theory

⟳ **Sequence**
△ **Measure**

LESSON 2
- cell wall • cell membrane
- nucleus • organelle • ribosome
- cytoplasm • mitochondria
- endoplasmic reticulum
- Golgi apparatus • vacuole
- chloroplast • lysosome
- multicellular • unicellular
- tissue • organ • organ system

⟳ **Identify the Main Idea**
△ **Make Models**

LESSON 3
- element • compound
- carbohydrate • lipid • protein
- enzyme • nucleic acid • DNA
- double helix

⟳ **Compare and Contrast**
△ **Draw Conclusions**

LESSON 4
- selectively permeable
- passive transport • diffusion
- osmosis • active transport
- endocytosis • exocytosis

⟳ **Relate Cause and Effect**
△ **Predict**

> VOCAB FLASH CARDS For extra help with vocabulary, visit **Vocab Flash Cards** and type in *Introduction to Cells.*

Discovering Cells

UNLOCK
THE BIG
?

🔑 **What Are Cells?**

🔑 **What Is the Cell Theory?**

🔑 **How Do Microscopes Work?**

my planet diary

Life at First Sight

Anton van Leeuwenhoek was the first researcher to see bacteria under a microscope. In his journal, he described how he felt after discovering this new and unfamiliar form of life.

"For me . . . no more pleasant sight has met my eye than this of so many thousand of living creatures in one small drop of water."

VOICES FROM HISTORY

Read the quote, and answer the question below.

Why do you think Leeuwenhoek was so excited about what he saw?

_____

_____

▶ PLANET DIARY Go to **Planet Diary** to learn more about studying cells.

A modern view of bacteria similar to those seen by Leeuwenhoek

Lab ® zone Do the Inquiry Warm-Up *What Can You See?*

What Are Cells?

What do you think a mushroom, a tree, a spider, a bird, and you have in common? All are living things, or organisms. Like all organisms, they are made of cells. **Cells** form the parts of an organism and carry out all of its functions. 🔑 **Cells are the basic units of structure and function in living things.**

Cells and Structure When you describe the structure of an object, you describe what it is made of and how its parts are put together. For example, the structure of a building depends on the way bricks, steel beams, or other materials are arranged. The structure of a living thing is determined by the amazing variety of ways its cells are put together.

Vocabulary
- cell
- microscope
- cell theory

Skills
- ⟳ Reading: Sequence
- △ Inquiry: Measure

Single Cell

Food

Water

Carbon dioxide

FIGURE 1 ....

Needs of Cells

A single cell has the same needs as an entire organism.

✏ **Classify** On each blank arrow, write the name of a material that moves as shown.

Organism

Wastes

Excess water

Oxygen

Lab® zone Do the Quick Lab Comparing Cells.

Cells and Function An organism's functions are the processes that enable it to live, grow, and reproduce. Those functions include obtaining oxygen, food, and water and getting rid of wastes. Cells are involved in all these functions. For example, cells in your digestive system absorb food. The food provides your body with energy and materials needed for growth. Cells in your lungs help you get oxygen. Your body's cells work together, keeping you alive. And for each cell to stay alive, it must carry out many of the same functions as the entire organism.

⌂ Assess Your Understanding

got it? ....

○ **I get it!** Now I know that a cell is the basic unit of_____

_____

○ **I need extra help with** _____

Go to MY SCIENCE ⬢ COACH online for help with this subject.

What Is the Cell Theory?

Until the 1600s, no one knew cells existed because there was no way to see them. Around 1590, the invention of the first microscope allowed people to look at very small objects. A **microscope** is an instrument that makes small objects look larger. Over the next 200 years, this new technology revealed cells and led to the development of the cell theory. The **cell theory** is a widely accepted explanation of the relationship between cells and living things.

Seeing Cells English scientist Robert Hooke built his own microscopes and made drawings of what he saw when he looked at the dead bark of certain oak trees. Hooke never knew the importance of what he saw. A few years later, Dutch businessman Anton van Leeuwenhoek (LAY von hook) was the first to see living cells through his microscopes.

FIGURE 2 ···

Growth of the Cell Theory

The cell theory describes how cells relate to the structure and function of living things. ✎ **Review** Answer the questions in the spaces provided.

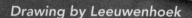

Drawing by Leeuwenhoek

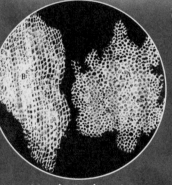

Hooke's drawing
of cork

Hooke's Microscope

In 1663, Robert Hooke used his microscope to observe a thin slice of cork. Cork, the bark of the cork oak tree, is made up of cells that are no longer alive. To Hooke, the empty spaces in the cork looked like tiny rectangular rooms. Therefore, Hooke called the empty spaces cells, which means "small rooms."

What was important about Hooke's work?

Leeuwenhoek's Microscope

Leeuwenhoek built microscopes in his spare time. Around 1674, he looked at drops of lake water, scrapings from teeth and gums, and water from rain gutters. Leeuwenhoek was surprised to find a variety of one-celled organisms. He noted that many of them whirled, hopped, or shot through water like fast fish. He called these moving organisms animalcules, meaning "little animals."

What did Leeuwenhoek's observations reveal?

What the Cell Theory Says

Figure 2 highlights people who made key discoveries in the early study of cells. Their work and the work of many others led to the development of the cell theory. 🔑 **The cell theory states the following:**

- **All living things are composed of cells.**
- **Cells are the basic units of structure and function in living things.**
- **All cells are produced from other cells.**

Living things differ greatly from one another, but all are made of cells. The cell theory holds true for all living things, no matter how big or how small. Because cells are common to all living things, cells can provide clues about the functions that living things perform. And because all cells come from other cells, scientists can study cells to learn about growth and reproduction.

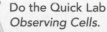

🔄 **Sequence** Fill in the circle next to the name of the person who was the first to see living cells through a microscope.
- ◯ Matthias Schleiden
- ◯ Robert Hooke
- ◯ Anton van Leeuwenhoek
- ◯ Rudolf Virchow
- ◯ Theodor Schwann

Schleiden, Schwann, and Virchow

In 1838, using his own research and the research of others, Matthias Schleiden concluded that all plants are made of cells. A year later, Theodor Schwann reached the same conclusion about animals. In 1855, Rudolf Virchow proposed that new cells are formed only from cells that already exist. "All cells come from cells," wrote Virchow.

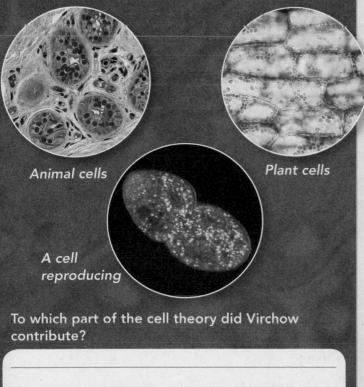

Animal cells

Plant cells

A cell reproducing

To which part of the cell theory did Virchow contribute?

_____

_____

Lab zone Do the Quick Lab *Observing Cells.*

🔑 Assess Your Understanding

1a. Relate Cause and Effect Why would Hooke's discovery have been impossible without a microscope?

_____

_____

_____

b. Apply Concepts Use Virchow's ideas to explain why plastic plants and stuffed animals are not alive.

_____

_____

_____

_____

got it? ....

◯ **I get it!** Now I know that the cell theory describes_____

_____

_____

◯ **I need extra help with** _____

Go to my science ⓢ coach *online for help with this subject.*

7

How Do Microscopes Work?

The cell theory could not have been developed without microscopes. 🗝 **Some microscopes focus light through lenses to produce a magnified image, and other microscopes use beams of electrons.** Both light microscopes and electron microscopes do the same job in different ways. For a microscope to be useful, it must combine two important properties—magnification and resolution.

Magnification and Lenses Have you ever looked at something through spilled drops of water? If so, did the object appear larger? Magnification is the condition of things appearing larger than they are. Looking through a magnifying glass has the same result. A magnifying glass consists of a convex lens, which has a center that is thicker than its edge. When light passes through a convex lens and into your eye, the image you see is magnified. Magnification changes how you can see objects and reveals details you may not have known were there, as shown in **Figure 3.**

Vocabulary Prefixes The prefix *magni-* means "great" or "large." Underline all the words in the paragraph at the right that you can find with this prefix.

❶ Leaf; green color and veins

❷

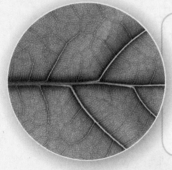

❸

❹

FIGURE 3 ·······································

Magnification

The images above have all been magnified, which makes them look unfamiliar. ✎ **Infer** On the lines, write what you think each photograph shows, and explain your reasoning. (One answer is completed for you.)

8 Introduction to Cells

Magnification With a Compound Microscope

Figure 4 shows a microscope that is similar to one you may use in your classroom. This type of instrument, called a compound microscope, magnifies the image using two lenses at once. One lens is fixed in the eyepiece. A second lens is chosen from a group of two or three lenses on the revolving nosepiece. Each of these lenses has a different magnifying power. By turning the nosepiece, you can select the lens you want. A glass slide on the stage holds the object to be viewed.

A compound microscope can magnify an object more than a single lens can. Light from a lamp (or reflecting off a mirror) passes through the object on the slide, the lower lens, and then the lens in the eyepiece. The total magnification of the object equals the magnifications of the two lenses multiplied together. For example, suppose the lower lens magnifies the object 10 times, and the eyepiece lens also magnifies the object 10 times. The total magnification of the microscope is 10 × 10, or 100 times, which is written as "100×."

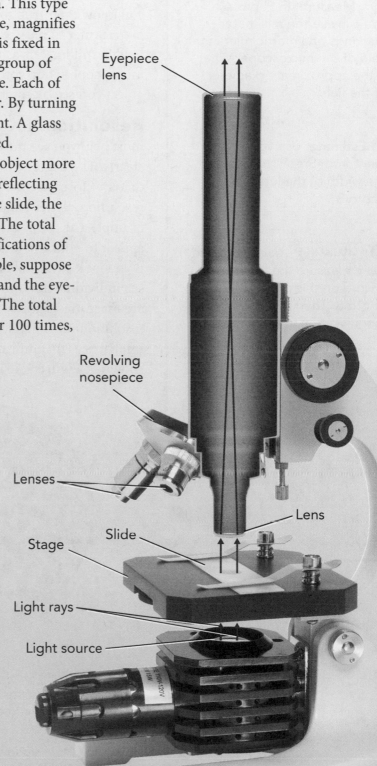

Eyepiece lens

Revolving nosepiece

Lenses

Slide

Stage

Light rays

Light source

Lens

FIGURE 4 ·····················

▷ VIRTUAL LAB **A Compound Microscope**

This microscope has a 10× lens in the eyepiece. The revolving nosepiece holds three different lenses: 4×, 10×, and 40×.

✎ **Complete these tasks.**

1. **Calculate** Calculate the three total magnifications possible for this microscope.

_____

_____

_____

2. **Predict** What would happen if the object on the slide were too thick for light to pass through it?

_____

_____

_____

apply it!

① ⚠ **Measure** In Photo A, you can see the millimeter markings of a metric ruler in the field of the microscope. What is the approximate diameter of the field?

_____

② **Estimate** Use your measurement from Step 1 to estimate the width of the letter in Photo B.

_____

③ [CHALLENGE] Using a metric ruler, measure the letter **e** in a word on this page and in Photo B. Then calculate the magnification in the photo.

_____

_____

A   B

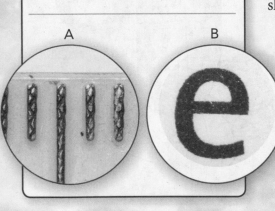

Measuring Microscopic Objects

When you see objects through a microscope, they look larger than they really are. How do you know their true size? One way is to use a metric ruler to measure the size of the circular field in millimeters as you see it through the microscope. Then you can estimate the size of the object you see by comparing it to the width of the field.

Resolution To create a useful image, a microscope must help you see the details of the object's structure clearly. The degree to which two separate structures that are close together can be distinguished is called resolution. Better resolution shows more details. For example, the colors of a newspaper photograph may appear to your eye to be solid patches of color. However, if you look at the colors through a microscope, you will see individual dots. You see the dots not only because they are magnified but also because the microscope improves resolution. In general, for light microscopes, resolution improves as magnification increases. Good resolution, as shown in **Figure 5,** makes it easier to study cells.

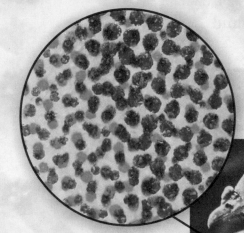

FIGURE 5 ··

Resolution
The images in colorful photographs actually consist of only a few ink colors in the form of dots.

✎ **Interpret Photos** What color dots does improved resolution allow you to see?

_____

_____

_____

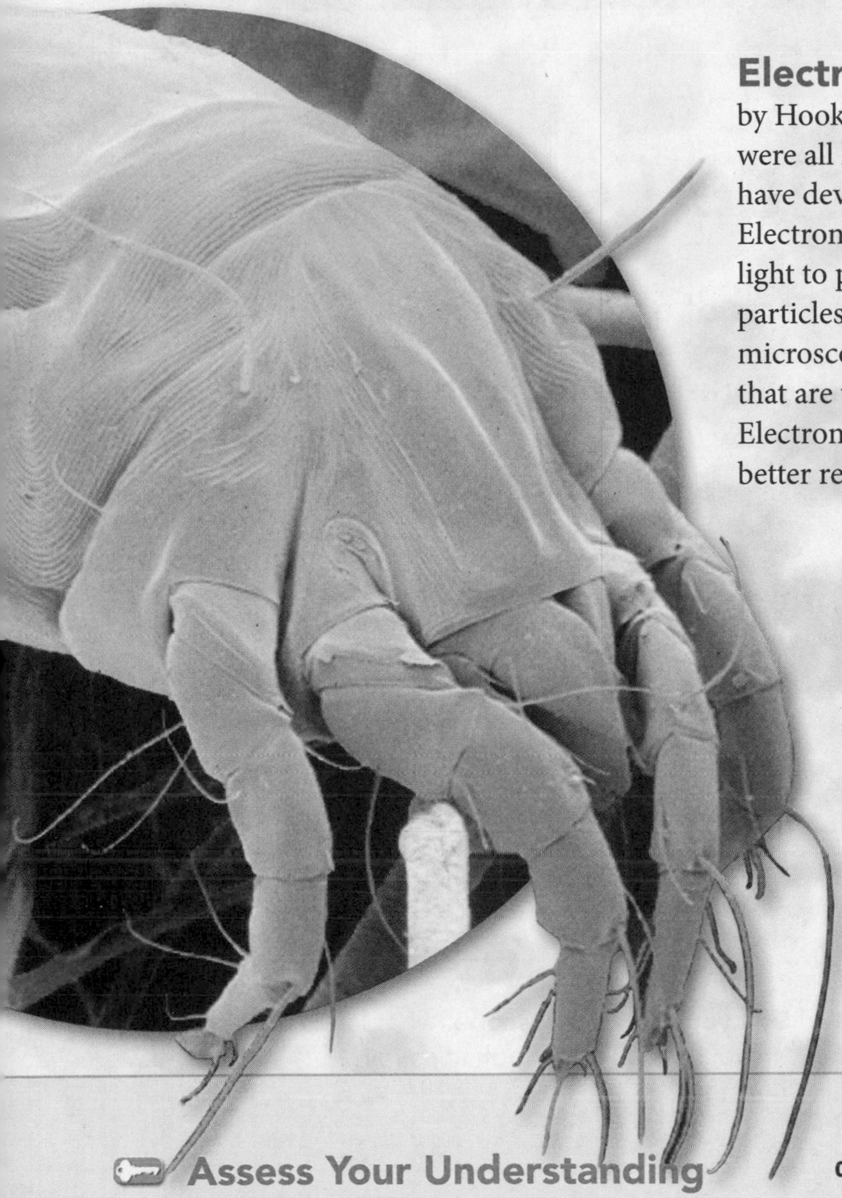

Electron Microscopes The microscopes used by Hooke, Leeuwenhoek, and other early researchers were all light microscopes. Since the 1930s, scientists have developed several types of electron microscopes. Electron microscopes use a beam of electrons instead of light to produce a magnified image. (Electrons are tiny particles that are smaller than atoms.) By using electron microscopes, scientists can obtain pictures of objects that are too small to be seen with light microscopes. Electron microscopes allow higher magnification and better resolution than light microscopes.

FIGURE 6 ·····································
A Dust Mite
Dust mites live in everyone's homes. A colorized image made with an electron microscope reveals startling details of a mite's body.

✎ **Observe** List at least three details that you can see in the photo.

_____

_____

_____

Lab® Do the Lab Investigation
zone *Design and Build a Microscope.*

Assess Your Understanding

2a. Define Magnification makes objects look (smaller/larger) than they really are.

b. Estimate The diameter of a microscope's field of view is estimated to be 0.9 mm. About how wide is an object that fills two thirds of the field? Circle your answer.

1.8 mm   0.6 mm   0.3 mm

c. Compare and Contrast How are magnification and resolution different?

_____

_____

_____

d. Explain How do the characteristics of electron microscopes make them useful for studying cells?

_____

_____

_____

_____

_____

got it? ·····································

○ **I get it!** Now I know that light microscopes

work by_____

○ **I need extra help with** _____

Go to **MY SCIENCE** ⑤ **COACH** online for help with this subject

11

Looking Inside Cells

UNLOCK THE BIG Q?

🔑 **How Do the Parts of a Cell Work?**

🔑 **How Do Cells Work Together in an Organism?**

MY PLANET DIARY

Glowing Globs

Do these cells look as if they're glowing? This photograph shows cells that have been stained with dyes that make cell structures easier to see. Scientists view such treated cells through a fluorescent microscope, which uses strong light to activate the dyes and make them glow. Here, each green area is a cell's nucleus, or control center. The yellow "fibers" form a kind of support structure for the cell.

Lab zone® Do the Inquiry Warm-Up *How Large Are Cells?*

TECHNOLOGY

Communicate Discuss these questions with a partner. Then write your answers below.

1. Why is staining useful when studying cells through a microscope?

_____

_____

2. If you had a microscope, what kinds of things would you like to look at? Why?

_____

_____

_____

▷ **PLANET DIARY** Go to **Planet Diary** to learn more about cell parts.

Vocabulary

- cell wall • cell membrane • nucleus • organelle
- ribosome • cytoplasm • mitochondria
- endoplasmic reticulum • Golgi apparatus • vacuole
- chloroplast • lysosome • multicellular • unicellular
- tissue • organ • organ system

Skills

⟳ **Reading: Identify the Main Idea**

△ **Inquiry: Make Models**

How Do the Parts of a Cell Work?

When you look at a cell through a microscope, you can usually see the outer edge of the cell. Sometimes you can also see smaller structures within the cell. 🔑 **Each kind of cell structure has a different function within a cell.** In this lesson, you will read about the structures that plant and animal cells have in common. You will also read about some differences between the cells.

Cell Wall The **cell wall** is a rigid layer that surrounds the cells of plants and some other organisms. The cells of animals, in contrast, do not have cell walls. A plant's cell wall helps protect and support the cell. The cell wall is made mostly of a strong material called cellulose. Still, many materials, including water and oxygen, can pass through the cell wall easily.

Cell Membrane Think about how a window screen allows air to enter and leave a room but keeps insects out. One of the functions of the cell membrane is something like that of a screen. The **cell membrane** controls which substances pass into and out of a cell. Everything a cell needs, such as food particles, water, and oxygen, enters through the cell membrane. Waste products leave the same way. In addition, the cell membrane prevents harmful materials from entering the cell.

All cells have cell membranes. In plant cells, the cell membrane is just inside the cell wall. In cells without cell walls, the cell membrane forms the border between the cell and its environment.

FIGURE 1 ···

A Typical Animal Cell

You will see this diagram of a cell again in this lesson.

✎ **Identify** Use a colored pencil to shade the cell membrane and fill in the box in the key.

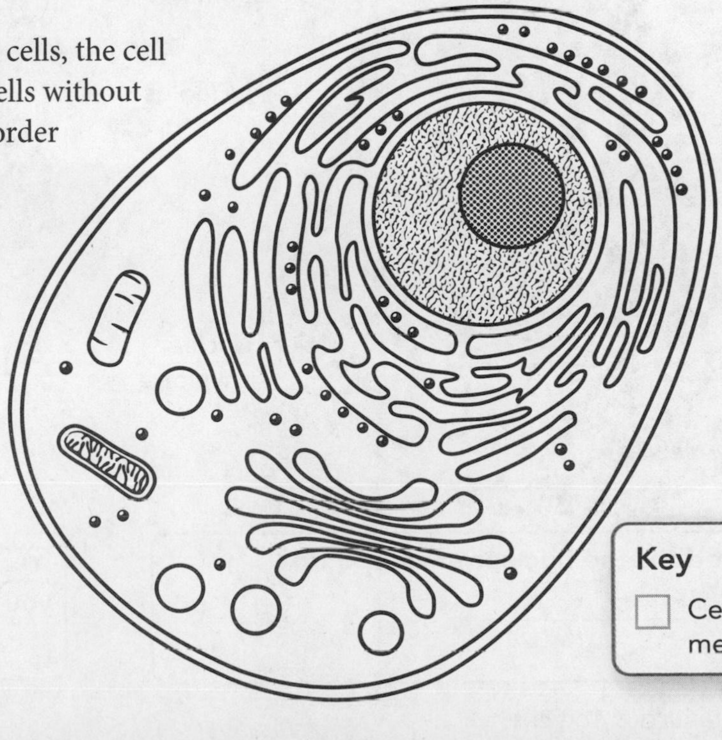

Key

☐ Cell membrane

Nucleus

A cell doesn't have a brain, but it has something that functions in a similar way. A large oval structure called the **nucleus** (NOO klee us) acts as a cell's control center, directing all of the cell's activities. The nucleus is the largest of many tiny cell structures, called **organelles,** that carry out specific functions within a cell. Notice in **Figure 2** that the nucleus is surrounded by a membrane called the nuclear envelope. Materials pass in and out of the nucleus through pores in the nuclear envelope.

Chromatin

You may wonder how the nucleus "knows" how to direct the cell. Chromatin, thin strands of material that fill the nucleus, contains information for directing a cell's functions. For example, the instructions in the chromatin ensure that leaf cells grow and divide to form more leaf cells.

Nucleolus

Notice the small, round structure in the nucleus. This structure, the nucleolus, is where ribosomes are made. **Ribosomes** are small grain-shaped organelles that produce proteins. Proteins are important substances in cells.

FIGURE 2 ······················

Organelles of a Cell
The structures of a cell look as different as their functions.

✎ **Complete each task.**

1. **Review** Answer the questions in the boxes.

2. **Relate Text and Visuals** In the diagram on the facing page, use different-colored pencils to color each structure and its matching box in the color key.

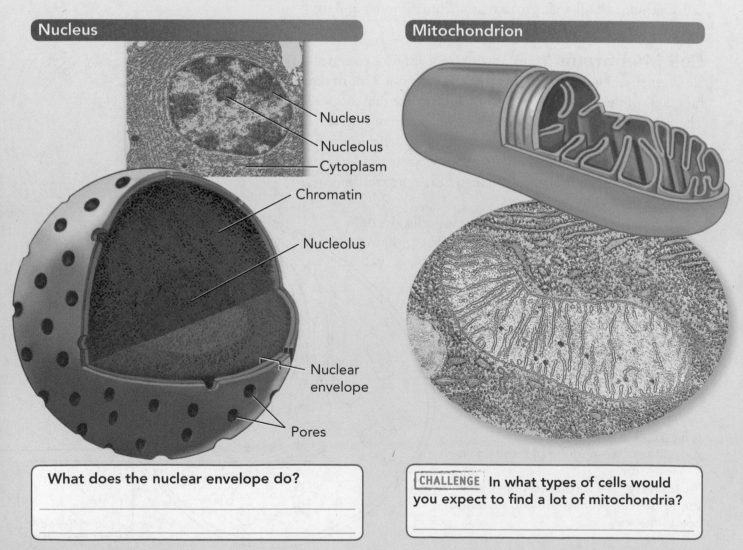

Nucleus

- Nucleus
- Nucleolus
- Cytoplasm
- Chromatin
- Nucleolus
- Nuclear envelope
- Pores

Mitochondrion

What does the nuclear envelope do?

_____

CHALLENGE In what types of cells would you expect to find a lot of mitochondria?

_____

14 Introduction to Cells

Organelles in the Cytoplasm

Most of a cell consists of a thick, clear, gel-like fluid. The **cytoplasm** fills the region between the cell membrane and the nucleus. The fluid of the cytoplasm moves constantly within a cell, carrying along the nucleus and other organelles that have specific jobs.

Mitochondria Floating in the cytoplasm are rod-shaped structures that are nicknamed the "powerhouses" of a cell. Look again at **Figure 2. Mitochondria** (myt oh KAHN dree uh; singular *mitochondrion*) convert energy stored in food to energy the cell can use to live and function.

Endoplasmic Reticulum and Ribosomes In **Figure 2,** you can see what looks something like a maze of passageways. The **endoplasmic reticulum** (en doh PLAZ mik rih TIK yuh lum), often called the ER, is an organelle with a network of membranes that produces many substances. Ribosomes dot some parts of the ER, while other ribosomes float in the cytoplasm. The ER helps the attached ribosomes make proteins. These newly made proteins and other substances leave the ER and move to another organelle.

Vocabulary Prefixes The prefix *endo-* is Greek for "within." If the word part *plasm* refers to the "body" of the cell, what does the prefix *endo-* tell you about the endoplasmic reticulum?

_____

_____

Endoplasmic Reticulum and Ribosomes

Ribosomes

What do ribosomes do?

_____

Key

- ☐ Nucleus
- ☐ Nucleolus
- ☐ Cytoplasm
- ☐ Mitochondria
- ☐ ER
- ☐ Ribosomes

CELLS IN LIVING THINGS

What are cells made of?

FIGURE 3 ....

▷ INTERACTIVE ART These illustrations show typical structures found in plant and animal cells. Other living things share many of these structures, too. ✎ **Describe** Describe the function of each structure in the boxes provided.

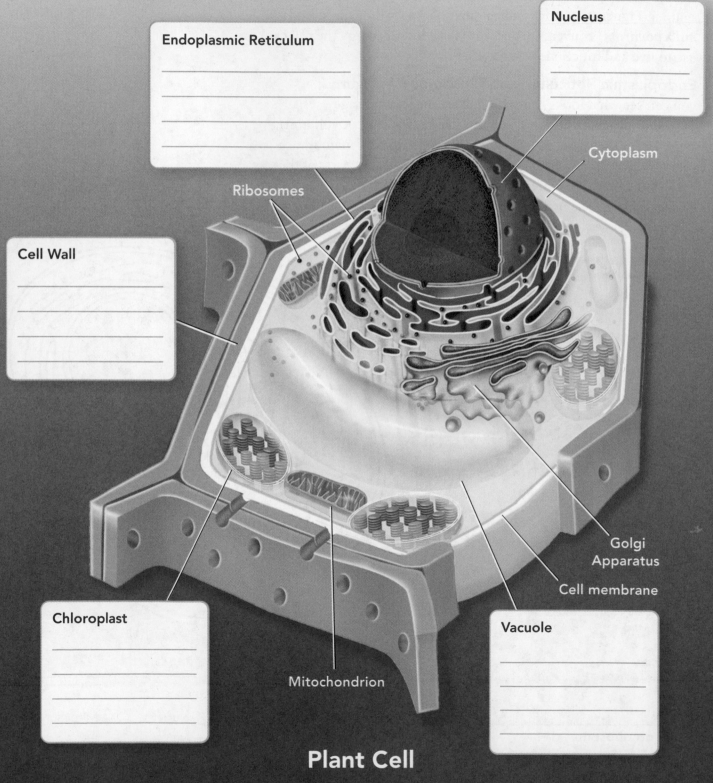

Nucleus

Endoplasmic Reticulum

Cytoplasm

Ribosomes

Cell Wall

Chloroplast

Golgi Apparatus

Cell membrane

Mitochondrion

Vacuole

Plant Cell

Check the box for each structure present in plant cells or animal cells.

Structure	Cell wall	Cell membrane	Cytoplasm	Nucleus	Mitochondria	Chloroplasts	Ribosomes	Endoplasmic reticulum	Vacuoles	Golgi apparatus	Lysosomes
Plant cells											
Animal cells											

Ribosomes

Cytoplasm

Mitochondria

Endoplasmic
Reticulum

Golgi Apparatus

Lysosomes

Cell Membrane

Vacuole

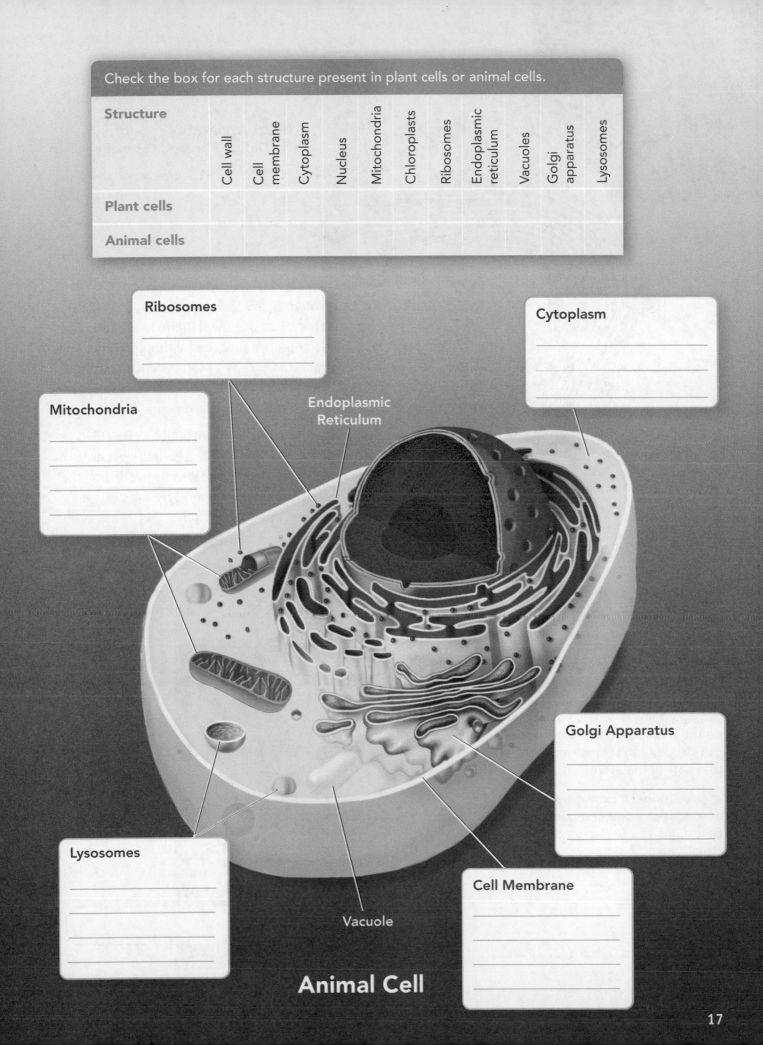

Animal Cell

FIGURE 4 ·······················

Golgi Apparatus

✎ **Define** The Golgi apparatus is an organelle that _____ and _____ materials made in the _____.

Golgi Apparatus As proteins leave the endoplasmic reticulum, they move to a structure that looks like the flattened sacs and tubes shown in **Figures 3 and 4.** This structure can be thought of as a cell's warehouse. The **Golgi apparatus** receives proteins and other newly formed materials from the ER, packages them, and distributes them to other parts of the cell or to the outside of the cell.

Vacuoles Plant cells often have one or more large, water-filled sacs floating in the cytoplasm. This type of sac, called a **vacuole** (VAK yoo ohl), stores water, food, or other materials needed by the cell. Vacuoles can also store waste products until the wastes are removed. Some animal cells do not have vacuoles, while others do.

apply it!

Can a store's building be a model for a cell? If so, how do the parts of a cell function in ways that are similar to the parts of a building? See if you can figure it out. In each blank space on the picture, write the name of a cell structure that functions most like that part of the store.

⚠ **Make Models** How do you think making real-world comparisons with cells helps you understand cell structure and function?

_____

_____

_____

_____

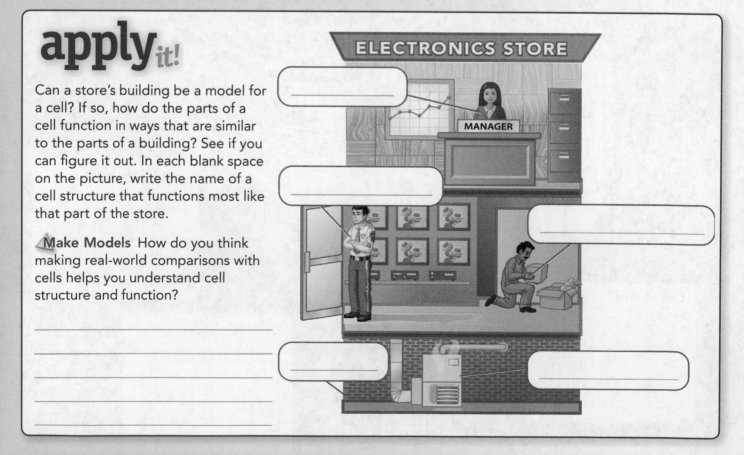

ELECTRONICS STORE

MANAGER

Chloroplasts A typical plant cell contains green structures, called chloroplasts, in the cytoplasm. A **chloroplast**, shown in **Figure 5,** captures energy from sunlight and changes it to a form of energy cells can use in making food. Animal cells don't have chloroplasts, but the cells of plants and some other organisms do. Chloroplasts make leaves green because leaf cells contain many chloroplasts.

Lysosomes Look again at the animal cell in **Figure 3**. Notice the saclike organelles, called **lysosomes** (LY suh sohmz), which contain substances that break down large food particles into smaller ones. Lysosomes also break down old cell parts and release the substances so they can be used again. You can think of lysosomes as a cell's recycling centers.

FIGURE 5 ···
A Chloroplast
✎ **Infer** In which part of a plant would you NOT expect to find cells with chloroplasts?

_____

_____

 Do the Quick Lab
Gelatin Cell Model.

🔑 Assess Your Understanding

1a. Interpret Tables Use the table you completed in **Figure 3** to summarize the differences between a plant cell and an animal cell.

_____

_____

_____

b. Make Generalizations How are the functions of the endoplasmic reticulum and the Golgi apparatus related?

_____

_____

_____

c. CHALLENGE A solar panel collects sunlight and converts it to heat or electrical energy. How is a solar panel similar to chloroplasts?

_____

_____

_____

d. ANSWER THE BIG ? What are cells made of?

_____

_____

_____

_____

got it? ·····································

○ **I get it!** Now I know that different kinds of organelles in a cell_____

○ **I need extra help with** _____

Go to MY SCIENCE ⓢ COACH *online for help with this subject.*

19

How Do Cells Work Together in an Organism?

Plants and animals (including you) are **multicellular,** which means "made of many cells." Single-celled organisms are called **unicellular.** In a multicellular organism, the cells often look quite different from one another. They also perform different functions.

Specialized Cells All cells in a multicellular organism must carry out key functions, such as getting oxygen, to remain alive. However, cells also may be specialized. That is, they perform specific functions that benefit the entire organism. These specialized cells share what can be called a "division of labor." One type of cell does one kind of job, while other types of cells do other jobs. For example, red blood cells carry oxygen to other cells that may be busy digesting your food. Just as specialized cells differ in function, they also differ in structure. **Figure 6** shows specialized cells from plants and animals. Each type of cell has a distinct shape. For example, a nerve cell has thin, fingerlike extensions that reach toward other cells. These structures help nerve cells transmit information from one part of your body to another. The nerve cell's shape wouldn't be helpful to a red blood cell.

> ◉ **Identify the Main Idea**
> Reread the paragraph about specialized cells. Then underline the phrases or sentences that describe the main ideas about specialized cells.

FIGURE 6 ....

▷ **INTERACTIVE ART** **The Right Cell for the Job**

Many cells in plants and animals carry out specialized functions.

✎ **Draw Conclusions** Write the number of each kind of cell in the circle of the matching function.

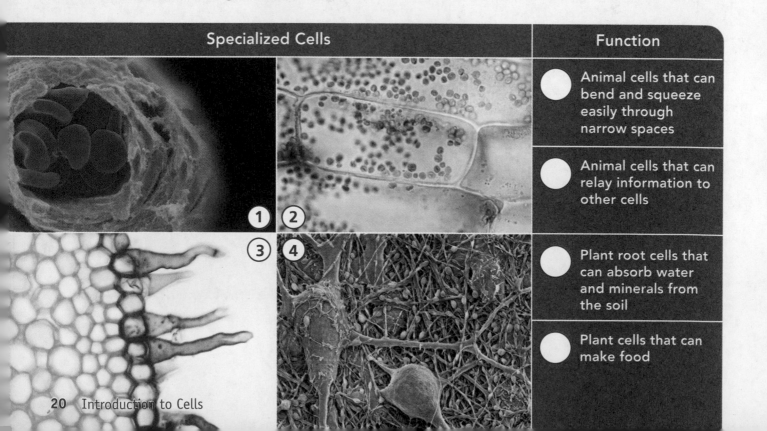

Specialized Cells	Function
① ② ③ ④	◯ Animal cells that can bend and squeeze easily through narrow spaces
	◯ Animal cells that can relay information to other cells
	◯ Plant root cells that can absorb water and minerals from the soil
	◯ Plant cells that can make food

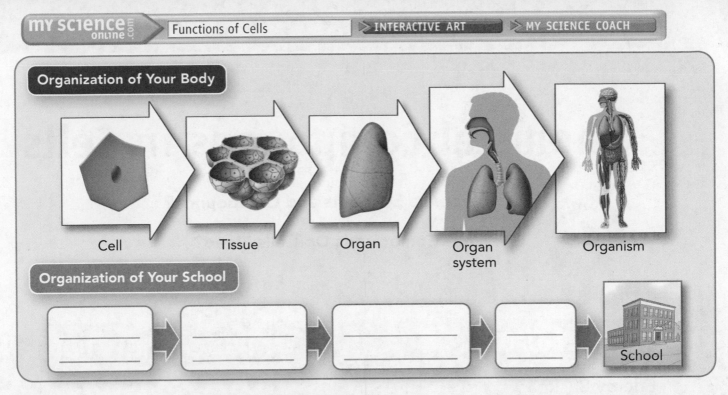

Organization of Your Body

Cell → Tissue → Organ → Organ system → Organism

Organization of Your School

_____ → _____ → _____ → _____ → School

Cells Working Together
A division of labor occurs among specialized cells in an organism. It also occurs at other levels of organization. 🗝 **In multicellular organisms, cells are organized into tissues, organs, and organ systems.** A *tissue* is a group of similar cells that work together to perform a specific function. For example, your brain is made mostly of nerve tissue, which consists of nerve cells that relay information to other parts of your body. An **organ,** such as your brain, is made of different kinds of tissues that function together. For example, the brain also has blood vessels that carry the blood that supplies oxygen to your brain cells. Your brain is part of your nervous system, which directs body activities and processes. An **organ system** is a group of organs that work together to perform a major function. As **Figure 7** shows, the level of organization in an organism becomes more complex from cell, to tissue, to organ, to organ systems.

FIGURE 7 ·······································
Levels of Organization
Living things are organized in levels of increasing complexity. Many nonliving things, like a school, have levels of organization, too.

✏ **Apply Concepts** On the lines above, write the levels of organization of your school building, from the simplest level, such as your desk, to the most complex.

Do the Quick Lab
Tissues, Organs, Systems.

🗝 Assess Your Understanding

2a. Describe What does the term *division of labor* mean as it is used in this lesson?

_____

_____

b. Infer Would a tissue or an organ have more kinds of specialized cells? Explain your answer.

_____

_____

got it? ·······································

○ **I get it!** Now I know that the levels of organization in a multicellular organism include_____

_____

○ **I need extra help with** _____

Go to my science ⑤ coach *online for help with this subject.*

21

3 Chemical Compounds in Cells

UNLOCK THE BIG ?

🔑 **What Are Elements and Compounds?**

🔑 **What Compounds Do Cells Need?**

MY PLANET DIARY

Energy Backpacks

Some people think a camel's humps carry water. Not true! They actually store fat. A hump's fatty tissue supplies energy when the camel doesn't eat. When a camel has enough food, the hump remains hard and round. But when food is scarce, the hump gets smaller and may sag to the side. If the camel then gets more food, the hump can regain its full size and shape in about three or four months.

MISCONCEPTION

Communicate Discuss this question with a group of classmates. Then write your answer below.

How do you think the camel might be affected if it didn't have humps?

_____

_____

_____

▷ **PLANET DIARY** Go to **Planet Diary** to learn more about chemical compounds in cells.

Lab zone® Do the Inquiry Warm-Up *Detecting Starch.*

What Are Elements and Compounds?

You are made of many substances. These substances supply the raw materials that make up your blood, bones, muscles, and more. They also take part in the processes carried out by your cells.

Elements You have probably heard of carbon, hydrogen, oxygen, and nitrogen—maybe phosphorus and sulfur, too. All of these are examples of **elements** found in your body. 🔑 **An element is any substance that cannot be broken down into simpler substances.** The smallest unit of an element is a particle called an atom. Any single element is made up of only one kind of atom.

Vocabulary

- element
- compound
- carbohydrate
- lipid
- protein
- enzyme
- nucleic acid
- DNA
- double helix

Skills

- ⟳ Reading: Compare and Contrast
- △ Inquiry: Draw Conclusions

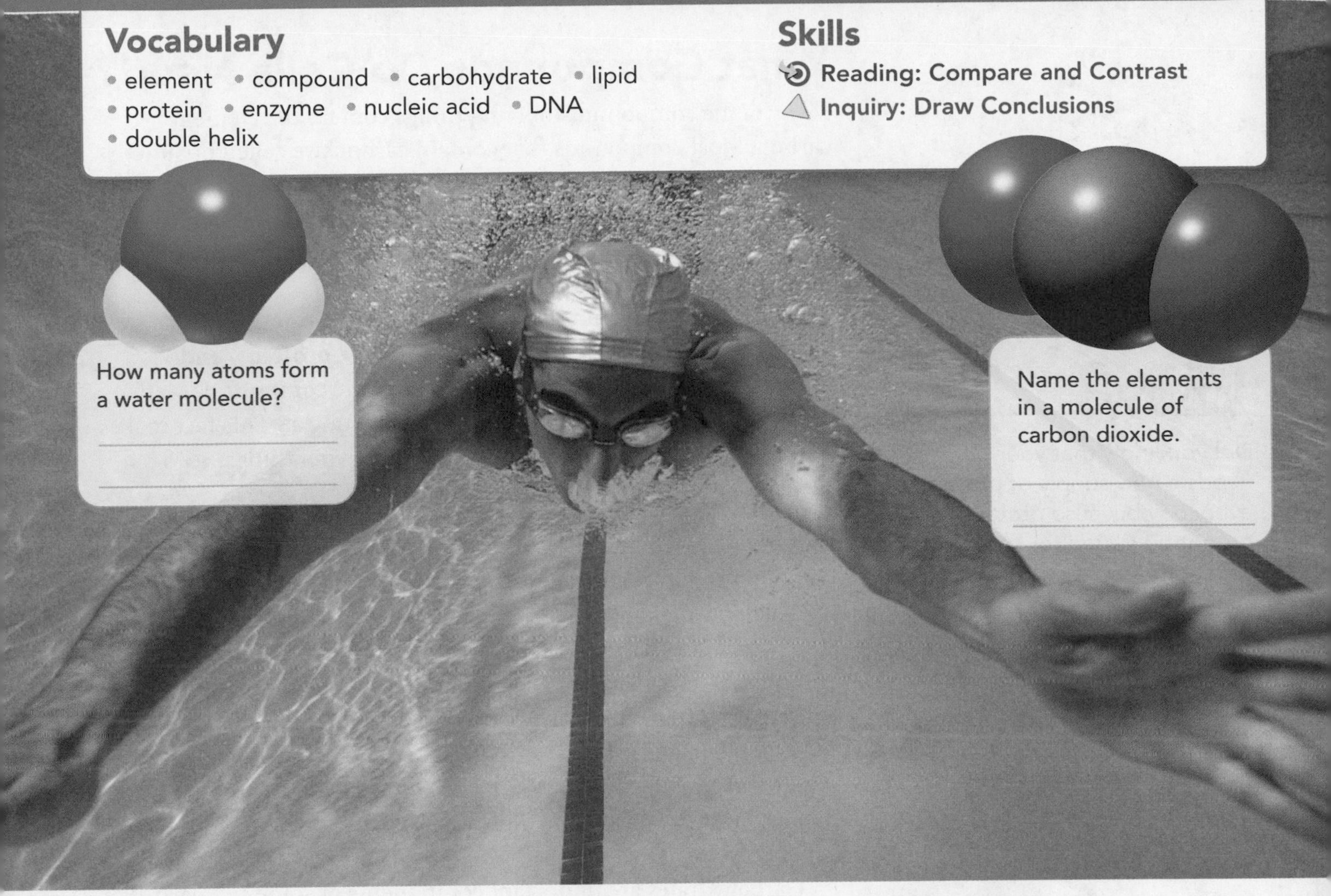

How many atoms form a water molecule?

_____

_____

Name the elements in a molecule of carbon dioxide.

_____

_____

Compounds

Carbon dioxide and water are examples of **compounds**. 🔑 **Compounds form when two or more elements combine chemically.** Most elements in living things occur in the form of compounds. For example, carbon dioxide is a compound made up of the elements carbon and oxygen.

The smallest unit of many compounds is a molecule. A molecule of carbon dioxide consists of one carbon atom and two oxygen atoms. Compare the diagrams of the carbon dioxide molecule and the water molecule in **Figure 1**.

FIGURE 1 ·····················

Molecules and Compounds

Carbon dioxide, in the air exhaled from the swimmer's lungs, is a compound. So is water.

✏ **Interpret Diagrams** Answer the questions in the boxes provided.

 Lab zone® Do the Quick Lab _What Is a Compound?_

🔑 Assess Your Understanding

got it? ···

○ I get it! Now I know that compounds form when _____

_____

○ I need extra help with _____

Go to **my science** 💬 **coach** online for help with this subject.

23

What Compounds Do Cells Need?

Many of the compounds in living things contain the element carbon. Most compounds that contain carbon are called organic compounds. Organic compounds that you may have heard of include nylon and polyester. Compounds that don't contain carbon are called inorganic compounds. Water and table salt are familiar examples of inorganic compounds.

Some important groups of organic compounds that living things need are carbohydrates, lipids, proteins, and nucleic acids. Water is a necessary inorganic compound. Many of these compounds are found in the foods you eat. This fact makes sense because the foods you eat come from living things.

did you **know?**

Did you know that your body needs a new supply of proteins every day because protein cannot be stored for later use, as fat or carbohydrates can?

Carbohydrates You have probably heard of sugars and starches. They are examples of **carbohydrates,** energy-rich organic compounds made of the elements carbon, hydrogen, and oxygen.

The food-making process in plants produces sugars. Fruits and some vegetables have a high sugar content. Sugar molecules can combine, forming larger molecules called starches, or complex carbohydrates. Plant cells store excess energy in molecules of starch. Many foods, such as potatoes, pasta, rice, and bread, come from plants and contain starch. When you eat these foods, your body breaks down the starch into glucose, a sugar your cells can use to get energy.

Carbohydrates are important components of some cell parts. For example, the cellulose found in the cell walls of plants is a type of carbohydrate. Carbohydrates are also found on cell membranes.

FIGURE 2

Energy-Rich Compounds

Cooked pasta served with olive oil, spices, and other ingredients makes an energy-packed meal.

Classify Label each food a starch or a lipid. Next to the label, write another example of a food that contains starch or lipids.

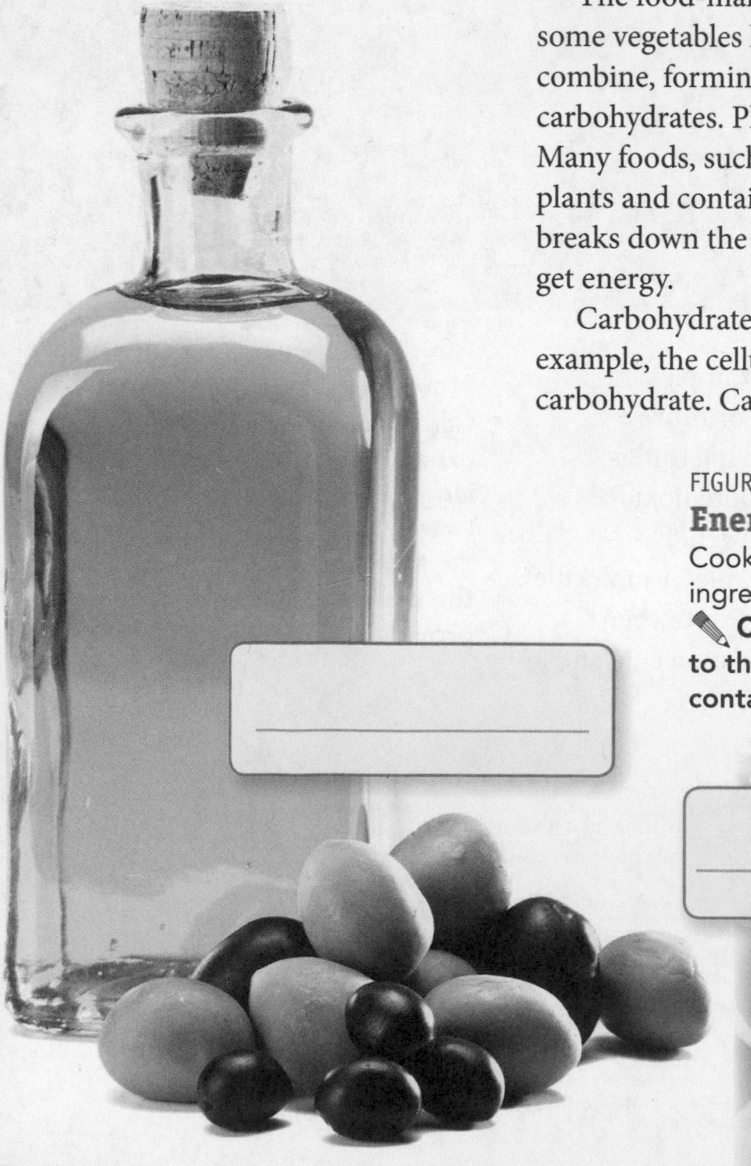

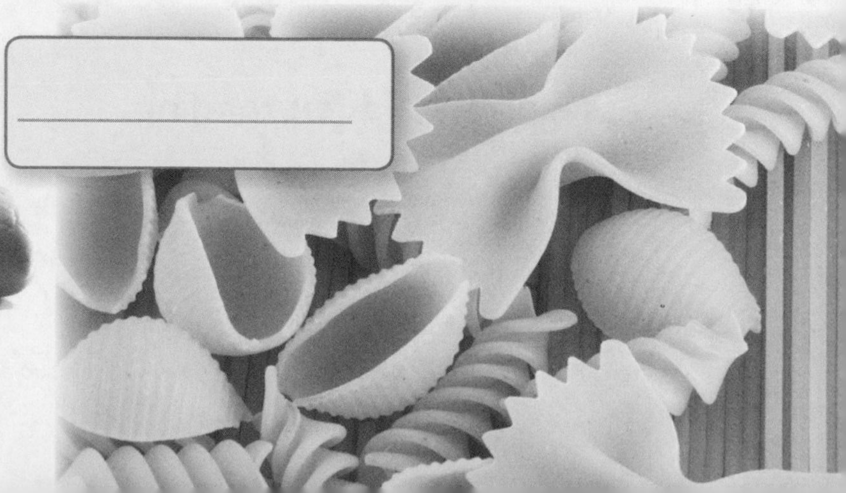

Lipids Have you ever seen a cook trim fat from a piece of meat before cooking it? The cook is trimming away one kind of lipid. **Lipids** are compounds that are made mostly of carbon and hydrogen and some oxygen. Cell membranes consist mainly of lipids.

Fats, oils, and waxes are all lipids. Gram for gram, fats and oils contain more energy than carbohydrates. Cells store energy from fats and oils for later use. For example, during winter, an inactive bear lives on the energy stored in its fat cells. Foods high in fats include whole milk, ice cream, and fried foods.

Proteins What do a bird's feathers, a spider's web, and a hamburger have in common? They consist mainly of proteins. **Proteins** are large organic molecules made of carbon, hydrogen, oxygen, nitrogen, and, in some cases, sulfur. Foods that are high in protein include meat, dairy products, fish, nuts, and beans.

Much of a cell's structure and function depends on proteins. Proteins form part of a cell's membrane. Proteins also make up parts of the organelles within a cell. A group of proteins known as **enzymes** speed up chemical reactions in living things. Without enzymes, the many chemical reactions that are necessary for life would take too long. For example, an enzyme in your saliva speeds up the digestion of starch. The starch breaks down into sugars while still in your mouth.

Compare and Contrast
As you read, complete the table below to compare carbohydrates, lipids, and proteins.

FIGURE 3
Proteins
A parrot's beak, feathers, and claws are made of proteins.
Apply Concepts What part of your body most likely consists of proteins similar to those of a parrot's claws?

Type of Compound	Elements	Functions
Carbohydrate		
Lipid		
Protein		

FIGURE 4 ·····················

DNA

Smaller molecules connect in specific patterns and sequences, forming DNA.

✏️ **Interpret Diagrams** In the diagram below, identify the pattern of colors. Then color in the ones that are missing.

Nucleic Acids

Nucleic acids are very long organic molecules. These molecules consist of carbon, oxygen, hydrogen, nitrogen, and phosphorus. Nucleic acids contain the instructions that cells need to carry out all the functions of life. Foods high in nucleic acids include red meat, shellfish, mushrooms, and peas.

One kind of nucleic acid is deoxyribonucleic acid (dee AHK see RY boh noo KLEE ik), or DNA. **DNA** is the genetic material that carries information about an organism and is passed from parent to offspring. This information directs a cell's functions. Most DNA is found in a cell's nucleus. The shape of a DNA molecule is described as a **double helix.** Imagine a rope ladder that's been twisted around a pole, and you'll have a mental picture of the double helix of DNA. The double helix forms from many small molecules connected together. The pattern and sequence in which these molecules connect make a kind of chemical code the cell can "read."

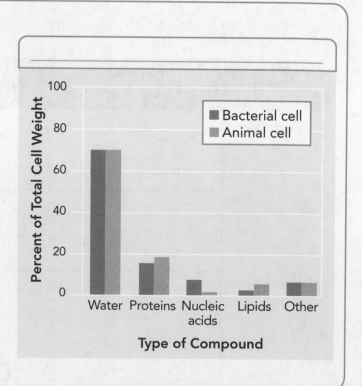

do the math!

Most cells contain the same compounds. The graph compares the percentages of some compounds found in a bacterial cell and in an animal cell. Write a title for the graph and answer the questions below.

❶ **Read Graphs** Put a check above the bar that shows the percentage of water in an animal cell. How does this number compare to the percentage of water in a bacterial cell?

_____

❷ **Read Graphs** (Proteins/Nucleic acids) make up a larger percentage of an animal cell.

❸ ⚠️ **Draw Conclusions** In general, how do you think a bacterial cell and an animal cell compare in their chemical composition?

_____

_____

FIGURE 5 ···

Mostly Water

About two thirds of the human body is water. But you know you don't really look like a tank of water with a fish! ✎ **Graph Complete and label the circle graph to show the percentage of water in your body.**

Water and Living Things
Water plays many important roles in cells. For example, most chemical reactions in cells depend on substances that must be dissolved in water to react. And water itself takes part in many chemical reactions in cells.

Water also helps cells keep their shape. A cell without water would be like a balloon without air! Think about how the leaves of a plant wilt when the plant needs water. After you add water to the soil, the cells absorb the water, and the leaves perk up.

Water changes temperature slowly, so it helps keep the temperature of cells from changing rapidly—a change that can be harmful. Water also plays a key role in carrying substances into and out of cells. Without water, life as we know it would not exist on Earth.

Lab® zone Do the Quick Lab
What's That Taste?

🦴 Assess Your Understanding

1a. Describe An organic compound that contains only the elements carbon, hydrogen, and oxygen is most likely (a carbohydrate/ a protein/DNA). Explain your answer.

_____

_____

b. Classify Which groups of organic compounds found in living things are NOT energy rich?

_____

_____

c. Review What is the function of DNA?

_____

_____

_____

d. CHALLENGE Describe ways a lack of water could affect cell functions.

_____

_____

_____

_____

got it? ···

○ **I get it!** Now I know that the important compounds in living things include _____

_____

○ I need extra help with _____

Go to MY SCIENCE ⓢ COACH online for help with this subject.

The Cell in Its Environment

🔑 **How Do Materials Move Into and Out of Cells?**

my planeT DiaRY

Something Good in the Air

You're in your bedroom studying, and you smell something good. Someone is cooking lunch! How did the smell travel from the kitchen to your nose? During cooking, molecules from soup and many other foods diffuse, or spread farther and farther apart. The molecules are also carried by air currents. Your nose sniffs in the molecules and sends a message to your brain. Even if only one molecule in ten million carries the odor, your nose will send a "smell" message! Amazingly, your brain can identify about ten thousand different smells.

FUN FACTS

Communicate Discuss this question with a classmate and write your answers below.

If the kitchen door is closed, how will that affect your ability to smell cooking odors in your room?

_____

_____

_____

_____

_____

▶ PLANET DIARY Go to **Planet Diary** to learn more about cells in their environments.

Lab ® Do the Inquiry Warm-Up
zone *Diffusion in Action.*

How Do Materials Move Into and Out of Cells?

Cells have structures that protect their contents from the world outside the cell. To live and function, however, cells must let certain materials enter and leave. Oxygen and water and particles of food must be able to move into a cell, while carbon dioxide and other waste materials must move out. Much as a gatekeeper controls the flow of traffic into and out of a parking lot, the cell membrane controls how materials move into or out of a cell.

Vocabulary

- selectively permeable • passive transport • diffusion
- osmosis • active transport • endocytosis
- exocytosis

Skills

- ◉ Reading: Relate Cause and Effect
- △ Inquiry: Predict

Importance of the Cell Membrane Every cell is surrounded by a cell membrane. In **Figure 1** you can see that the cell membrane consists of a double layer of lipid molecules lined up side by side. Remember that lipids are a group of organic compounds found in living things. Here and there in the double layer of lipid molecules, you can see proteins, some with chains of carbohydrates attached. Other carbohydrate chains sit on the surface of the membrane. All these molecules play important roles in helping materials move through the cell membrane.

Some materials move freely across the cell membrane. Others move less freely or not at all. The cell membrane is **selectively permeable,** which means that some substances can cross the membrane while others cannot. ⚷ **Substances that can move into and out of a cell do so by means of one of two processes: passive transport or active transport.**

FIGURE 1 ·······························

A Selective Barrier

✎ **Make Models** In what way is the cell membrane like a gatekeeper?

_____

_____

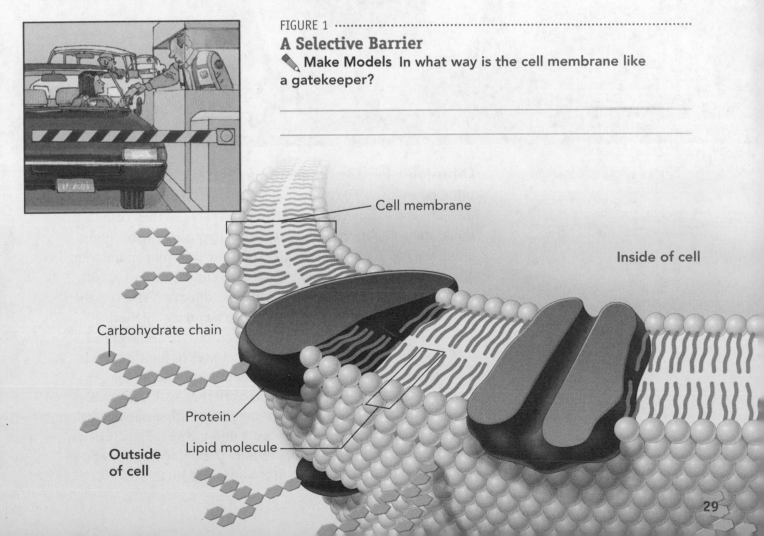

Cell membrane

Inside of cell

Carbohydrate chain

Protein

Lipid molecule

Outside of cell

29

Diffusion and Osmosis: Forms of Passive Transport

If you have ever ridden a bicycle down a hill, you know that it takes hardly any of your energy to go fast. But you do have to use energy to pedal back up the hill. Moving materials across the cell membrane sometimes requires the cell to use its own energy. At other times, the cell uses no energy. The movement of dissolved materials across a cell membrane without using the cell's energy is called **passive transport.**

FIGURE 2 ···

Diffusion

A drop of food coloring in a plate of gelatin gradually spreads as molecules of the dye diffuse. ✎ **Predict In the third plate, draw how you think the plate would look if diffusion continues.**

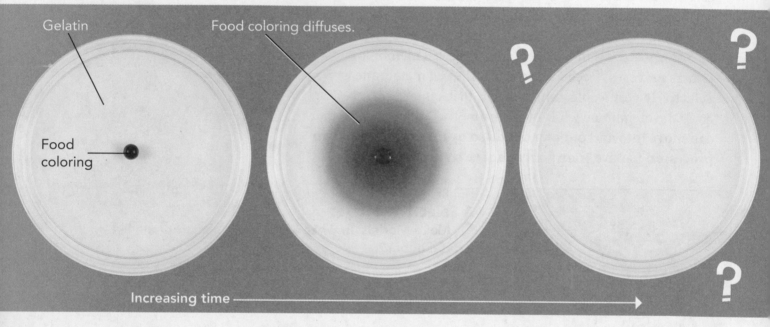

Gelatin

Food coloring diffuses.

Food coloring

?

?

?

Increasing time ⟶

◑ Relate Cause and Effect

Diffusion causes molecules to move from areas of _____ concentration to areas of _____ concentration.

Diffusion Molecules are always moving. As they move, they bump into one another. The more molecules there are in a space, the more they are said to be concentrated in that space. So they collide more often. Collisions cause molecules to push away from one another. Over time, as molecules continue colliding and moving apart, they become less concentrated. Eventually, they spread evenly throughout the space. **Diffusion** (dih FYOO zhun) is the process by which molecules move from an area of higher concentration to an area of lower concentration. See **Figure 2.**

Consider a unicellular organism that lives in pond water. It gets oxygen from that water. Many more molecules of oxygen are dissolved in the water outside the cell than inside the cell. In other words, the concentration of oxygen is higher outside the cell. What happens? Oxygen moves easily into the cell. The diffusion of oxygen into the cell does not require the cell to use any of its energy. Diffusion is one form of passive transport.

Osmosis Like oxygen, water passes easily into and out of a cell across the cell membrane. **Osmosis** is the diffusion of water molecules across a selectively permeable membrane. Because cells cannot function properly without adequate water, many cellular processes depend on osmosis. Osmosis is a form of passive transport.

Osmosis can have important effects on cells and entire organisms. The plant cells in the top photo of **Figure 3** have a healthy flow of water both into and out of each cell. Under certain conditions, osmosis can cause water to move out of the cells more quickly than it moves in. When that happens, the cytoplasm shrinks and the cell membrane pulls away from the cell wall, as shown in the bottom photo. If conditions do not change, the cells can die.

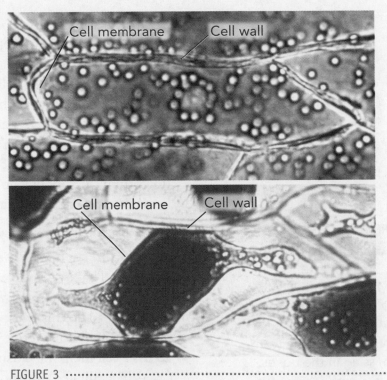

FIGURE 3 ···

Effects of Osmosis
Cells shrink and die when they lose too much water.

✎ **Infer** Using a colored pencil, shade the cells in the bottom photo to show how they would change if the flow of water was reversed.

apply it!

Most cells are too small to be seen without a microscope. What does cell size have to do with moving materials into and out of a cell? Suppose the diagrams at the right represent two cells. One cell is three times the width of the other cell. Think about how this difference could affect processes in the cells.

❶ **Infer** Cytoplasm streams within a cell, moving materials somewhat as ocean currents move a raft. In which cell will materials move faster from the cell membrane to the center of the cell? Why?

_____

_____

❷ **Predict** Wastes are poisonous to a cell and must be removed from the cytoplasm. Predict how cell size could affect the removal process and the survival of a cell.

_____

_____

_____

Large cell

Small cell

Facilitated Diffusion Oxygen and carbon dioxide diffuse freely across a cell membrane. Other molecules, such as sugar, do not. Sugars cannot cross easily through the membrane's lipid molecules. In a process called facilitated diffusion, proteins in the cell membrane form channels through which the sugars can pass. The word *facilitate* means "to make easier." As shown in **Figure 4,** these proteins provide a pathway for the sugars to diffuse. The proteins function much the way downspouts guide water that flows from the roof of a house to the ground. Facilitated diffusion uses no cell energy and is another form of passive transport.

Active Transport Molecules in cells must often move in the opposite direction from the way they would naturally move due to diffusion. That is, the molecules move from a place of *lower* concentration to a place of *higher* concentration. Cells have to supply the energy to do this work—just as you would supply the energy to pedal a bike uphill. **Active transport** is the movement of materials across a cell membrane using cellular energy.

As in facilitated diffusion, proteins within the cell membrane play a key role in active transport. Using the cell's energy, transport proteins "pick up" specific molecules and carry them across the membrane. Substances that are carried into and out of cells by this process include calcium, potassium, and sodium.

FIGURE 4 ··
> ART IN MOTION **Crossing the Cell Membrane**
✎ Molecules move into and out of a cell by means of passive or active transport.

1. **Name** Fill in the words missing in the boxes.
2. CHALLENGE On the diagram, write an "H" where the concentration of each substance is high and an "L" where the concentration is low.

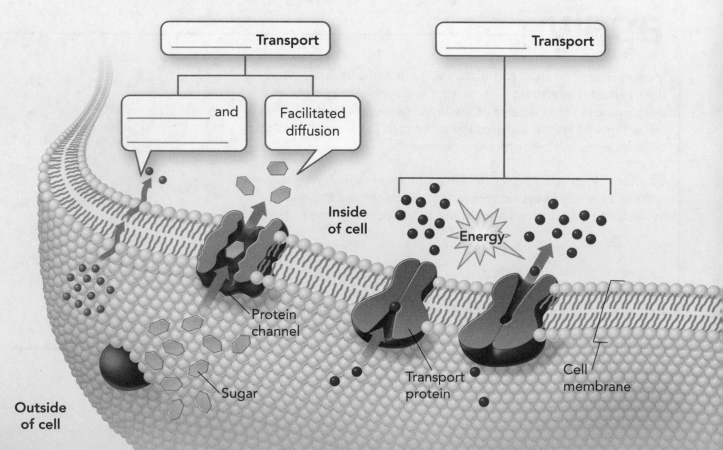

Moving Large Particles

Some materials, such as food particles, are too large to cross the cell membrane. In a process called **endocytosis** (ehn doh sigh TOH sihs), the cell membrane changes shape and engulfs the particle. You can see this process happening in **Figure 5.** Once the food particle is engulfed, the cell membrane fuses, pinching off a vacuole within the cell. The reverse process, called **exocytosis** (ehk soh sigh TOH sihs), allows large particles to leave a cell. During exocytosis, a vacuole first fuses with the cell membrane. Then the cell membrane forms an opening to the outside and spills out the contents of the vacuole. Both endocytosis and exocytosis require energy from the cell.

FIGURE 5 ·····················
Amoeba Engulfing Food
A single-celled amoeba slowly surrounds bits of food.

✏ **Observe Look at these photographs. They show** (endocytosis/exocytosis).

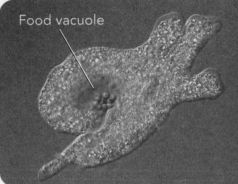

❶ Amoeba's cytoplasm streams toward food particles.

❷ Cytoplasm surrounds food particles as vacuole begins to form.

❸ Cell membrane fuses, trapping food particles in new vacuole.

Lab zone® Do the Quick Lab *Effect of Concentration on Diffusion.*

🔑 Assess Your Understanding

1a. Review Use diffusion to tell what happens when you drop a sugar cube into water.

_____
_____
_____

b. ✏ **Predict** Draw an arrow to show the overall direction water will travel as a result of osmosis. (The yellow line is the cell membrane.)

Water molecule

c. Identify Active transport depends on (sugars/proteins) to move molecules across the cell membrane.

d. Compare and Contrast How does active transport differ from passive transport?

_____
_____
_____
_____

got it? ·····································

○ **I get it!** Now I know that a key function of the cell membrane is to _____
_____
_____

○ **I need extra help with** _____

Go to **MY SCIENCE** Ⓢ **COACH** online for help with this subject.

1 Study Guide

All living things are made of _____, which are the smallest units of _____

and _____

LESSON 1 Discovering Cells

🔑 Cells are the basic units of structure and function in living things.

🔑 All living things are composed of cells, and all cells come from other cells.

🔑 Some microscopes focus light through lenses to produce a magnified image, and other microscopes use beams of electrons.

Vocabulary
• cell   • microscope   • cell theory

LESSON 2 Looking Inside Cells

🔑 Each kind of cell structure has a different function within a cell.

🔑 In multicellular organisms, cells are organized into tissues, organs, and organ systems.

Vocabulary
• cell wall   • cell membrane   • nucleus   • organelle
• ribosome   • cytoplasm   • mitochondria
• endoplasmic reticulum   • Golgi apparatus   • vacuole
• chloroplast   • lysosome   • multicellular   • unicellular
• tissue   • organ   • organ system

LESSON 3 Chemical Compounds in Cells

🔑 Elements are the simplest substances. Compounds form when elements combine.

🔑 Important compounds in living things include carbohydrates, lipids, proteins, nucleic acids, and water.

Vocabulary
• element   • compound   • carbohydrate
• lipid   • protein   • enzyme
• nucleic acid   • DNA   • double helix

LESSON 4 The Cell in Its Environment

🔑 Substances move into and out of a cell by one of two processes: passive transport or active transport.

Vocabulary
• selectively permeable   • passive transport
• diffusion   • osmosis   • active transport
• endocytosis   • exocytosis

Review and Assessment

LESSON 1 Discovering Cells

1. Which tool could help you see a plant cell?

   a. a filter **b.** a microscope

   c. a microwave **d.** an electromagnet

2. The _____ states that all living things are made of cells.

3. **Classify** Your cells take in oxygen, water, and food. What is one waste product that leaves your cells?

   _____

   _____

4. **Compare and Contrast** How is a light microscope similar to an electron microscope? How do the two types of microscopes differ?

   _____

   _____

   _____

5. **Estimate** Using a microscope, you see the one-celled organism shown below. The diameter of the microscope's field of view is 0.8 mm. Estimate the cell's length and width, and write your answer in the space provided.

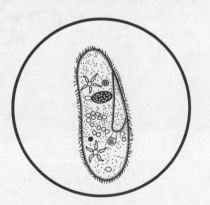

_____

_____

LESSON 2 Looking Inside Cells

6. Which cellular structures are found in plant cells but NOT in animal cells?

   a. chloroplast and cell wall

   b. Golgi apparatus and vacuole

   c. mitochondrion and ribosome

   d. endoplasmic reticulum and nucleus

7. Mitochondria and chloroplasts are two types of _____

8. **Interpret Diagrams** What is the function of the cell structure shown in purple in the cell at the right?

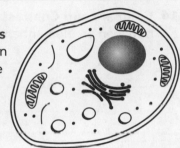

   _____

   _____

9. **Sequence** Arrange the following, from smallest to largest level of organization: organ system, tissue, cell, organ.

   _____

   _____

10. **Infer** A certain cell can no longer package and release materials out of the cell. Which of the cell's organelles is not working?

    _____

    _____

11. **Write About It** Imagine you are a tour guide. You and the tour group have shrunk to the size of water molecules. You are now ready to start a tour of the cell! Write a narrative of your tour that you could give a new tour guide to use.

Chemical Compounds in Cells

12. Starch is an example of a

   a. lipid.   **b.** protein.

   c. nucleic acid.   **d.** carbohydrate.

13. Which type of organic molecule is found primarily in a cell's nucleus?

_____

14. Compare and Contrast What is the difference between an element and a compound?

_____

_____

_____

15. Infer How may a lack of proteins in a person's diet affect the body?

_____

_____

_____

16. math! The graph below shows the amounts of different compounds that make up an animal cell. What percentage of the total cell weight is made up of lipids?

Compounds in Animal Cells

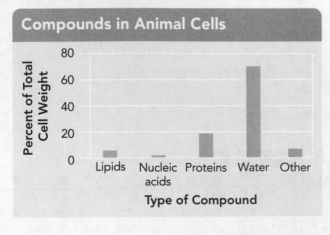

_____

The Cell in Its Environment

17. The process by which water moves across a cell's membrane is called

   a. osmosis.   **b.** exocytosis.

   c. resolution.   **d.** active transport.

18. Some substances but not others can cross the _____ membrane of a cell.

19. Compare and Contrast How are facilitated diffusion and active transport similar? How are they different?

_____

_____

_____

_____

APPLY THE BIG Q

What are cells made of?

20. At right is a photograph of a multicellular plant called a primrose. List three conclusions you can make about the primrose as a living thing.

_____

_____

_____

_____

_____

_____

_____

_____

Standardized Test Prep

Multiple Choice

Circle the letter of the best answer.

1. Which transport process is shown in the illustration below?

   A osmosis   B diffusion

   C endocytosis   D exocytosis

2. Which of the following types of cells have cell walls?

   A plant cells   B muscle cells

   C blood cells   D animal cells

3. A compound microscope has two lenses. One lens has a magnification of 15× and the other has a magnification of 40×. What is the total magnification?

   A 25×   B 55×

   C 150×   D 600×

4. Which of the following is an example of an element?

   A cell   B water

   C hydrogen   D starch

5. The cell membrane is made mostly of a double layer of molecules called

   A lipids   B proteins

   C nucleic acids   D carbohydrates

Constructed Response

Use the diagram below and your knowledge of cells to help you answer Question 6 on a separate sheet of paper.

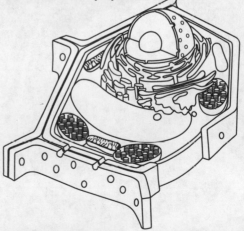

6. Identify this drawing as a plant cell or an animal cell. Justify your answer by describing how the structures of this cell compare to those of plant cells and animal cells.

ElectronEYES

▼ Looking through a TEM gives a close-up view of the cells of an onion.

▼ Samples of bread mold as captured by an SEM

The invention of the optical microscope around the year 1600 caused a revolution in science. For the first time, scientists were able to see the cells that make up living things. However, even the most modern optical microscopes that focus light through lenses to produce an enlarged image can magnify an object only about 1,000 times.

Beginning in the early 1930s, new kinds of microscopes have caused new revolutions in science. The electron microscope uses electrons, instead of light, to make very detailed images of specimens. Today, powerful microscopes can magnify images up to 1,000,000 times—enough to enable scientists to see individual atoms!

Scientists use three main types of very powerful microscopes:

Transmission Electron Microscope (TEM) A TEM focuses a beam of electrons so that they pass through a very thinly sliced specimen. They are very useful for studying the interior structures of cells.

Scanning Electron Microscope (SEM) An SEM uses an electron beam to scan the surface of the specimen. The electron beam excites the electrons on the object's surface. The excited electrons are used to make a three-dimensional image of the specimen.

Scanning Tunneling Microscope (STM) An STM works by passing an electrically charged probe very close to the surface of a specimen. As the probe passes over the specimen, the probe moves up and down to keep the current in the probe constant. The path of the probe is recorded and is used to create an image of the specimen's surface.

Design It Research to find images taken by electron or scanning tunneling microscopes. Create a gallery or slide presentation of amazing microscope images to share with your class. See if your classmates can guess what object is shown in each image!

THE GENOGRAPHIC PROJECT

Have you ever wondered where your earliest ancestors came from? Archaeologists have worked for years to uncover evidence of ancient human migrations. They study the things people left behind, such as arrowheads, beads, and tools. Yet some of the most promising evidence is not found in archaeological sites. It is found in the cells that make up our bodies! The Genographic Project is a research project that uses DNA samples to help uncover the history of the human species.

Participants in the Genographic Project receive a kit that allows them to provide a DNA sample. To give a sample, participants use a cotton swab to gather cells from the inside of their cheek. This sample is mailed to a lab that analyzes the DNA contained in the cells. The DNA in the cells is compared with other DNA samples from around the world.

Then participants receive a report that describes the history of their earliest ancestors. The report includes a map that shows the migration route that these ancestors may have followed. Participants may choose to have their genetic information anonymously added to a genetic database. This database will help researchers build a very detailed map of ancient and modern human migration.

Explore It What has the Genographic Project discovered so far? Research the project, and create a map that shows what it has revealed about ancient human migration.

▲ People who want to help the Genographic Project collect cells from their cheeks.

▲ Scientists trace ancestry by determining which individuals share specific genes or sequences of genes called genetic markers.

HOW DO THESE GIANTS GROW?

How do living things get energy?

Looking straight up into the sky from the ground, you can see the tallest trees on Earth. These giant California redwoods can grow up to 110 meters tall, about the size of a 35-story skyscraper! To grow this big takes energy and raw materials from food. These trees don't eat food as you do. But they do get water through their roots, gases from the air, and lots of sunlight. **Develop Hypotheses** How do these trees get the energy they need to grow?

_____

_____

_____

_____

_____

> **UNTAMED SCIENCE** Watch the **Untamed Science** video to learn more about living things and energy.

Cell Processes and Energy

2 Getting Started

Check Your Understanding

1. **Background** Read the paragraph below and then answer the question.

In science class, we looked at both plant and animal cells under the microscope. I could see the **nucleus** in many cells. In plant cells, we could see green-colored **chloroplasts.** Both plant and animal cells have **mitochondria,** but they were too small for us to see with the microscopes we had.

The **nucleus** is the organelle that acts as the cell's control center and directs the cell's activities.

Chloroplasts are organelles that capture energy from sunlight and use it to produce food for the cell.

Mitochondria are organelles that convert energy in food to energy the cell can use to carry out its functions.

• Circle the names of the organelles found only in plant cells. Underline the organelles found in both plant and animal cells.

nucleus   mitochondria   chloroplasts

> MY READING WEB If you had trouble completing the question above, visit **My Reading Web** and type in *Cell Processes and Energy.*

Vocabulary Skill

Greek Word Origins The table below shows English word parts that have Greek origins. Learning the word parts can help you understand some of the vocabulary in this chapter.

Greek Word Part	Meaning	Example
auto-	self	**autotroph,** *n.* an organism that makes its own food; a producer
hetero-	other, different	**heterotroph,** *n.* an organism that cannot make its own food; a consumer

State Standards Right Justified TK

2. **Quick Check** The word part *-troph* comes from the Greek word *trophe,* which means "food." Circle the word part in two places in the chart above. How does the Greek word relate to the meaning of the terms?

_____

_____

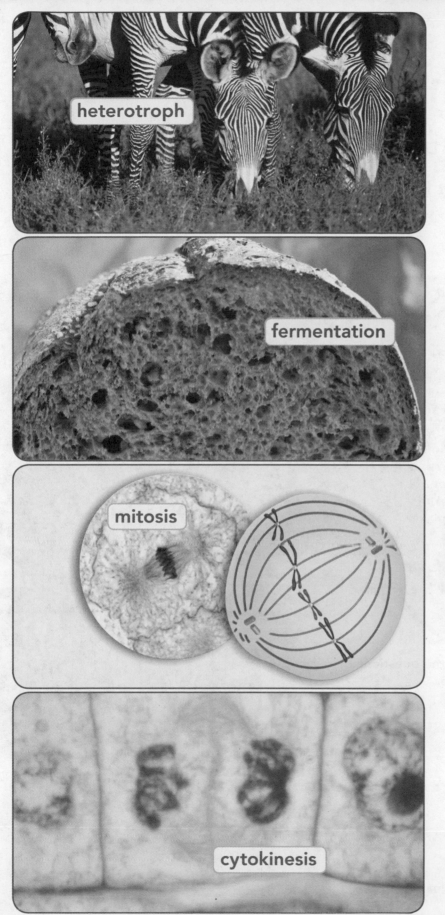

heterotroph

fermentation

mitosis

cytokinesis

Chapter Preview

LESSON 1
- photosynthesis
- autotroph
- heterotroph
- chlorophyll
- ↻ **Sequence**
- △ **Classify**

LESSON 2
- cellular respiration
- fermentation
- ↻ **Summarize**
- △ **Control Variables**

LESSON 3
- cell cycle
- interphase
- replication
- chromosome
- mitosis
- cytokinesis
- ↻ **Ask Questions**
- △ **Interpret Data**

> VOCAB FLASH CARDS   For extra help with vocabulary, visit **Vocab Flash Cards** and type in *Cell Processes and Energy.*

🔑 **How Do Living Things Get Energy From the Sun?**

🔑 **What Happens During Photosynthesis?**

my planet diary

MISCONCEPTION

When Is Food Not Food?

Misconception: Some people think that the plant food they give to house and garden plants is food for the plants. It isn't.

Plants make their own food—in the form of sugars—using water, carbon dioxide, and sunlight. So what is the "food" that people add to plants? It's fertilizer. Fertilizer is a mixture of minerals, such as potassium, calcium, and phosphorus. It helps plants grow but doesn't supply them with energy as food does. Farmers add fertilizer to soil to grow better quality crops. People do the same to grow bigger and healthier plants at home.

Communicate Write your answers to the questions below. Then discuss Question 2 with a partner.

1. What is "plant food"?

_____

_____

2. Why do you think people may feed their houseplants more often than farmers fertilize crops?

_____

_____

> PLANET DIARY Go to **Planet Diary** to learn more about photosynthesis.

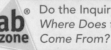 **Lab zone** Do the Inquiry Warm-Up *Where Does the Energy Come From?*

Vocabulary
- photosynthesis
- autotroph
- heterotroph
- chlorophyll

Skills
- ⤷ Reading: Sequence
- △ Inquiry: Classify

How Do Living Things Get Energy From the Sun?

On a plain in Africa, a herd of zebras peacefully eats grass. But watch out! A group of lions is about to attack the herd. The lions will kill one of the zebras and eat it.

Both the zebras and the lion you see in **Figure 1** use the food they eat to obtain energy. Every living thing needs energy. All cells need energy to carry out their functions, such as making proteins and transporting substances into and out of the cell. Like the raw materials used within a cell, energy used by living things comes from their environment. Zebra meat supplies the lion's cells with energy. Similarly, grass provides the zebra's cells with energy. But where does the energy in the grass come from? Plants and certain other organisms, such as algae and some bacteria, obtain their energy in a different way. These organisms use the energy in sunlight to make their own food.

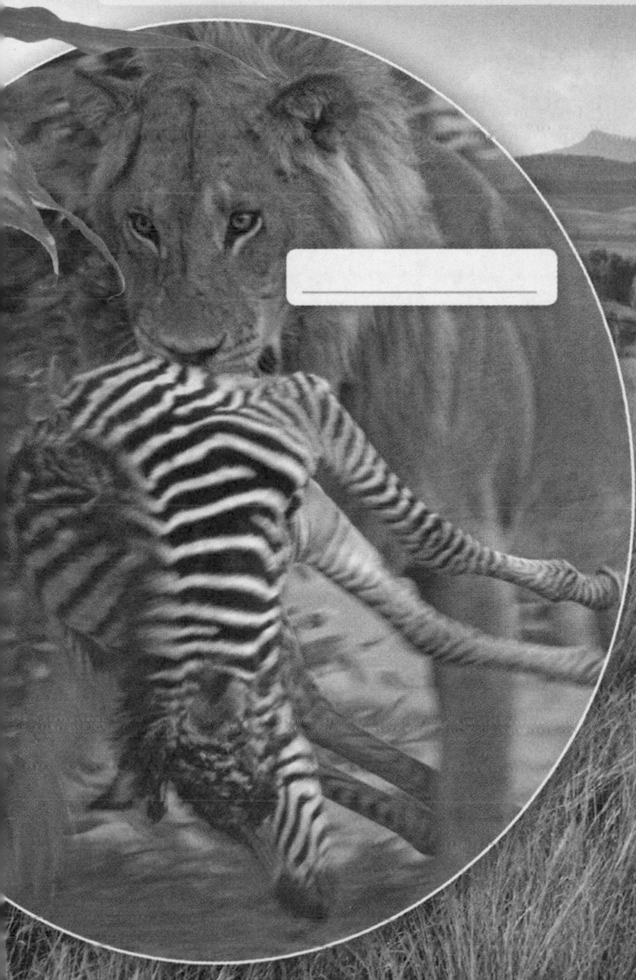

FIGURE 1 ....
An Energy Chain
All living things need energy.

✎ **Interpret Photos** In the boxes, write the direct source of energy for each organism. Which organism shown does not depend on another organism for food?

45

apply it!

A spider catches and eats a caterpillar that depends on plant leaves for food.

1 ⟳ **Sequence** Draw a diagram of your own that tracks how the sun's energy gets to the spider.

2 △ **Classify** In your diagram, label each organism as a heterotroph or an autotroph.

The Sun as an Energy Source

The process by which a cell captures energy in sunlight and uses it to make food is called **photosynthesis** (foh toh SIN thuh sis). The term *photosynthesis* comes from the Greek words *photos*, which means "light," and *syntithenai*, which means "putting together."

 Nearly all living things obtain energy either directly or indirectly from the energy of sunlight that is captured during photosynthesis. Grass obtains energy directly from sunlight because grass makes its own food during photosynthesis. When the zebra eats grass, it gets energy from the sun that has been stored in the grass. Similarly, the lion obtains energy stored in the zebra. The zebra and lion both obtain the sun's energy indirectly from the energy that the grass obtained through photosynthesis.

Producers and Consumers

Plants make their own food through the process of photosynthesis. An organism that makes its own food is called a producer, or an **autotroph** (AWT oh trohf). An organism that cannot make its own food, including animals such as the zebra and the lion, is called a consumer, or a **heterotroph** (HET ur oh trohf). Many heterotrophs obtain food by eating other organisms. Some heterotrophs, such as fungi, absorb their food from other organisms.

Lab zone ® Do the Quick Lab *Energy From the Sun.*

Assess Your Understanding

1a. Identify An organism that makes its own food is a(n) (autotroph/heterotroph).

b. Explain Why do living things need energy?

_____

c. Apply Concepts Give an example of how energy from the sun gets into your cells.

_____

_____

_____

got it?

○ **I get it!** Now I know that living things get energy directly from the sun by _____

or indirectly by _____

○ I need extra help with _____

Go to MY SCIENCE COACH online for help with this subject.

What Happens During Photosynthesis?

You've just read that plants make their own food. So how do they do that? 🔑 **During photosynthesis, plants and some other organisms absorb energy from the sun and use the energy to convert carbon dioxide and water into sugars and oxygen.** You can think of photosynthesis as taking place in two stages. First, plants capture the sun's energy. Second, plants produce sugars.

Stage 1: Capturing the Sun's Energy
In the first stage of photosynthesis, energy from sunlight is captured. In plants, this process occurs mostly in the leaves. Recall that chloroplasts are green organelles inside plant cells. The green color comes from pigments, colored chemical compounds that absorb light. The main pigment for photosynthesis in chloroplasts is **chlorophyll**.

Chlorophyll functions something like the solar cells in a solar-powered calculator. Solar cells capture the energy in light and convert it to a form that powers the calculator. Similarly, chlorophyll captures light energy and converts it to a form that is used in the second stage of photosynthesis.

During Stage 1, water in the chloroplasts is split into hydrogen and oxygen, as shown in **Figure 2.** The oxygen is given off as a waste product. The hydrogen is used in Stage 2.

Vocabulary Greek Word Origins The Greek word part *chloros-* means "pale green." Circle two words in the text that begin with this word part. Which word means "a green compound that absorbs light"?
- ○ Chloroplast
- ○ Chlorophyll

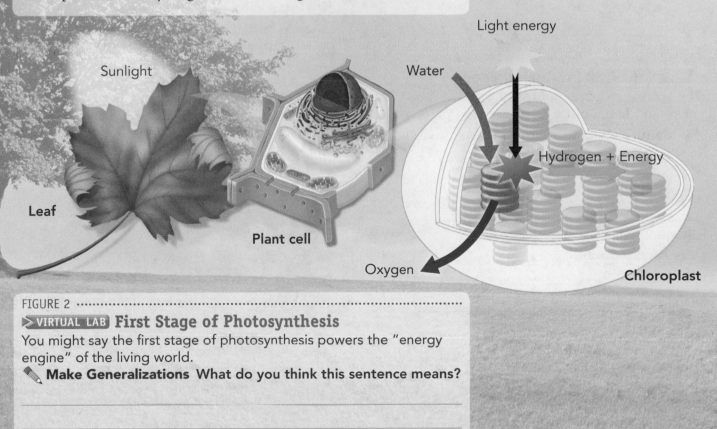

Light energy

Sunlight

Water

Hydrogen + Energy

Leaf

Plant cell

Oxygen

Chloroplast

FIGURE 2 ....
> VIRTUAL LAB First Stage of Photosynthesis
You might say the first stage of photosynthesis powers the "energy engine" of the living world.

✎ **Make Generalizations** What do you think this sentence means?

_____

_____

Stage 2: Using Energy to Make Food

In the second stage of photosynthesis, cells produce sugars. As shown in **Figure 3,** cells use hydrogen (H) that came from the splitting of water in Stage 1. Cells also use carbon dioxide (CO_2) from the air. Carbon dioxide enters the plant through small openings on the undersides of the leaves and moves into the chloroplasts.

Powered by the energy captured in Stage 1, hydrogen and carbon dioxide undergo a series of reactions that result in sugars. One important sugar produced is glucose. It has the chemical formula $C_6H_{12}O_6$. You may know that sugars are a type of carbohydrate. Cells can use the energy in glucose to carry out vital cell functions.

The other product of photosynthesis is oxygen gas (O_2). Recall that oxygen forms during the first stage when water molecules are split apart. Oxygen gas exits a leaf through the openings on its underside. Almost all the oxygen in Earth's atmosphere is produced by living things through the process of photosynthesis.

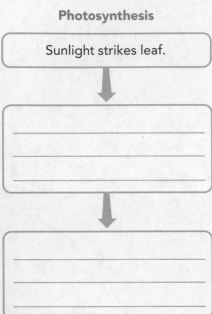

Photosynthesis

Sunlight strikes leaf.

FIGURE 3 ·······················

> INTERACTIVE ART **Producing Food**
The second stage of photosynthesis makes food for a plant.

Identify Fill in the missing terms in the spaces provided.

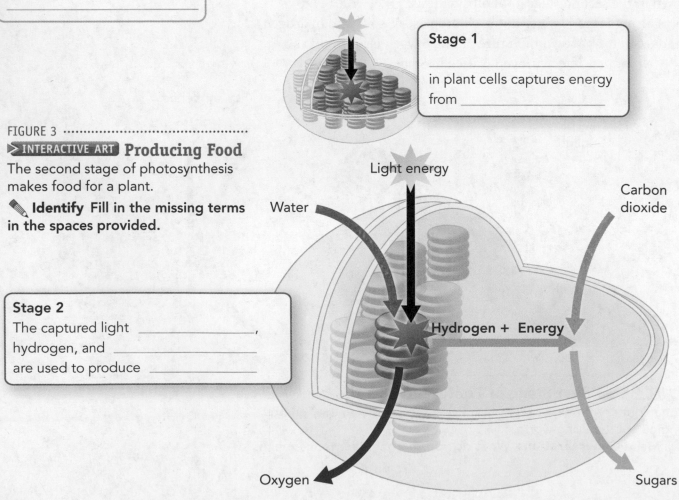

Stage 1
_____
in plant cells captures energy
from _____

Light energy

Water

Carbon dioxide

Hydrogen + Energy

Stage 2
The captured light _____,
hydrogen, and _____
are used to produce _____

Oxygen

Sugars

The Photosynthesis Equation

The events of photosynthesis that lead to the production of glucose can be summed up by the following chemical equation:

$$\text{light energy} + 6\ CO_2 \text{ (carbon dioxide)} + 6\ H_2O \text{ (water)} \longrightarrow C_6H_{12}O_6 \text{ (glucose)} + 6\ O_2 \text{ (oxygen)}$$

Notice that six molecules of carbon dioxide and six molecules of water are on the left side of the equation. These compounds are raw materials. One molecule of glucose and six molecules of oxygen are on the right side. These compounds are products. An arrow, meaning "yields," points from the raw materials to the products. Energy is not a raw material, but it is written on the left side of the equation to show that it is used in the reaction.

What happens to the sugars produced in photosynthesis? Plant cells use some of the sugars for food. The cells break down these molecules in a process that releases energy. This energy can then be used to carry out the plant's functions, such as growing and making seeds. Some sugar molecules are made into other compounds, such as cellulose for cell walls. Other sugar molecules may be stored in the plant's cells for later use. When you eat food from plants, such as potatoes or carrots, you are eating the plant's stored energy.

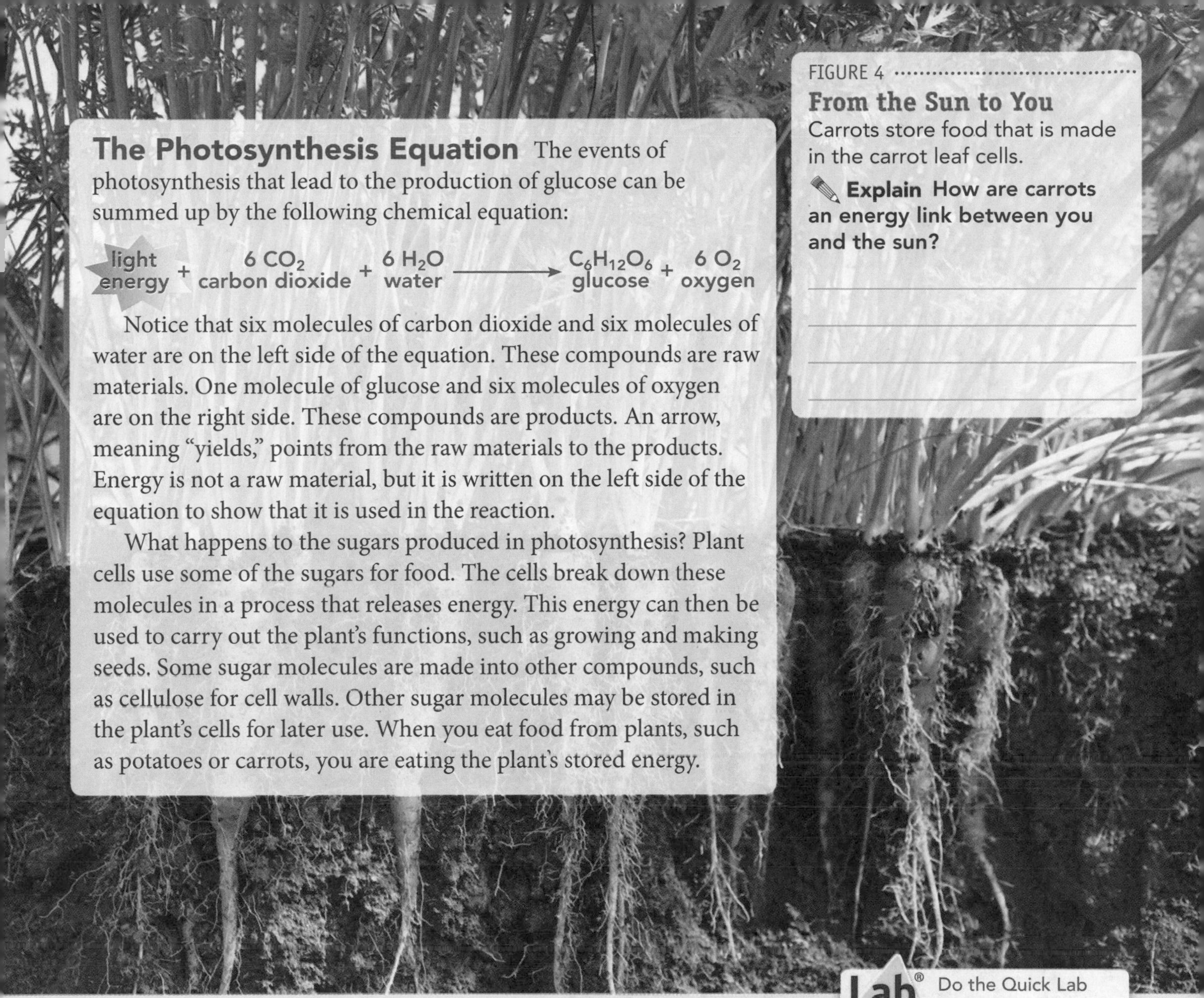

FIGURE 4 ·······

From the Sun to You
Carrots store food that is made in the carrot leaf cells.

✎ **Explain** How are carrots an energy link between you and the sun?

_____

_____

_____

Lab zone® Do the Quick Lab
Looking at Pigments.

⬚ Assess Your Understanding

2a. Name Circle two products of photosynthesis.
glucose/carbon dioxide/oxygen/chlorophyll

b. Interpret Diagrams Refer to **Figure 3** on the facing page. Where does the hydrogen that is used in Stage 2 of photosynthesis come from?

_____

_____

c. [CHALLENGE] Would you expect a plant to produce more oxygen on a sunny day or a cloudy day? Explain your answer.

_____

_____

_____

_____

got it? ·······

○ **I get it!** Now I know that during photosynthesis _____

_____

○ **I need extra help with** _____

Go to MY SCIENCE 🔊 COACH *online for help with this subject.*

Cellular Respiration

UNLOCK THE BIG

🔑 **What Happens During Cellular Respiration?**

🔑 **What Happens During Fermentation?**

my planet Diary

FUN FACTS

Going to Extremes

You may not know it, but there are organisms living in rocks deep below Earth's surface. Other organisms hang out in steaming hot lakes, like Grand Prismatic Spring in Yellowstone National Park, shown here. The water in this lake can be as hot as 86°C! Still other organisms nestle inside nuclear waste. All of these organisms are extremophiles, organisms that thrive in extreme habitats. These life forms can get energy in strange ways. Some make food from ocean minerals. Others break down compounds in radioactive rocks!

Pose Questions Write a question about something else you would like to learn about extremophiles.

_____

_____

_____

_____

▶ **PLANET DIARY** Go to **Planet Diary** to learn more about extremophiles.

Lab zone® Do the Inquiry Warm-Up *Cellular Respiration.*

What Happens During Cellular Respiration?

You and your friend have been hiking all morning. You look for a flat rock to sit on, so you can eat the lunch you packed. The steepest part of the trail is ahead. You'll need a lot of energy to get to the top of the mountain! That energy will come from food.

Vocabulary
- cellular respiration
- fermentation

Skills
- ↻ Reading: Summarize
- △ Inquiry: Control Variables

What Is Cellular Respiration?
After you eat a meal, your body breaks down the food and releases the sugars in the food. The most common sugar in foods is glucose ($C_6H_{12}O_6$). **Cellular respiration** is the process by which cells obtain energy from glucose. 🗝 **During cellular respiration, cells break down glucose and other molecules from food in the presence of oxygen, releasing energy.** Living things need a constant supply of energy. The cells of living things carry out cellular respiration continuously.

Storing and Releasing Energy
Imagine you have money in a savings account. If you want to buy something, you withdraw some money. Your body stores and uses energy in a similar way, as shown in **Figure 1.** When you eat a meal, you add to your body's energy savings account by storing glucose. When cells need energy, they "withdraw" it by breaking down glucose through cellular respiration.

Breathing and Respiration
You may have already heard of the word *respiration*. It can mean "breathing"—or moving air in and out of your lungs. Breathing brings oxygen into your lungs, which is then carried to cells for cellular respiration. Breathing also removes the waste products of cellular respiration from your body.

FIGURE 1 ·······························
Getting Energy
Your body runs on the energy it gets from food.

✎ **Complete each task.**

1. **Infer** Color in the last three energy scales to show how the hiker's energy changes.

2. **CHALLENGE** How do you think the hiker's breathing rate changes as she climbs?

_____

_____

_____

| Distance to top 10 km | Distance to top 6 km | | Welcome to the top |

| Low — Energy Scale — High | Low — High | Low — High | Low — High |

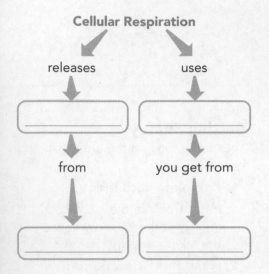

The Two Stages of Cellular Respiration Like photosynthesis, cellular respiration is a two-stage process. See **Figure 2.** The first stage occurs in the cytoplasm of a cell. There, molecules of glucose are broken down into smaller molecules. Oxygen is not involved in this stage, and only a small amount of energy is released.

The second stage takes place in the mitochondria. There, the small molecules are broken down even more. This change requires oxygen and releases a great deal of energy that the cell can use for all its activities. No wonder mitochondria are sometimes called the "powerhouses" of the cell!

The Cellular Respiration Equation Although respiration occurs in a series of complex steps, the overall process can be summarized in the following equation:

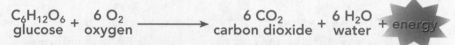

$$\underset{\text{glucose}}{C_6H_{12}O_6} + \underset{\text{oxygen}}{6\,O_2} \longrightarrow \underset{\text{carbon dioxide}}{6\,CO_2} + \underset{\text{water}}{6\,H_2O} + \text{energy}$$

Notice that the raw materials for cellular respiration are glucose and oxygen. Animals get glucose from the foods they consume. Plants and other organisms that carry out photosynthesis are able to produce their own glucose. The oxygen needed for cellular respiration is in the air or water surrounding the organism.

FIGURE 2 ⋯⋯⋯⋯⋯⋯⋯⋯⋯⋯⋯⋯⋯⋯⋯⋯⋯⋯⋯⋯⋯⋯⋯⋯

> INTERACTIVE ART **Releasing Energy**
Cellular respiration takes place in two stages.

Identify Fill in the missing terms in the spaces provided.

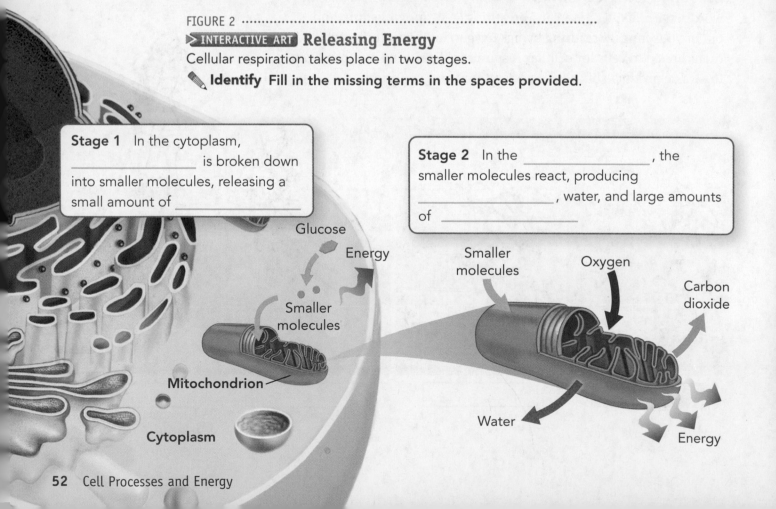

Stage 1 In the cytoplasm, _____ is broken down into smaller molecules, releasing a small amount of _____

Glucose

Energy

Smaller molecules

Mitochondrion

Cytoplasm

Stage 2 In the _____, the smaller molecules react, producing _____, water, and large amounts of _____

Smaller molecules

Oxygen

Carbon dioxide

Water

Energy

Comparing Two Energy Processes

If you think the equation for cellular respiration is the opposite of the one for photosynthesis, you're right! Photosynthesis and cellular respiration can be thought of as opposite processes. Together, these two processes form a cycle that keeps the levels of oxygen and carbon dioxide fairly constant in Earth's atmosphere. As you can see from **Figure 3,** living things cycle both gases over and over again. The energy released through cellular respiration is used or lost as heat.

FIGURE 3 ·······························
Opposite Processes
Producers carry out photosynthesis, but producers and consumers both carry out cellular respiration.

✎ **Name** Use the word bank to fill in the missing terms. Words can be used more than once.

Word Bank	
Oxygen	Energy
Carbon dioxide	Glucose
Water	

Photosynthesis

+

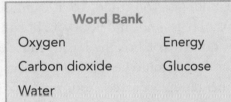

+

Cellular Respiration

Lab zone Do the Lab Investigation
Exhaling Carbon Dioxide.

🔑 Assess Your Understanding

1a. Interpret Diagrams Look at **Figure 2** on the facing page. How does Stage 2 of cellular respiration benefit a cell?

_____

_____

_____

b. Relate Cause and Effect Why does cellular respiration add carbon dioxide to the atmosphere, but photosynthesis does not?

_____

_____

_____

got it? ···

○ **I get it!** Now I know that during cellular respiration, cells _____

_____

○ **I need extra help with** _____

Go to MY SCIENCE ⬤ COACH online for help with this subject.

What Happens During Fermentation?

Some organisms can live in the presence or absence of oxygen. If not enough oxygen is present to carry out cellular respiration, these organisms switch to another process. **Fermentation** is an energy-releasing process that does not require oxygen. 🔑 **During fermentation, cells release energy from food without using oxygen.** One drawback to fermentation is that it releases far less energy than cellular respiration does.

Alcoholic Fermentation Did you know that when you eat a slice of bread, you are eating a product of fermentation? Alcoholic fermentation occurs in yeast and other single-celled organisms. This type of fermentation produces alcohol, carbon dioxide, and a small amount of energy. These products are important to bakers and brewers. Carbon dioxide produced by yeast creates gas pockets in bread dough, causing it to rise. Carbon dioxide is also the source of bubbles in alcoholic drinks such as beer and sparkling wine.

Lactic Acid Fermentation Think of a time when you ran as fast and as long as you could. Your leg muscles were pushing hard against the ground, and you were breathing quickly. But, no matter how quickly you breathed, your muscle cells used up the oxygen faster than it could be replaced. Because your cells lacked oxygen, fermentation occurred. Your muscle cells got energy, but they did so by breaking down glucose without using oxygen. One product of this type of fermentation is a compound known as lactic acid. When lactic acid builds up, you may feel a painful burning sensation in your muscles. Lactic acid was once thought to be the cause of muscle soreness. Scientists have learned that lactic acid is gone from muscles shortly after exercising and is not responsible for the soreness you feel in the days after you exercise. Instead, the soreness is likely caused by microscopic damage to muscles that occurred during the exercise.

apply it!

A ball of bread dough mixed with yeast is left in a bowl at room temperature. As time passes, the dough increases in size.

❶ Compare and Contrast How does fermentation that causes dough to rise differ from fermentation in muscles?

_____

_____

_____

_____

_____

❷ Control Variables How would you show that yeast was responsible for making the dough rise?

_____

_____

_____

_____

_____

_____

EXPLORE THE BIG ?

Energy for Life

How do living things get energy?

FIGURE 4 ······························

> ART IN MOTION Energy processes in living things include photosynthesis, cellular respiration, and fermentation.

✎ **Review** Circle the correct answers and complete the sentences in the spaces provided.

Producers
Plant cells capture energy by way of (photosynthesis/fermentation/cellular respiration).

Plants are autotrophs because

_____

_____

Plant cells release energy for cell function by way of (photosynthesis/fermentation/cellular respiration).

Plants get this energy when oxygen reacts with

_____

_____

Consumers
A runner on an easy jog through the woods gets energy by way of (photosynthesis/fermentation/cellular respiration).

The runner is a heterotroph because she gets energy from

_____

If the runner makes a long, fast push to the finish, her muscle cells may get energy by way of (photosynthesis/fermentation/cellular respiration).

This process releases less energy and _____

_____

Lab® zone Do the Quick Lab Observing Fermentation.

🔑 Assess Your Understanding

2a. Develop Hypotheses When a race ends, why do you think runners continue to breathe quickly and deeply for a few minutes?

_____

_____

b. ANSWER THE BIG ? How do living things get energy?

_____

_____

_____

_____

_____

got it?

○ **I get it!** Now I know fermentation is a way for cells to _____

_____

_____

_____

○ **I need extra help with** _____

_____

Go to my science ⑤ coach *online for help with this subject.*

3 Cell Division

🗝 **What Are the Functions of Cell Division?**

🗝 **What Happens During the Cell Cycle?**

my planet Diary

Cycling On

How long do you think it takes a cell to grow and reproduce, that is, to complete one cell cycle? The answer depends on the type of cell and the organism. Some cells, such as the frog egg cells shown here, divide every 30 minutes, and others take as long as a year! The table below compares the length of different cell cycles.

Comparing Cell Cycles			
Frog Egg Cells	**Yeast Cells**	**Fruit Fly Wing Cells**	**Human Liver Cells**
30 minutes	90 minutes	9–10 hours	Over 1 year

SCIENCE STATS

Interpret Data Use the table to help you answer the following questions.

1. Which type of cell completes a cell cycle fastest?

_____

2. With each cell cycle, two cells form from one cell. In three hours, how many cells could form from one frog egg cell?

_____

▷ **PLANET DIARY** Go to **Planet Diary** to learn more about cell division.

Lab ® Do the Inquiry Warm-Up *What*
zone *Are the Yeast Cells Doing?*

What Are the Functions of Cell Division?

How do tiny frog eggs become big frogs? Cell division allows organisms to grow larger. One cell splits into two, two into four, and so on, until a single cell becomes a multicellular organism.

How does a broken bone heal? Cell division produces new healthy bone cells that replace the damaged cells. Similarly, cell division can replace aging cells and those that die from disease.

Vocabulary

- cell cycle
- interphase
- replication
- chromosome
- mitosis
- cytokinesis

Skills

- ⟳ Reading: Ask Questions
- △ Inquiry: Interpret Data

Growth and repair are two functions of cell division. A third function is reproduction. Some organisms reproduce simply through cell division. Many single-celled organisms, such as amoebas, reproduce this way. Other organisms can reproduce when cell division leads to the growth of new structures. For example, a cactus can grow new stems and roots. These structures can then break away from the parent plant and become a separate plant.

Most organisms reproduce when specialized cells from two different parents combine, forming a new cell. This cell then undergoes many divisions and grows into a new organism.

Cell division has more than one function in living things, as shown in **Figure 1**. ⟞ **Cell division allows organisms to grow, repair damaged structures, and reproduce.**

FIGURE 1 ·····················

Cell Division

Each photo represents at least one function of cell division.

✏ **Answer these questions.**

1. **Identify** Label each photo as
   (A) growth,
   (B) repair, or
   (C) reproduction.

2. **CHALLENGE** Which photo(s) represents more than one function and what are they?

_____

_____

 Do the Quick Lab
Observing Mitosis.

⟞ Assess Your Understanding

got it? ···

○ **I get it!** Now I know the functions of cell division are _____

○ **I need extra help with** _____

Go to **MY SCIENCE ⑤ COACH** online for help with this subject.

What Happens During the Cell Cycle?

The regular sequence of growth and division that cells undergo is known as the **cell cycle**. 🔑 **During the cell cycle, a cell grows, prepares for division, and divides into two new cells, which are called "daughter cells."** Each of the daughter cells then begins the cell cycle again. The cell cycle consists of three main stages: interphase, mitosis, and cytokinesis.

Stage 1: Interphase

The first stage of the cell cycle is **interphase.** This stage is the period before cell division. During interphase, the cell grows, makes a copy of its DNA, and prepares to divide into two cells.

Growing Early during interphase, a cell grows to its full size and produces the organelles it needs. For example, plant cells make more chloroplasts. And all cells make more ribosomes and mitochondria. Cells also make more enzymes, substances that speed up chemical reactions in living things.

Copying DNA Next, the cell makes an exact copy of the DNA in its nucleus in a process called **replication.** You may know that DNA holds all the information that a cell needs to carry out its functions. Within the nucleus, DNA and proteins form threadlike structures called **chromosomes.** At the end of replication, the cell contains two identical sets of chromosomes.

Preparing for Division Once the DNA has replicated, preparation for cell division begins. The cell produces structures that will help it to divide into two new cells. In animal cells, but not plant cells, a pair of centrioles is duplicated. You can see the centrioles in the cell in **Figure 2.** At the end of interphase, the cell is ready to divide.

FIGURE 2 ·······················

Interphase: Preparing to Divide

The changes in a cell during interphase prepare the cell for mitosis.

✏️ **List Make a list of the events that occur during interphase.**

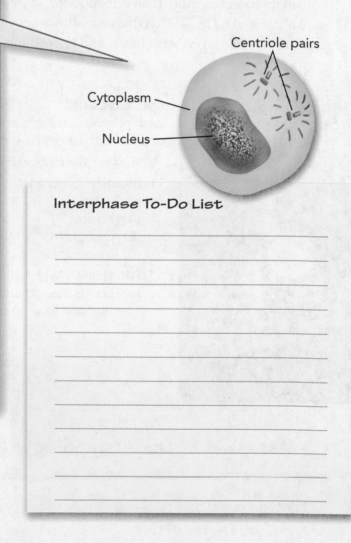

Centriole pairs

Cytoplasm

Nucleus

Interphase To-Do List

apply it!

When one cell splits in half during cell division, the result is two new cells. Each of those two cells can divide into two more, and so on.

1 Calculate How many cell divisions would it take to produce at least 1,000 cells from one cell?

_____

2 Describe What happens to the number of cells after each division?

_____

3 [CHALLENGE] Do you think all human cells divide at the same rate throughout life? Justify your answer.

_____

_____

_____

Stage 2: Mitosis

Once interphase ends, the second stage of the cell cycle begins. During **mitosis** (my TOH sis), the cell's nucleus divides into two new nuclei and one set of DNA is distributed into each daughter cell.

Scientists divide mitosis into four parts, or phases: prophase, metaphase, anaphase, and telophase. During prophase, the chromosomes condense into shapes that can be seen under a microscope. In **Figure 3** you can see that a chromosome consists of two rod-like parts, called chromatids. Each chromatid is an exact copy of the other, containing identical DNA. A structure known as a centromere holds the chromatids together until they move apart later in mitosis. One copy of each chromatid will move into each daughter cell during the final phases of mitosis. When the chromatids separate they are called chromosomes again. Each cell then has a complete copy of DNA. **Figure 4** on the next page summarizes the events of mitosis.

FIGURE 3 ·······························

Mitosis: Prophase

Mitosis begins with prophase, which involves further changes to the cell.

✎ **Compare and Contrast** How does prophase look different from interphase?

_____

_____

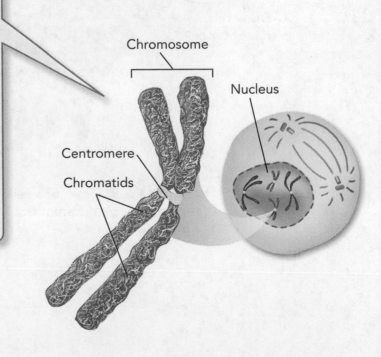

Chromosome

Nucleus

Centromere

Chromatids

FIGURE 4 ·······················

> INTERACTIVE ART **The Cell Cycle**

Cells undergo an orderly sequence of events as they grow and divide. The photographs show cells of a developing whitefish.

✎ **Interpret Diagrams** Answer the questions and draw the missing parts of the stages in the spaces provided.

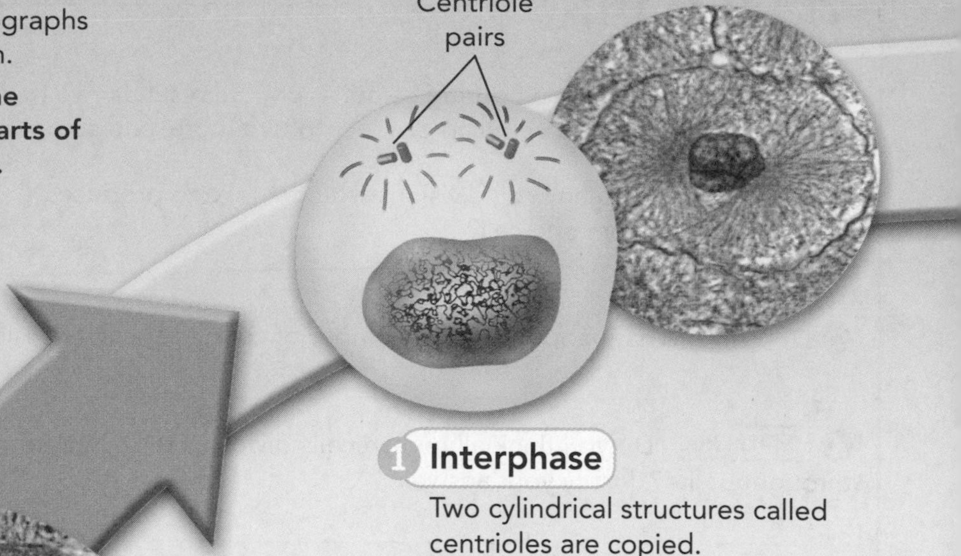

Centriole pairs

1 Interphase

Two cylindrical structures called centrioles are copied.
Identify two other changes that happen in interphase.

_____

_____

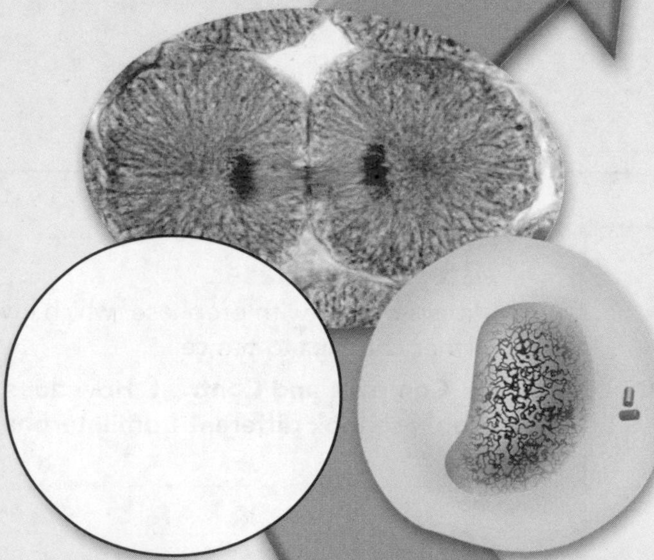

3 Cytokinesis

Cytokinesis begins during mitosis. As cytokinesis continues, the cell splits into two daughter cells. Each daughter cell ends up with an identical set of chromosomes and about half the organelles of the parent cell.

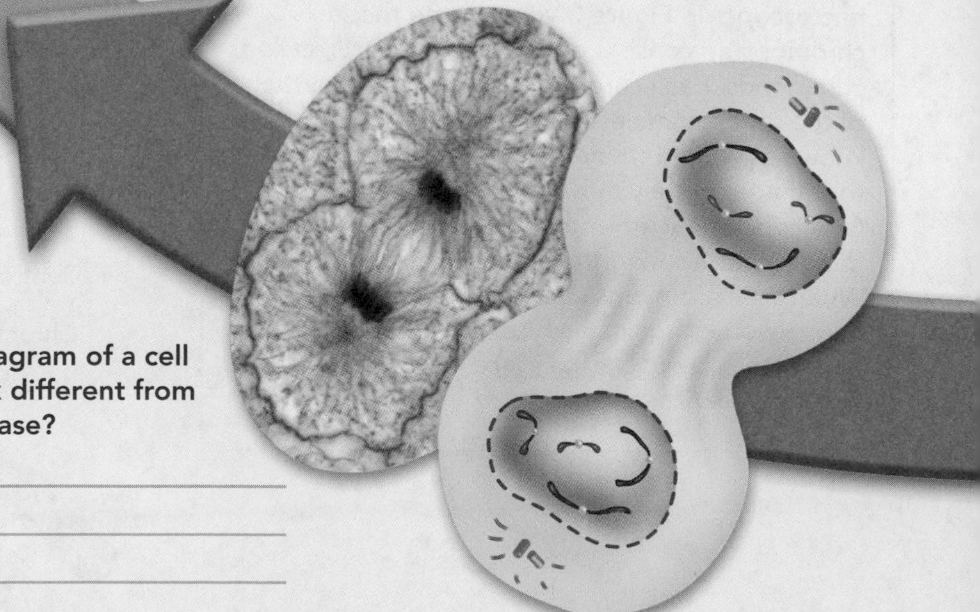

Draw this daughter cell.

Telophase
How does the diagram of a cell in telophase look different from the one in anaphase?

_____

_____

_____

Spindle fiber

Centromere

Chromatids

② Mitosis

Prophase
Chromosomes in the nucleus condense. The pairs of centrioles move to opposite sides of the nucleus. Spindle fibers form a bridge between the ends of the cell. The nuclear envelope breaks down.

Metaphase
Each chromosome attaches to a spindle fiber at its centromere. **What is missing from the cell? What happened to the chromosomes?**

_____

_____

_____

Anaphase
The centromere of each chromosome splits, pulling the chromatids apart. Each chromatid is now called a chromosome. These chromosomes are drawn by their spindle fibers to opposite ends of the cell. The cell stretches out.
Draw the missing structures.

Stage 3: Cytokinesis

The final stage of the cell cycle, which is called **cytokinesis** (sy toh kih NEE sis), completes the process of cell division. During cytokinesis, the cytoplasm divides. The structures are then distributed into each of the two new cells. Cytokinesis usually starts at about the same time as telophase. When cytokinesis is complete, each daughter cell has the same number of chromosomes as the parent cell. At the end of cytokinesis, each cell enters interphase, and the cycle begins again.

Cytokinesis in Animal Cells During cytokinesis in animal cells, the cell membrane squeezes together around the middle of the cell, as shown here. The cytoplasm pinches into two cells. Each daughter cell gets about half of the organelles of the parent cell.

Cytokinesis in Plant Cells Cytokinesis is somewhat different in plant cells. A plant cell's rigid cell wall cannot squeeze together in the same way that a cell membrane can. Instead, a structure called a cell plate forms across the middle of the cell, as shown in **Figure 5.** The cell plate begins to form new cell membranes between the two daughter cells. New cell walls then form around the cell membranes.

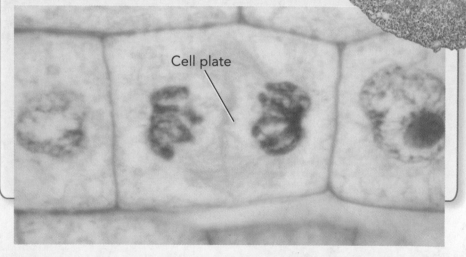

Plant cells ▼　　　　　　**Animal cells ▶**

Cell plate

FIGURE 5 ···

Cytokinesis
Both plant and animal cells undergo cytokinesis.

✎ **Compare and Contrast** How does cytokinesis differ in plant and animal cells?

_____

_____

_____

✐ **Ask Questions** Before you read details about cytokinesis, write a question that asks something you would like to learn.

_____

_____

_____

_____

_____

_____

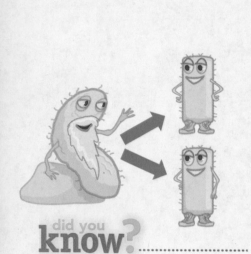

do the math! Analyzing Data

Length of a liver cell cycle

How long does it take for a cell to go through one cell cycle? It depends on the cell. Human liver cells generally reproduce less than once per year. At other times, they can complete one cell cycle in about 22 hours, as shown in the circle graph. Study the graph and answer the following questions.

1 **Read Graphs** What do the three curved arrows outside of the circle represent?

_____

2 **Read Graphs** The wedge representing growth is in which stage of the cell cycle?

_____

3 **Interpret Data** About what percentage of the cell cycle is shown for DNA replication?

_____

4 **Interpret Data** What stage in the cell cycle takes the shortest amount of time? How do you know?

_____

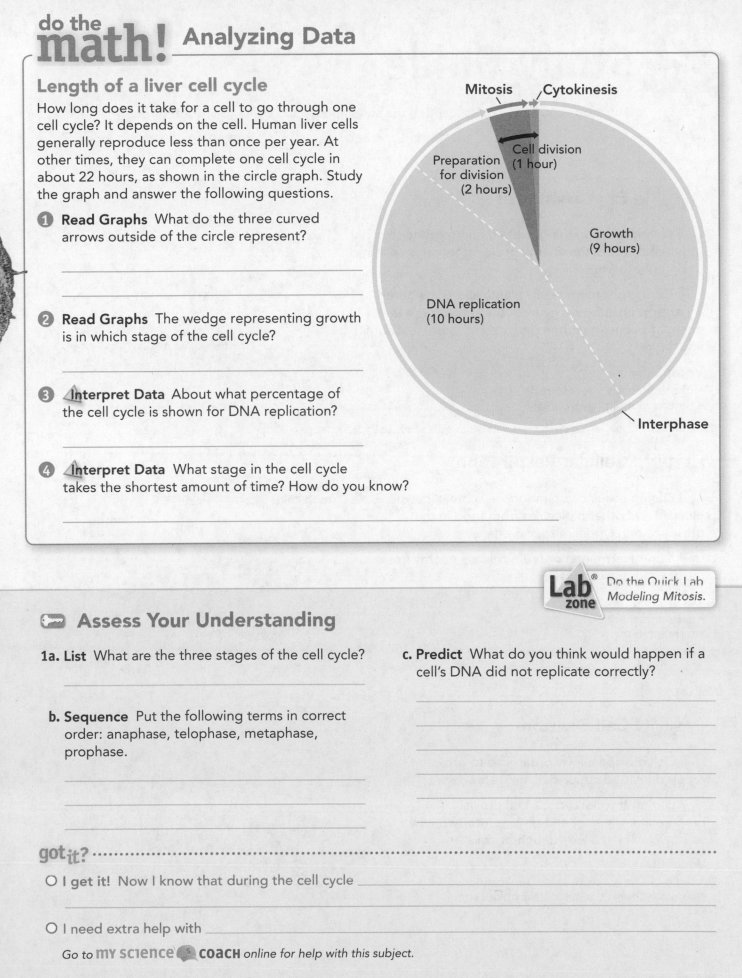

Mitosis Cytokinesis

Cell division
(1 hour)

Preparation
for division
(2 hours)

Growth
(9 hours)

DNA replication
(10 hours)

Interphase

Lab zone Do the Quick Lab
Modeling Mitosis.

Assess Your Understanding

1a. List What are the three stages of the cell cycle?

_____

b. Sequence Put the following terms in correct order: anaphase, telophase, metaphase, prophase.

_____

_____

c. Predict What do you think would happen if a cell's DNA did not replicate correctly?

_____

_____

_____

_____

_____

got it?

○ **I get it!** Now I know that during the cell cycle _____

○ **I need extra help with** _____

Go to **MY SCIENCE COACH** *online for help with this subject.*

2 Study Guide

Autotrophs, such as plants, capture the sun's energy and make their food through
_____, while _____ get energy by eating food.

LESSON 1 Photosynthesis

🔑 Nearly all living things obtain energy either directly or indirectly from the energy of sunlight that is captured during photosynthesis.

🔑 During photosynthesis, plants and some other organisms absorb energy from the sun and use the energy to convert carbon dioxide and water into sugars and oxygen.

Vocabulary
- photosynthesis
- autotroph
- heterotroph
- chlorophyll

Light energy

Cell energy

LESSON 2 Cellular Respiration

🔑 During cellular respiration, cells break down glucose and other molecules from food in the presence of oxygen, releasing energy.

🔑 During fermentation, cells release energy from food without using oxygen.

Vocabulary
- cellular respiration
- fermentation

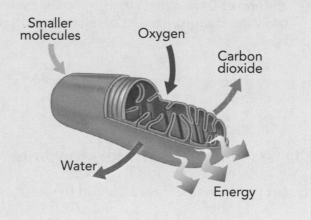

Smaller molecules

Oxygen

Carbon dioxide

Water

Energy

LESSON 3 Cell Division

🔑 Cell division allows organisms to grow, repair damaged structures, and reproduce.

🔑 During the cell cycle, a cell grows, prepares for division, and divides into two new cells, which are called "daughter cells."

Vocabulary
- cell cycle
- interphase
- replication
- chromosome
- mitosis
- cytokinesis

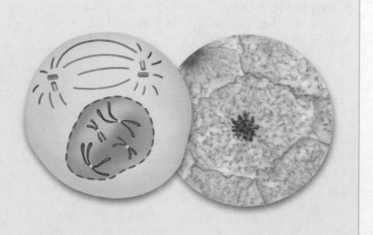

Review and Assessment

LESSON 1 Photosynthesis

1. Which of the following organisms are autotrophs?

  a. fungi   **b.** rabbits

  c. humans   **d.** oak trees

2. Plants are green because of

_____, the main

photosynthetic pigment in chloroplasts.

3. **Interpret Diagrams** Fill in the missing labels in the diagram below.

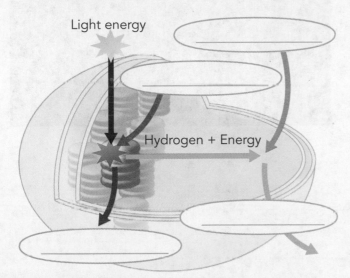

Light energy

Hydrogen + Energy

4. **Predict** Suppose a volcano threw so much ash into the air that it blocked much of the sunlight. How might this event affect the ability of animals to obtain energy to live?

_____

_____

_____

_____

5. **Write About It** How do you get energy? Describe the path of energy from the sun to you, using at least two vocabulary terms you learned in this lesson.

LESSON 2 Cellular Respiration

6. In which organelle does cellular respiration take place?

  a. nucleus   **b.** chloroplast

  c. chlorophyll   **d.** mitochondrion

7. _____ is a process that releases energy in cells without using oxygen.

8. What is one common food that is made with the help of fermentation?

_____

9. **Explain** Write a word equation for cellular respiration in cells.

_____

_____

_____

_____

10. **Summarize** In one or two sentences, summarize what happens during each of the two stages of cellular respiration.

_____

_____

_____

_____

_____

_____

_____

_____

11. **Apply Concepts** How is breathing related to cellular respiration?

_____

_____

_____

_____

_____

65

LESSON 3 **Cell Division**

12. During which phase of the cell cycle does DNA replication occur?

    a. mitosis   **b.** division

    c. interphase   **d.** cytokinesis

13. During _____, a cell's nucleus divides into two new nuclei.

14. Make Generalizations Why is cell division a necessary function of living things?

_____

_____

_____

15. Relate Cause and Effect Why is replication a necessary step in cell division?

_____

_____

_____

16. Sequence Fill in the diagram below with descriptions of each part of the cell cycle.

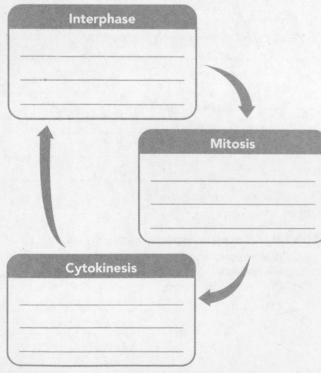

Interphase

Mitosis

Cytokinesis

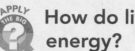
How do living things get energy?

17. All living things need energy. Use the terms *autotroph* and *heterotroph* to describe how each of the organisms in the illustration below obtains energy.

Fox

Grass

Rabbit

_____

_____

_____

_____

_____

_____

_____

_____

_____

_____

_____

_____

Standardized Test Prep

Multiple Choice

Circle the letter of the best answer.

1. Choose the name and cellular process that match the organelle shown below.

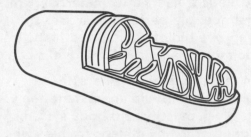

   A chloroplast; cellular respiration
   B mitochondrion; cellular respiration
   C chloroplast; photosynthesis
   D mitochondrion; photosynthesis

2. What is the result of cell division?

   A one daughter cell with double the DNA of the parent cell
   B two daughter cells with double the DNA of the parent cell
   C one daughter cell with half the DNA of the parent cells
   D two daughter cells with the same DNA as the parent cell

3. What is the source of energy used in photosynthesis?

   A glucose
   B sunlight
   C chlorophyll
   D DNA

4. What is one main difference between fermentation and cellular respiration?

   A Fermentation does not require oxygen, while cellular respiration does.
   B Fermentation does not release energy, while cellular respiration does.
   C Fermentation does not occur in animals, while cellular respiration does.
   D Fermentation does not depend on the sun, while cellular respiration does.

5. Which statement best applies to chromosomes?

   A They carry out respiration.
   B They consist mostly of the pigment chlorophyll.
   C Their structure is visible only during interphase.
   D They become visible during the mitosis stage of the cell cycle.

Constructed Response

Copy the table below onto a separate piece of paper. Use your table to answer Question 6.

	Photosynthesis	Cellular Respiration
Raw materials	Water and carbon dioxide	a. _____
Products	b. _____	c. _____
Energy released?	d. _____	e. _____

6. Complete the table to compare and contrast photosynthesis and cellular respiration.

Athletic Trainer

Athletic trainers at commercial gyms help people perform exercises to improve their health. But athletic trainers do more than play at the gym all day.

In reality, athletic trainers are professionals who understand the ways in which muscles and body systems work together. Many athletic trainers who work with elite athletes study biology, anatomy and physiology, or physical education in college. They are often athletes too, and may gain experience as a trainer at a commercial gym.

An athletic trainer must apply scientific discoveries to people's fitness training. For example, have you ever felt a burning sensation in your muscles after a workout? People sometimes think this feeling is caused by a buildup of lactic acid in the muscles. However, scientists think that cells use lactic acid to produce energy when glucose supplies are low. An athletic trainer may suggest that an athlete use endurance training. Endurance training helps train muscles to efficiently burn lactic acid, which improves the athlete's performance.

Athletic trainers work in an exciting and constantly changing field. As scientists learn more about human biology, athletic trainers apply these lessons. They help athletes continue to push the limits of human performance.

Research It Find out about an athletic trainer, and create a profile of that person. Describe where he or she works, why he or she chose this career, and whether the trainer performs any research. Then, identify where in your community an athletic trainer might be able to help people.

WHY HEARTS Don't Get Cancer

You've probably heard of heartburn and heart attacks, and even heartbreak. But have you heard of heart cancer? Heart cancer occurs very rarely, and the tumors usually do not grow the way most cancer tumors do. So why doesn't the heart usually develop cancer? The answer may lie with cell division.

Every moment of your life, cells in your body are dividing. During cell division, a cell's genetic material is copied, and a new cell forms. However, mistakes in how genes are copied can occur during cell division. Occasionally, these mistakes can lead to certain forms of cancer.

In a healthy heart, cell division slows significantly by the time a person reaches adulthood. Cell division is slow and rare in the adult heart because the cells of the heart are active every minute of life. Therefore, heart cells do not mutate very often, so the risk of a mutation causing cancer is very low.

Present It Find out more about rare cancers. Then, create a multimedia presentation that describes why these types of cancer are uncommon. Be sure to cite your sources of information.

This colored transmission electron micrograph (TEM) shows muscle cells from a healthy heart. The hardworking cells in your heart rarely rest long enough for cell division to occur. ▶

WHAT MAKES THIS BABY KOALA DIFFERENT?

THE BIG ?

Why don't offspring always look like their parents?

Even though this young koala, or joey, has two fuzzy ears, a long nose, and a body shaped like its mom's, you can see that the two are different. You might expect a young animal to look exactly like its parents, but think about how varied a litter of kittens or puppies can look. This joey is an albino—an animal that lacks the usual coloring in its eyes, fur, and skin.

△ **Observe** Describe how this joey looks different from its mom.

_____

_____

_____

_____

▶ **UNTAMED SCIENCE** Watch the **Untamed Science** video to learn more about heredity.

Genetics: The Science of Heredity

CHAPTER

3

3 Getting Started

Check Your Understanding

1. **Background** Read the paragraph below and then answer the question.

Kent's cat just had six kittens. All six kittens look different from one another—and from their two parents! Kent knows each kitten is unique because cats reproduce through **sexual reproduction,** not **asexual reproduction.** Before long, the kittens will grow bigger and bigger as their cells divide through **mitosis.**

- In what way are the two daughter cells that form by mitosis and cell division identical?

> **Sexual reproduction** involves two parents and combines their genetic material to produce a new organism that differs from both parents.

> **Asexual reproduction** involves only one parent and produces offspring that are identical to the parent.

During **mitosis,** a cell's nucleus divides into two new nuclei, and one copy of DNA is distributed into each daughter cell.

> **MY READING WEB** If you had trouble completing the question above, visit **My Reading Web** and type in *Genetics: The Science of Heredity*.

Vocabulary Skill

Suffixes A suffix is a word part that is added to the end of a word to change its meaning. For example, the suffix *-tion* means "process of." If you add the suffix *-tion* to the verb *fertilize*, you get the noun *fertilization*. *Fertilization* means "the process of fertilizing." The table below lists some other common suffixes and their meanings.

Suffix	Meaning	Example
-ive	performing a particular action	recessive allele, *n.* an allele that is masked when a dominant allele is present
-ance or *-ant*	state, condition of	codominance, *n.* occurs when both alleles are expressed equally

2. **Quick Check** Fill in the blank with the correct suffix.

- A domin_____ allele can mask a recessive allele.

trait

Tall

Short

phenotype

incomplete dominance

meiosis

Chapter Preview

LESSON 1
- heredity
- trait
- genetics
- fertilization
- purebred
- gene
- allele
- dominant allele
- recessive allele
- hybrid

🔁 **Identify Supporting Evidence**
△ **Predict**

LESSON 2
- probability
- Punnett square
- phenotype
- genotype
- homozygous
- heterozygous

🔁 **Identify the Main Idea**
△ **Draw Conclusions**

LESSON 3
- incomplete dominance
- codomInance
- multiple alleles
- polygenic inheritance

🔁 **Compare and Contrast**
△ **Interpret Data**

LESSON 4
- meiosis

🔁 **Relate Cause and Effect**
△ **Design Experiments**

▸ **VOCAB FLASH CARDS** For extra help with vocabulary, visit **Vocab Flash Cards** and type in *Genetics: The Science of Heredity.*

What Is Heredity?

UNLOCK THE BIG

🔑 **What Did Mendel Observe?**

🔑 **How Do Alleles Affect Inheritance?**

my planet diary

Almost Forgotten

When scientists make great discoveries, sometimes their work is praised, criticized, or even forgotten. Gregor Mendel was almost forgotten. He spent eight years studying pea plants, and he discovered patterns in the way characteristics pass from one generation to the next. For almost 40 years, people overlooked Mendel's work. When it was finally rediscovered, it unlocked the key to understanding heredity.

BIOGRAPHY

Communicate Discuss the question below with a partner. Then write your answer.

Did you ever rediscover something of yours that you had forgotten? How did you react?

_____

_____

_____

▷ **PLANET DIARY** Go to **Planet Diary** to learn more about heredity.

Lab zone Do the Inquiry Warm-Up *What Does the Father Look Like?*

What Did Mendel Observe?

In the mid-nineteenth century, a priest named Gregor Mendel tended a garden in a central European monastery. Mendel's experiments in that peaceful garden would one day transform the study of heredity. **Heredity** is the passing of physical characteristics from parents to offspring.

Mendel wondered why different pea plants had different characteristics. Some pea plants grew tall, while others were short. Some plants produced green seeds, while others had yellow seeds. Each specific characteristic, such as stem height or seed color, is called a **trait.** Mendel observed that the forms of the pea plants' traits were often similar to those of their parents. Sometimes, however, the forms differed.

Vocabulary

- heredity • trait • genetics • fertilization
- purebred • gene • allele • dominant allele
- recessive allele • hybrid

Skills

- Reading: Identify Supporting Evidence
- Inquiry: Predict

Mendel's Experiments Mendel experimented with thousands of pea plants. Today, Mendel's discoveries form the foundation of **genetics,** the scientific study of heredity. **Figure 1** shows the parts of a pea plant's flower. The pistil produces female sex cells, or eggs. The stamens produce pollen, which contains the male sex cells, or sperm. A new organism begins to form when egg and sperm cells join in the process called **fertilization.** Before fertilization can happen in pea plants, pollen must reach the pistil of a pea flower. This process is called pollination.

Pea plants are usually self-pollinating. In self-pollination, pollen from a flower lands on the pistil of the same flower. Mendel developed a method by which he cross-pollinated, or "crossed," pea plants. **Figure 1** shows his method.

Mendel decided to cross plants that had contrasting forms of a trait—for example, tall plants and short plants. He started with purebred plants. A **purebred** organism is the offspring of many generations that have the same form of a trait. For example, purebred tall pea plants always come from tall parent plants.

FIGURE 1 ···

Crossing Pea Plants

Mendel devised a way to cross-pollinate pea plants.

✎ Use the diagram to answer the questions about Mendel's procedure.

1. Observe How does flower B differ from flower A?

_____

_____

2. Infer Describe how Mendel cross-pollinated pea plants.

_____

_____

_____

_____

B

A

Pistil

Stamens

Pollen

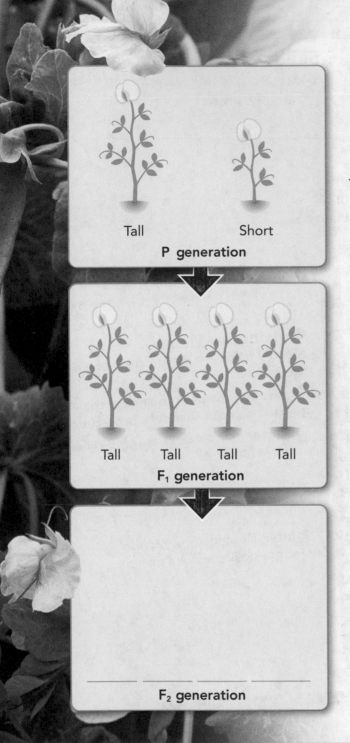

Tall   Short
P generation

Tall   Tall   Tall   Tall
F₁ generation

_____ _____ _____ _____
F₂ generation

The F₁ and F₂ Offspring

Mendel crossed purebred tall plants with purebred short plants. Today, scientists call these plants the parental, or P, generation. The resulting offspring are the first filial (FIL ee ul), or F₁, generation. The word *filial* comes from *filia* and *filius*, the Latin words for "daughter" and "son."

Look at **Figure 2** to see the surprise Mendel found in the F₁ generation. All the offspring were tall. The shortness trait seemed to have disappeared!

When these plants were full-grown, Mendel allowed them to self-pollinate. The F₂ (second filial) generation that followed surprised Mendel even more. He counted the plants of the F₂ generation. About three fourths were tall, while one fourth were short.

Experiments With Other Traits

Mendel repeated his experiments, studying other pea-plant traits, such as flower color and seed shape. 🔑 **In all of his crosses, Mendel found that only one form of the trait appeared in the F₁ generation. However, in the F₂ generation, the "lost" form of the trait always reappeared in about one fourth of the plants.**

FIGURE 2 ···
Results of a Cross
In Mendel's crosses, some forms of a trait were hidden in one generation but reappeared in the next.

✏️ **Interpret Diagrams** Draw and label the offspring in the F₂ generation.

 Do the Quick Lab *Observing Pistils and Stamens.*

🔑 Assess Your Understanding

1a. Define What happens during fertilization?

_____

_____

b. Compare and Contrast In Mendel's cross for stem height, how did the plants in the F₂ generations differ from the F₁ plants?

_____

How Do Alleles Affect Inheritance?

Mendel reached several conclusions from his experimental results. He reasoned that individual factors, or sets of genetic "information," must control the inheritance of traits in peas. The factors that control each trait exist in pairs. The female parent contributes one factor, while the male parent contributes the other factor. Finally, one factor in a pair can mask, or hide, the other factor. The tallness factor, for example, masked the shortness factor.

Genes and Alleles Today, scientists use the word **gene** to describe the factors that control a trait. **Alleles** (uh LEELZ) are the different forms of a gene. The gene that controls stem height in peas has one allele for tall stems and one allele for short stems. Each pea plant inherits two alleles—one from the egg and the other from the sperm. A plant may inherit two alleles for tall stems, two alleles for short stems, or one of each.

🔑 **An organism's traits are controlled by the alleles it inherits from its parents. Some alleles are dominant, while other alleles are recessive.** A **dominant allele** is one whose trait always shows up in the organism when the allele is present. A **recessive allele,** on the other hand, is hidden whenever the dominant allele is present. **Figure 3** shows dominant and recessive alleles of the traits in Mendel's crosses.

FIGURE 3 ···
Alleles in Pea Plants
Mendel studied the inheritance of seven different traits in pea plants.

✏️ **Use the table to answer the questions.**

1. **Draw Conclusions** Circle the picture of each dominant form of the trait in the P generation.

2. **Predict** Under what conditions would the recessive form of one of these traits reappear?

_____

_____

Inheritance of Pea Plants Studied by Mendel

	Seed Shape	Seed Color	Pod Shape	Pod Color	Flower Color	Flower Position	Stem Height
P	Wrinkled X Round	Yellow X Green	Pinched X Smooth	Green X Yellow	Purple X White	Tip of stem X Side of stem	Tall X Short
F₁	Round	Yellow	Smooth	Green	Purple	Side of stem	Tall

FIGURE 4 ·······························

VIRTUAL LAB **Dominant and Recessive Alleles**

Symbols serve as a shorthand way to identify alleles.

✎ **Complete each row of the diagram.**

1. **Identify** Fill in the missing allele symbols and descriptions.

2. **Summarize** Use the word bank to complete the statements. (Terms will be used more than once.)

3. **Relate Cause and Effect** Draw the two possible ways the F₂ offspring could look.

Alleles in Mendel's Crosses In Mendel's cross for stem height, the purebred tall plants in the P generation had two alleles for tall stems. The purebred short plants had two alleles for short stems. But each F_1 plant inherited one allele for tall stems and one allele for short stems. The F_1 plants are called hybrids. A **hybrid** (HY brid) organism has two different alleles for a trait. All the F_1 plants are tall because the dominant allele for tall stems masks the recessive allele for short stems.

Symbols for Alleles Geneticists, scientists who study genetics, often use letters to represent alleles. A dominant allele is symbolized by a capital letter. A recessive allele is symbolized by the lowercase version of the same letter. For example, T stands for the allele for tall stems, and t stands for the allele for short stems. When a plant has two dominant alleles for tall stems, its alleles are written as TT. When a plant has two recessive alleles for short stems, its alleles are written as tt. These plants are the P generation shown in **Figure 4**. Think about the symbols that would be used for F_1 plants that all inherit one allele for tall stems and one for short stems.

P

Tall
T____
Purebred

Short
t____
Purebred

Word Bank
dominant
recessive

F₁

____
T____
____

All plants inherit one _____ allele and one _____ allele. These plants are all tall.

F₂

Plants may inherit two _____ alleles. These plants are tall.

Plants may inherit one _____ allele and one _____ allele. These plants are tall.

Plants may inherit two _____ alleles. These plants are short.

apply it!

In fruit flies, long wings are dominant over short wings. A scientist crossed a purebred long-winged fruit fly with a purebred short-winged fruit fly.

1 If *W* stands for long wings, write the symbols for the alleles of each parent fly.

_____

2 ◢Predict What will be the wing length of the F_1 offspring?

_____

3 ◢Predict If the scientist crosses a hybrid male F_1 fruit fly with a hybrid F_1 female, what will their offspring probably be like?

_____

_____

_____

Significance of Mendel's Contribution
Mendel's discovery of genes and alleles eventually changed scientists' ideas about heredity. Before Mendel, most people thought that the traits of an individual organism were simply a blend of the parents' characteristics. Mendel showed that offspring traits are determined by individual, separate alleles inherited from each parent. Unfortunately, the value of Mendel's discovery was not known during his lifetime. But when scientists in the early 1900s rediscovered Mendel's work, they quickly realized its importance. Because of his work, Mendel is often called the Father of Genetics.

◢ **Identify Supporting Evidence** What evidence showed Mendel that traits are determined by separate alleles?

_____

_____

_____

_____

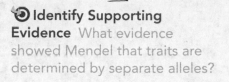 Do the Quick Lab *Inferring the Parent Generation.*

🗝 Assess Your Understanding

2a. Relate Cause and Effect Why is a pea plant that is a hybrid for stem height tall?

_____

_____

_____

b. [CHALLENGE] Can a short pea plant be a hybrid for the trait of stem height? Why or why not?

_____

_____

_____

got it?

○ **I get it!** Now I know that an organism's traits are controlled by _____

_____

_____

_____

○ **I need extra help with** _____

Go to **my science coach** online for help with this subject.

Probability and Heredity

UNLOCK THE BIG

🔑 **How Is Probability Related to Inheritance?**

🔑 **What Are Phenotype and Genotype?**

MY PLANET DiARY

Storm on the Way?

Have you ever watched a hurricane form? Weather forecasters at the National Hurricane Center (NHC) in Miami, Florida, have. From May 15 to November 30, the NHC Operations Area is staffed around the clock with forecasters. They study data from aircraft, ocean buoys, and satellites to develop computer models. These models predict the probable paths of a storm. If the probability of a certain path is high, the NHC issues a warning that helps save lives and reduce damage.

FIELD TRIP

Communicate Answer the question below. Then discuss your answer with a partner.

Local weather forecasters often talk about the percent chance for rainfall. What do you think they mean?

_____

_____

_____

_____

_____

▶ **PLANET DIARY** Go to **Planet Diary** to learn more about probability and weather.

Lab® Do the Inquiry Warm-Up
zone *What's the Chance?*

How Is Probability Related to Inheritance?

Before the start of a football game, the team captains stand with the referee for a coin toss. The team that wins the toss chooses whether to kick or receive the ball. As the referee tosses the coin, the visiting team captain calls "heads." What is the chance that the visitors will win the toss? To answer this question, you need to understand the principles of probability.

Vocabulary
- probability
- phenotype
- homozygous
- Punnett square
- genotype
- heterozygous

Skills
- Reading: Identify the Main Idea
- Inquiry: Draw Conclusions

What Is Probability? Each time you toss a coin, there are two possible ways it can land—heads up or tails up. **Probability** is a number that describes how likely it is that an event will occur. In mathematical terms, you can say the probability that a tossed coin will land heads up is 1 in 2. There's also a 1 in 2 probability that the coin will land tails up. A 1 in 2 probability is expressed as the fraction $\frac{1}{2}$ or as 50 percent.

The laws of probability predict what is *likely* to occur, not what *will* occur. If you toss a coin 20 times, you may expect it to land heads up 10 times and tails up 10 times. But you may get 11 heads and 9 tails, or 8 heads and 12 tails. The more tosses you make, the closer your actual results will be to those predicted by probability.

Do you think the result of one toss affects the result of the next toss? Not at all. Each event occurs independently. Suppose you toss a coin five times and it lands heads up each time. What is the probability that it will land heads up on the next toss? If you said the probability is still 1 in 2, or 50 percent, you're right. The results of the first five tosses do not affect the result of the sixth toss.

do the math!

Percentage

One way to express probability is as a percentage. A percentage is a number compared to 100. For example, 50 percent, or 50%, means 50 out of 100. Suppose you want to calculate percentage from the results of a series of basketball free throws in which 3 out of 5 free throws go through the hoop.

STEP 1 Write the comparison as a fraction.

$$3 \text{ out of } 5 = \frac{3}{5}$$

STEP 2 Calculate the number value of the fraction.

$$3 \div 5 = 0.6$$

STEP 3 Multiply this number by 100%.

$$0.6 \times 100\% = 60\%$$

.... Practice! ....

1 Calculate Suppose 5 out of 25 free throws go through the hoop. Write this result as a fraction.

_____

2 Calculate Express your answer in Question 1 as a percentage.

_____

_____

_____

Probability and Genetics How is probability related to genetics? Think back to Mendel's experiments. He carefully counted the offspring from every cross. When he crossed two plants that were hybrid for stem height (*Tt*), about three fourths of the F$_2$ plants had tall stems. About one fourth had short stems.

Each time Mendel repeated the cross, he observed similar results. He realized that the principles of probability applied to his work. He found that the probability of a hybrid cross producing a tall plant was 3 in 4. The probability of producing a short plant was 1 in 4. Mendel was the first scientist to recognize that the principles of probability can predict the results of genetic crosses.

Punnett Squares

A tool that can help you grasp how the laws of probability apply to genetics is called a Punnett square. A **Punnett square** is a chart that shows all the possible ways alleles can combine in a genetic cross. Geneticists use Punnett squares to see these combinations and to determine the probability of a particular outcome, or result. ⚷ **In a genetic cross, the combination of alleles that parents can pass to an offspring is based on probability.**

Figure 1 shows how to make a Punnett square. In this case, the cross is between two hybrid pea plants with round seeds (*Rr*). The allele for round seeds (*R*) is dominant over the allele for wrinkled seeds (*r*). Each parent can pass either one allele or the other to an offspring. The boxes in the Punnett square show the possible combinations of alleles that the offspring can inherit.

FIGURE 1 ·······························
▶ **INTERACTIVE ART** **How to Make a Punnett Square**

You can use a Punnett square to find the probabilities of a genetic cross.

✎ **Follow the steps in the figure to fill in the Punnett square.**

1. **Predict** What is the probability that an offspring will have wrinkled seeds?

   _____

2. **Interpret Tables** What is the probability that an offspring will have round seeds? Explain your answer.

   _____

   _____

   _____

1 Start by drawing a box and dividing it into four squares.

2 The male parent's alleles are written along the top of the square. Fill in the female parent's alleles along the left side.

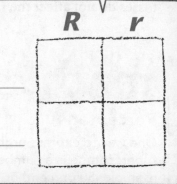

5 The completed square shows all the possible allele combinations the offspring can have.

	R	r
R	**RR**	**Rr**
r	**Rr**	**rr**

4 Copy the male parent's alleles into the boxes beneath them.

	R	r
R	**R___**	**R___**
r	**___ r**	**___ r**

3 Copy the female parent's alleles into the boxes to their right. The first one is done for you.

	R	r
R	**R**	___
r	___	___

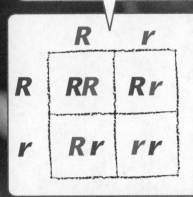

✏️ **Identify the Main Idea** In your own words, describe what a Punnet square shows you about combinations of alleles.

_____

_____

_____

_____

_____

Relating Punnett Squares to Mendel Mendel did not know about alleles. But a Punnett square shows why he got the results he saw in the F₂ generations. Plants with alleles *RR* would have round seeds. So would plants with alleles *Rr*. Only plants with alleles *rr* would have wrinkled seeds.

 Lab zone® Do the Quick Lab *Coin Crosses.*

🗝 **Assess Your Understanding**

1a. Review What is probability?

_____

_____

b. Apply Concepts What is the probability that a cross between a hybrid pea plant with round seeds and one with wrinkled seeds will produce offspring with wrinkled seeds? (Draw a Punnett square on other paper to find the answer.)

_____

got it?

○ **I get it!** Now I know that the combination of

alleles parents can pass to offspring _____

_____

○ **I need extra help with** _____

Go to **MY SCIENCE** 🔊 **COACH** online for help with this subject.

What Are Phenotype and Genotype?

Two terms that geneticists use are **phenotype** (FEE noh typ) and **genotype** (JEE noh typ). **An organism's phenotype is its physical appearance, or visible traits. An organism's genotype is its genetic makeup, or alleles.** In other words, genotype is an organism's alleles. Phenotype is how a trait looks or is expressed.

To compare phenotype and genotype, look at **Figure 2**. The allele for smooth pea pods (*S*) is dominant over the allele for pinched pea pods (*s*). All the plants with at least one *S* allele have the same phenotype. That is, they all produce smooth pods. However, these plants can have two different genotypes—*SS* or *Ss*. If you were to look at the plants with smooth pods, you would not be able to tell the difference between those that have the genotype *SS* and those with the genotype *Ss*. The plants with pinched pods, on the other hand, would all have the same phenotype—pinched pods—as well as the same genotype—*ss*.

Geneticists use two additional terms to describe an organism's genotype. An organism that has two identical alleles for a trait is said to be **homozygous** (hoh moh ZY gus) for that trait. A smooth-pod plant that has the alleles *SS* and a pinched-pod plant with the alleles *ss* are both homozygous. An organism that has two different alleles for a trait is **heterozygous** (het ur oh ZY gus) for that trait. A smooth-pod plant with the alleles *Ss* is heterozygous. Recall that Mendel used the term *hybrid* to describe heterozygous pea plants.

Vocabulary Suffixes The suffix *-ous* means "having." Circle this suffix in the highlighted terms *homozygous* and *heterozygous* in the paragraph at the right. These terms describe the organism as having

_____

_____

_____

FIGURE 2 ·················

Describing Inheritance

An organism's phenotype is its physical appearance. Its genotype is its genetic makeup.

✎ **Based on what you have read, answer these questions.**

1. **Classify** Fill in the missing information in the table.

2. **Interpret Tables** How many genotypes are there for the smooth-pod phenotype?

_____

Phenotypes and Genotypes		
Phenotype	Genotype	Homozygous or Heterozygous
Smooth pods	_____	_____
Smooth pods	_____	_____
Pinched pods	_____	_____

apply it!

Mendel's principles of heredity apply to many other organisms. For example, in guinea pigs, black fur color (*B*) is dominant over white fur color (*b*). Suppose a pair of black guinea pigs produces several litters of pups during their lifetimes. The graph shows the phenotypes of the pups. Write a title for the graph.

❶ Read Graphs How many black pups were produced? How many white pups were produced?

_____

❷ Infer What are the possible genotypes of the offspring?

_____

❸ Draw Conclusions What can you conclude about the genotypes of the parent guinea pigs? Explain your answer.

_____
_____
_____
_____
_____

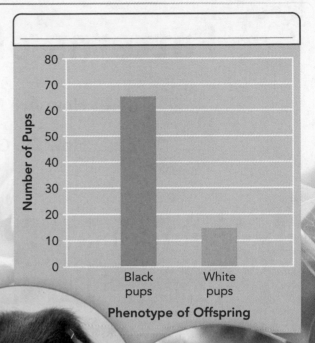

Phenotype of Offspring

Number of Pups / Black pups / White pups

Lab zone ® Do the Lab Investigation *Make the Right Call!*

🔑 Assess Your Understanding

2a. Relate Cause and Effect Explain how two organisms can have the same phenotype but different genotypes.

_____
_____
_____

b. **CHALLENGE** In their lifetimes, two guinea pigs produce 40 black pups and 40 white pups. On a separate paper, make a Punnett square and find the likely genotypes of these parents.

_____

got it?

◯ **I get it!** Now I know that phenotype and genotype are terms that describe _____
_____
_____
_____

◯ **I need extra help with** _____

Go to **my science** **coach** *online for help with this subject.*

Patterns of Inheritance

🔑 **How Are Most Traits Inherited?**

🔑 **How Do Genes and the Environment Interact?**

MY PLANET DIARY

Cold, With a Chance of Males

Is it a male or a female? If you're a red-eared slider turtle, the answer might depend on the temperature! These slider turtles live in the calm, fresh, warm waters of the southeastern United States. For these turtles and some other reptiles, the temperature of the environment determines the sex of their offspring. At 26°C, the eggs of red-eared slider turtles all hatch as males. But at 31°C, the eggs all hatch as females. Only at about 29°C is there a 50% chance of hatching turtles of either sex.

Predict Discuss the question below with a partner. Then write your answer.

What do you think might happen to a population of red-eared slider turtles in a place where the temperature remains near or at 26°C?

_____

_____

_____

_____

▶ **PLANET DIARY** Go to **Planet Diary** to learn more about patterns of inheritance.

Lab zone® Do the Inquiry Warm-Up *Observing Traits.*

How Are Most Traits Inherited?

The traits that Mendel studied are controlled by genes with only two possible alleles. These alleles are either dominant or recessive. Pea flower color is either purple or white. Peas are either yellow or green. Can you imagine if all traits were like this? If people were either short or tall? If cats were either black or yellow?

Studying two-allele traits is a good place to begin learning about genetics. But take a look around at the variety of living things in your surroundings. As you might guess, most traits do not follow such a simple pattern of inheritance. 🔑 **Most traits are the result of complex patterns of inheritance.** Four complex patterns of inheritance are described in this lesson.

Vocabulary

- incomplete dominance
- codominance • multiple alleles
- polygenic inheritance

Skills

➲ Reading: Compare and Contrast
△ Inquiry: Interpret Data

Incomplete Dominance

Some traits result from a pattern of inheritance known as incomplete dominance. **Incomplete dominance** occurs when one allele is only partially dominant. For example, look at **Figure 1.** The flowers shown are called snapdragons. A cross between a plant with red flowers and one with white flowers produces pink offspring.

Snapdragons with alleles *RR* produce a lot of red color in their flowers. It's no surprise that their flowers are red. A plant with two white alleles (*WW*) produces no red color. Its flowers are white. Both types of alleles are written as capital letters because neither is totally dominant. If a plant has alleles *RW*, only enough color is produced to make the flowers just a little red. So they look pink.

Codominance

The chickens in **Figure 1** show a different pattern of inheritance. **Codominance** occurs when both alleles for a gene are expressed equally. In the chickens shown, neither black feathers nor white feathers are dominant. All the offspring of a black hen and a white rooster have both black and white feathers.

Here, F^B stands for the allele for black feathers. F^W stands for the allele for white feathers. The letter *F* tells you the trait is feathers. The superscripts *B* for black and *W* for white tell you the color.

FIGURE 1 ··································

Other Patterns of Inheritance

Many crosses do not follow the patterns Mendel discovered.

✎ **Apply Concepts** Fill in the missing pairs of alleles.

apply it!

An imaginary insect called the blingwing has three alleles for wing color: *R* (red), *B* (blue), and *Y* (yellow).

1 List If an organism can inherit only two alleles for a gene, what are the six possible allele pairs for wing color in blingwings? One answer is given.

RB,

_____

2 ⚠ Interpret Data Suppose wing color results from incomplete dominance. What wing color would each pair of alleles produce? One answer is given.

RB: purple

_____

_____

_____

_____

_____

Multiple Alleles

Some genes have **multiple alleles,** which means that three or more possible alleles determine the trait. Remember that an organism can only inherit two alleles for a gene—one from each parent. Even if there are four, five, or more possible alleles, an individual can only have two. However, more genotypes can occur with multiple alleles than with just two alleles. For example, four alleles control the color of fur in some rabbits. Depending on which two alleles a rabbit inherits, its coat color can range from brownish gray to all white.

Polygenic Inheritance

The traits that Mendel studied were each controlled by a single gene. **Polygenic inheritance** occurs when more than one gene affects a trait. The alleles of the different genes work together to produce these traits.

Polygenic inheritance results in a broad range of phenotypes, like human height or the time it takes for a plant to flower. Imagine a field of sunflowers that were all planted the same day. Some might start to flower after 45 days. Most will flower after around 60 days. The last ones might flower after 75 days. The timing of flowering is a characteristic of polygenic traits.

Do the Quick Lab
Patterns of Inheritance.

🔒 Assess Your Understanding

1a. Describe How are the symbols written for alleles that share incomplete dominance?

_____

b. [CHALLENGE] How is polygenic inheritance different from the patterns described by Mendel?

_____

_____

got it?

○ **I get it!** Now I know that most traits are

produced by _____

_____

○ **I need extra help with** _____

Go to MY SCIENCE ⑤ COACH online for help with this subject.

How Do Genes and the Environment Interact?

You were not born knowing how to skateboard, but maybe you can skateboard now. Many traits are learned, or acquired. Unlike inherited traits, acquired traits are not carried by genes or passed to offspring. Although inherited traits are determined by genes, they also can be affected by factors in the environment. The phenotypes you observe in an organism result both from genes and from interactions of the organism with its environment.

Inherited and Acquired Traits Humans are born with inherited traits, such as vocal cords and tongues that allow for speech. But humans are not born speaking Spanish, or Mandarin, or English. The languages that a person speaks are acquired traits. Do you have a callus on your finger from writing with your pencil? That is an acquired trait. Skills you learn and physical changes that occur, such as calluses and haircuts, are acquired traits. See if you can tell the inherited traits from the acquired traits in **Figure 2.**

FIGURE 2 ·······················

Inherited or Acquired?
Which traits shown are carried in the genes, and which are not?

✏ **Classify** Identify each trait shown as inherited or acquired.

Their heights

Dyed hair color

Fish body color

These hedge shapes

Her freckles

Genes and the Environment Think again about sunflowers. Genes control when the plants flower. But sunlight, temperature, soil nutrients, and water also affect a plant's flowering time. ⊙**Environmental factors can influence the way genes are expressed.** Like sunflowers, you have factors in your environment that can affect how your genes are expressed. For example, you may have inherited the ability to play a musical instrument. But without an opportunity to learn, you may never develop the skill.

Some environmental factors can change an organism's genes. For example, tobacco smoke and other pollutants can affect genes in a person's body cells in a way that may result in lung cancer and other cancers. Still other genetic changes happen by chance.

Changes in body cells cannot be passed to offspring. Only changes in the sex cells—eggs and sperm—can be passed to offspring. Not all genetic changes have negative effects. Genetic change in sex cells is an important source of life's variety.

↺ **Compare and Contrast**
Underline two sentences that tell how changes to genes in body cells differ from changes to genes in egg and sperm cells.

Patterns of Inheritance

EXPLORE THE BIG ?

Why don't offspring always look like their parents?

FIGURE 3

▶ INTERACTIVE ART The traits you see in organisms result from their genes and from interactions of genes with the environment.

✎ **Summarize** Match the terms in the word bank with the examples shown.

Word Bank

Incomplete dominance	Dominant and recessive traits
Environmental factors	Polygenic inheritance
Multiple alleles	Codominance
Acquired traits	

_____
_____

_____
_____

_____
_____

_____
_____

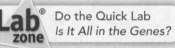
Do the Quick Lab
Is It All in the Genes?

🔑 Assess Your Understanding

2a. Review Only genetic changes in (sex cells/ body cells) can be passed to offspring.

b. Describe Give one example of how environmental factors affect gene expression.

_____
_____
_____

c. ANSWER THE BIG ? Why don't offspring always look like their parents?

_____
_____
_____
_____
_____

got**it?** ....

○ **I get it!** Now I know that the environment can affect _____

_____

○ **I need extra help with** _____

Go to **MY SCIENCE** ⑤ **COACH** online for help with this subject.

Chromosomes and Inheritance

🔑 **How Are Chromosomes, Genes, and Inheritance Related?**

🔑 **What Happens During Meiosis?**

my planeT DiaRY

Chromosome Sleuth

Finding answers about how chromosomes relate to disease is one job of genetic technologists. These scientists analyze chromosomes from cells. The analysis may pinpoint genetic information that can cause disease or other health problems. In their work, genetic technologists use microscopes, computer-imaging photography, and lab skills. They report data that are used in research and in treating patients affected by genetic diseases.

Communicate Answer these questions. Then discuss Question 2 with a partner.

1. Would you like to be a genetic technologist? Why or why not?

_____

_____

_____

_____

2. If you were a genetic technologist, what would you like to research?

_____

_____

_____

_____

▷ **PLANET DIARY** Go to **Planet Diary** to learn more about genetic technologists.

Lab zone® Do the Inquiry Warm-Up *Which Chromosome Is Which?*

Vocabulary
- meiosis

Skills
- Reading: Relate Cause and Effect
- Inquiry: Design Experiments

How Are Chromosomes, Genes, and Inheritance Related?

Mendel's work showed that genes exist. (Remember that he called them "factors.") But scientists in the early twentieth century did not know what structures in cells contained genes. The search for the answer was something like a mystery story. The story could be called "The Clue in the Grasshopper's Cells."

At the start of the 1900s, Walter Sutton, an American geneticist, studied the cells of grasshoppers. He wanted to understand how sex cells (sperm and eggs) form. Sutton focused on how the chromosomes moved within cells during the formation of sperm and eggs. He hypothesized that chromosomes are the key to learning how offspring have traits similar to those of their parents.

apply it!

⚠ **Design Experiments** Different types of organisms have different numbers of chromosomes, and some organisms are easier to study than others. Suppose you are a scientist studying chromosomes and you have to pick an organism from those shown below to do your work. Which one would you pick and why?

_____

_____

_____

_____

_____

did you know?

The organism with the highest known number of chromosomes is a plant in the fern family. The netted adderstongue fern has more than 1,200 chromosomes!

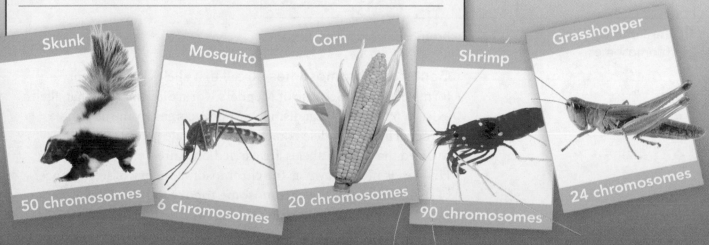

Skunk — 50 chromosomes

Mosquito — 6 chromosomes

Corn — 20 chromosomes

Shrimp — 90 chromosomes

Grasshopper — 24 chromosomes

Chromosomes and Inheritance

Sutton needed evidence to support his hypothesis. Look at **Figure 1** to see how he found this evidence in grasshopper cells. To his surprise, he discovered that grasshopper sex cells have exactly half the number of chromosomes found in grasshopper body cells.

Chromosome Pairs Sutton observed what happened when a sperm cell and an egg cell joined. The fertilized egg that formed had 24 chromosomes. It had the same number of chromosomes as each parent. These 24 chromosomes existed as 12 pairs. One chromosome in each pair came from the male parent. The other chromosome came from the female parent.

FIGURE 1 ·······························

Paired Up

Sutton studied grasshopper cells through a microscope. He concluded that genes are carried on chromosomes.

✎ **Relate Text and Visuals** Answer the questions in the spaces provided.

1 Body Cell

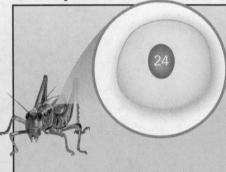

Each grasshopper body cell has 24 chromosomes.

2 Sex Cells

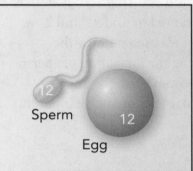
Sperm   Egg

Sutton found that grasshopper sex cells each have 12 chromosomes.

3 Fertilization

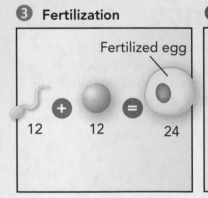
Fertilized egg
12   12   24

The fertilized egg cell has 24 chromosomes.

4 Grasshopper Offspring

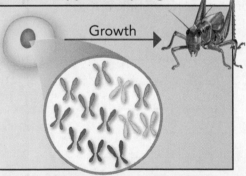
Growth

The 24 chromosomes exist as 12 pairs.

1. How does the number of chromosomes in grasshopper sex cells compare to the number in body cells?

_____

_____

_____

_____

2. How is the inheritance of chromosomes similar to what you know about alleles?

_____

_____

_____

_____

Genes on Chromosomes Recall that alleles are different forms of a gene. Because of Mendel's work, Sutton knew that alleles exist in pairs in an organism. One allele comes from the female parent. The other allele comes from the male parent. Sutton realized that paired alleles are carried on paired chromosomes. His idea is now known as the chromosome theory of inheritance.

🔑 **According to the chromosome theory of inheritance, genes pass from parents to their offspring on chromosomes.**

A Lineup of Genes The body cells of humans contain 46 chromosomes that form 23 pairs. Chromosomes are made up of many genes joined together like beads on a string. Although you have only 23 pairs of chromosomes, your body cells each contain between 20,000 and 25,000 genes. Genes control traits.

Figure 2 shows a pair of chromosomes from an organism. One chromosome is from the female parent. The other chromosome is from the male parent. Notice that each chromosome has the same genes. The genes are lined up in the same order on both chromosomes. However, the alleles for some of the genes are not identical. For example, one chromosome has allele *A,* and the other chromosome has allele *a.* As you can see, this organism is heterozygous for some traits and homozygous for others.

⤺ **Relate Cause and Effect**
Suppose gene A on the left chromosome is damaged and no longer functions. What form of the trait would show? Why?

_____

_____

_____

_____

FIGURE 2 ⋯⋯⋯⋯⋯⋯⋯⋯⋯⋯⋯⋯

A Pair of Chromosomes
Chromosomes in a pair may have different alleles for some genes and the same alleles for others.

✎ **Interpret Diagrams** For each pair of alleles, tell whether the organism is homozygous or heterozygous. The first two answers are shown.

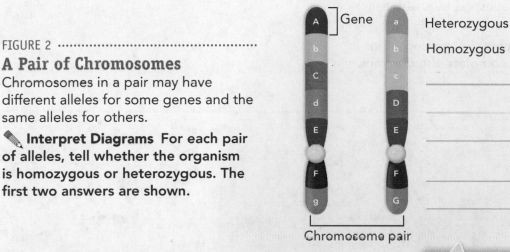

Heterozygous

Homozygous

_____

_____

_____

_____

_____

Chromosome pair

 Do the Quick Lab *Chromosomes and Inheritance.*

⎯ **Assess Your Understanding**

1a. Describe When two grasshopper sex cells join, the chromosome number in the new cell is (half/double) the number in the sex cells.

b. Summarize Describe the arrangement of genes on a pair of chromosomes.

_____

_____

_____

c. Relate Evidence and Explanation How do Sutton's observations support the chromosome theory of inheritance?

_____

_____

_____

_____

_____

got it? ⋯⋯⋯⋯⋯⋯⋯⋯⋯⋯⋯⋯⋯⋯⋯⋯⋯⋯⋯⋯⋯⋯⋯⋯⋯⋯⋯⋯⋯

○ **I get it!** Now I know that genes are passed from parents to offspring _____

○ **I need extra help with** _____

Go to my SCIENCE Ⓢ COACH *online for help with this subject.*

What Happens During Meiosis?

How do sex cells end up with half the number of chromosomes as body cells? The answer to this question is a form of cell division called meiosis. **Meiosis** (my OH sis) is the process by which the number of chromosomes is reduced by half as sex cells form. You can trace the events of meiosis in **Figure 3.** Here, the parent cell has four chromosomes arranged in two pairs. ⚭ **During meiosis, the chromosome pairs separate into two different cells. The sex cells that form later have only half as many chromosomes as the other cells in the organism.**

FIGURE 3 ···

▶ ART IN MOTION **Meiosis**

During meiosis, a cell produces sex cells with half the number of chromosomes.

✎ **Interpret Diagrams** Fill in the missing terms in the spaces provided, and complete the diagram.

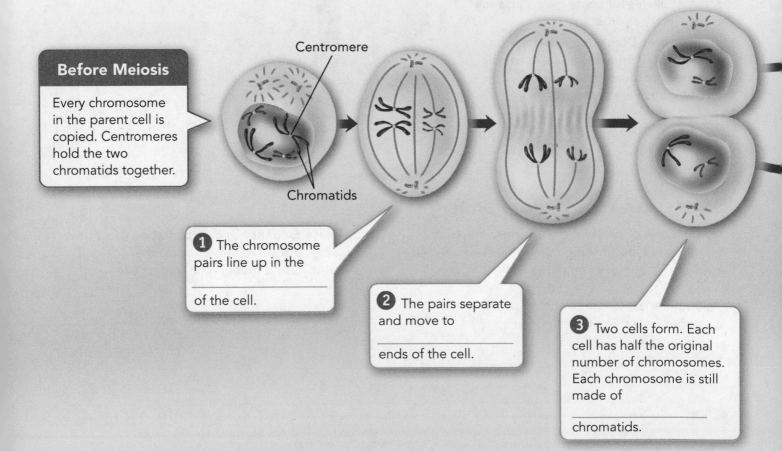

Before Meiosis

Every chromosome in the parent cell is copied. Centromeres hold the two chromatids together.

Centromere

Chromatids

❶ The chromosome pairs line up in the
_____
of the cell.

❷ The pairs separate and move to
_____
ends of the cell.

❸ Two cells form. Each cell has half the original number of chromosomes. Each chromosome is still made of
_____
chromatids.

During meiosis, a cell divides into two cells. Then each of these cells divides again, forming a total of four cells. The chromosomes duplicate only before the first cell division.

Each of the four sex cells shown below receives two chromosomes—one chromosome from each pair in the original cell. When two sex cells join at fertilization, the new cell that forms has the full number of chromosomes. In this case, the number is four. The organism that grows from this cell got two of its chromosomes from one parent and two from the other parent.

5 The centromeres split, and the _____ separate. They become single chromosomes and move to opposite ends of the cell.

4 In each cell, the _____ move to the center.

After Meiosis

Four sex cells are produced. Each cell has _____ the number of chromosomes of the_____ cell. Each sex cell has only _____chromosome from an original pair.

[CHALLENGE] How many chromosomes are in each cell in Step 3?

_____

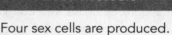
Do the Quick Lab
Modeling Meiosis.

Assess Your Understanding

got it? ....

○ **I get it!** Now I know that during meiosis, the number of chromosomes_____

_____

○ **I need extra help with** _____

Go to MY SCIENCE COACH online for help with this subject.

97

Study Guide

Offspring inherit different forms of genes called _____ from each parent. Traits are affected by patterns of inheritance and interactions with the _____.

LESSON 1 What Is Heredity?

In all of his crosses, Mendel found that only one form of the trait appeared in the F_1 generation. However, in the F_2 generation, the "lost" form of the trait always reappeared in about one fourth of the plants.

An organism's traits are controlled by the alleles it inherits from its parents. Some alleles are dominant, while other alleles are recessive.

Vocabulary
- heredity • trait • genetics • fertilization • purebred
- gene • allele • dominant allele • recessive allele • hybrid

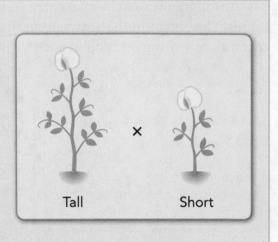

Tall   Short

LESSON 2 Probability and Heredity

In a genetic cross, the combination of alleles that parents can pass to an offspring is based on probability.

An organism's phenotype is its physical appearance, or visible traits. An organism's genotype is its genetic makeup, or alleles.

Vocabulary
- probability • Punnett square • phenotype • genotype
- homozygous • heterozygous

	R	r
R	RR	Rr
r	Rr	rr

LESSON 3 Patterns of Inheritance

Most traits are the result of complex patterns of inheritance.

Environmental factors can influence the way genes are expressed.

Vocabulary
- incomplete dominance
- codominance
- multiple alleles
- polygenic inheritance

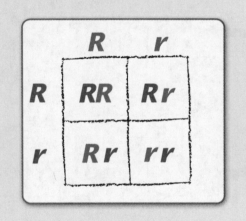

LESSON 4 Chromosomes and Inheritance

The chromosome theory of inheritance states that genes pass from parents to their offspring on chromosomes.

Meiosis produces sex cells that have half as many chromosomes as body cells.

Vocabulary
- meiosis

Review and Assessment

What Is Heredity?

1. Different forms of a gene are called

   a. alleles.   **b.** hybrids.

   c. genotypes.   **d.** chromosomes.

2. _____ is the scientific study of heredity.

3. Explain Mendel crossed two pea plants: one with green pods and one with yellow pods. The F_1 generation all had green pods. What color pods did the F_2 generation have? Explain your answer.

_____

_____

_____

_____

4. Predict The plant below is purebred for height (tall). Write the alleles of this plant. In any cross for height, what kind of offspring will this plant produce? Why?

_____

_____

_____

_____

_____

5. Compare and Contrast How do dominant alleles and recessive alleles differ?

_____

_____

_____

_____

6. **Write About It** Write a diary entry as if you are Gregor Mendel. You may describe any part of his experiences, experiments, or observations.

Probability and Heredity

7. Which of the following represents a heterozygous genotype?

   a. YY **b.** yy

   c. Yy **d.** $Y^H Y^H$

8. An organism's _____ is the way its genotype is expressed.

9. Make Models Fill in the Punnett square below to show a cross between two guinea pigs that are heterozygous for coat color. B is for black coat color, and b is for white coat color.

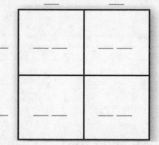

10. Interpret Tables What is the probability that an offspring from the cross above has each of the following genotypes?

BB _____

Bb _____

bb _____

11. Apply Concepts What kind of cross might tell you if a black guinea pig is BB or Bb? Why?

_____

_____

_____

12. **do the math!** A garden has 80 pea plants. Of this total, 20 plants have short stems and 60 plants have tall stems. What percentage of the plants have short stems? What percentage have tall stems?

99

CHAPTER 3 Review and Assessment

LESSON 3 Patterns of Inheritance

13. Which of the following terms describes a pattern of inheritance in which one allele is only partially dominant?

  a. codominance

  b. acquired traits

  c. multiple alleles

  d. incomplete dominance

14. Traits that have three or more phenotypes may be the result of _____ alleles.

15. Compare and Contrast How is codominance different from incomplete dominance?

_____

_____

_____

_____

_____

16. Relate Cause and Effect Human height is a trait with a very broad range of phenotypes. Which pattern of inheritance could account for human height? Explain your answer.

_____

_____

_____

_____

_____

17. Identify Faulty Reasoning Neither of Josie's parents plays a musical instrument. Josie thinks that she won't be able to play an instrument because her parents can't. Is she right? Why or why not?

_____

_____

_____

_____

LESSON 4 Chromosomes and Inheritance

18. Genes are carried from parents to offspring on structures called

  a. alleles.   **b.** chromosomes.

  c. phenotypes.   **d.** genotypes.

19. The process of _____ results in the formation of sex cells.

20. Summarize If an organism's body cells have 12 chromosomes, how many chromosomes will the sex cells have? Explain your answer.

_____

_____

_____

_____

_____

 APPLY THE BIG Q

Why don't offspring always look like their parents?

21. A species of butterfly has three alleles for wing color: blue, orange, and pale yellow. A blue butterfly mates with an orange butterfly. The following offspring result: about 25% are blue and 25% are orange. However, another 25% are speckled blue and orange, and 25% are yellow. Explain how these results could occur.

Offspring of blue butterfly and orange butterfly

_____

_____

_____

_____

Standardized Test Prep

Multiple Choice

Circle the letter of the best answer.

1. The Punnett square below shows a cross between two pea plants, each with round seeds. What is the missing genotype in the empty square?

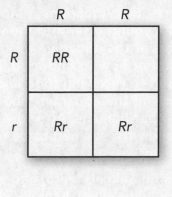

	R	R
R	RR	
r	Rr	Rr

   A   rr
   B   rR
   C   Rr
   D   RR

2. A particular trait has multiple alleles: A, B, and C. How many different genotypes are possible?

   A   2
   B   3
   C   4
   D   6

3. The scientific study of heredity is called

   A   meiosis.
   B   genetics.
   C   probability.
   D   fertilization.

4. For a particular plant, leaf texture is either fuzzy or smooth. A purebred fuzzy plant is crossed with a purebred smooth plant. All offspring are smooth. Which sentence best describes the alleles for this trait?

   A   Fuzzy is dominant over smooth.
   B   Smooth is dominant over fuzzy.
   C   The alleles are codominant.
   D   The alleles have incomplete dominance.

5. Which of the following traits is acquired?

   A   the number of petals that grow in a plant's flowers
   B   the wing shape of a wild bird
   C   the ability of some gorillas to use sign language
   D   a cheetah's ability to run faster than any other land animal

Constructed Response

Use the diagram below and your knowledge of genetics to answer Question 6. Write your answer on a separate piece of paper.

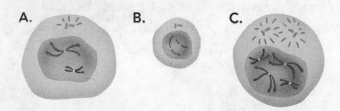

6. One of the cells shown is a parent cell about to undergo meiosis. Another cell is in the process of meiosis. A third cell is a sex cell that results from meiosis. Identify which cell is which, and explain your reasoning.

Nature vs. *Nurture*

In 1990, the Monterey Bay Aquarium in Monterey, California, released a young otter into the wild. Wildlife rehabilitators at the aquarium raised the otter and taught her how to find food. But, because she was used to receiving food and affection from people at the aquarium, she did not know to avoid other humans. After the otter pestered some local divers, she had to be returned to live at the aquarium.

So, which behaviors do animals learn, and which behaviors "just come naturally"? Actually, the line between inherited behaviors and learned behaviors is rarely clear. Although wild otters are naturally shy around humans, the otter at the Monterey Bay Aquarium had learned to expect food and affection from humans. As a result, wildlife rehabilitators commonly use puppets or animal costumes to keep the animals they care for from becoming too familiar with humans.

▼ This photograph shows a pair of otters, one of the species wildlife rehabilitators try to reintroduce into the wild.

Design It Choose a species, such as deer, otter, or panda, that is raised in captivity and returned to the wild. Design a rehabilitation activity to help orphaned animals learn a skill that they will need to survive in the wild. Explain the features of your rehabilitation activity to your class.

Seeing Spots

You would probably recognize a Dalmatian if you saw one—Dalmatians typically have white coats with distinctive black or brown spots. Spots are a defining characteristic of the Dalmatian breed. These spots can be large or small, but all Dalmatians have them.

In Dalmatians, spots are a dominant trait. When two Dalmatians breed, each parent contributes a gene for spots. The trait for spots is controlled by one set of genes with only two possible alleles. No matter how many puppies are in a litter, they will all develop spots.

But what if a Dalmatian breeds with another dog that isn't a Dalmatian? While the puppies won't develop the distinctive Dalmatian pattern, they will have spots, because the allele for spots is dominant. Some puppies will have many tiny spots and some will have large patches! Dalmatians, like leopards, cannot change their spots.

Newborn Dalmatian puppies are white—their spots develop when the puppies are about a week old. ▼

Predict It! Dalmatians' spots may be black or liver (brown), but never both on the same dog. Liver is a recessive allele. Use a Punnett square to predict the color of the spots on the offspring of a liver Dalmatian and a black Dalmatian with a recessive liver allele. Display your prediction on a poster.

103

WHY IS THIS LOBSTER BLUE?

THE BIG ?

What does DNA do?

American lobsters are usually dark green in color. But, most people see only red lobsters. Lobsters turn red after they have been cooked. The chance of finding a blue lobster is about one in a million.

Infer Why might a lobster have a blue shell?

▶ **UNTAMED SCIENCE** Watch the **Untamed Science** video to learn more about DNA.

_____

_____

_____

_____

_____

_____

_____

_____

DNA: The Code of Life

4 Getting Started

Check Your Understanding

1. **Background** Read the paragraph below and then answer the question.

Leo's sister likes to joke that Leo inherited his dad's **genes** for playing the piano. Leo knows that **heredity** may not be that simple. But there are other **traits**—like the widow's peak on his forehead—that he did inherit from his father.

> A segment of DNA on a chromosome that codes for a specific trait is a **gene**.
>
> **Heredity** is the passing of traits from parent to offspring.
>
> A **trait** is a characteristic that an organism can pass on through its genes.

- Why couldn't Leo inherit his dad's piano skills?

_____

_____

> **MY READING WEB** If you had trouble completing the question above, visit **My Reading Web** and type in *DNA: The Code of Life.*

Vocabulary Skill

Latin Word Parts Some vocabulary in this chapter contains word parts with Latin origins. Look at the Latin words below, and the example derived from each word.

Latin Word	Meaning of Latin Word	Example
mutare	to change	mutation, *n.* any change in the DNA of a gene or chromosome
tumere	to swell	tumor, *n.* a mass of abnormal cells that develops when cells divide and grow uncontrollably

2. **Quick Check** The meaning of the Latin word *mutare* appears in the definition of *mutation*. Circle the word in both places that it appears in the table above.

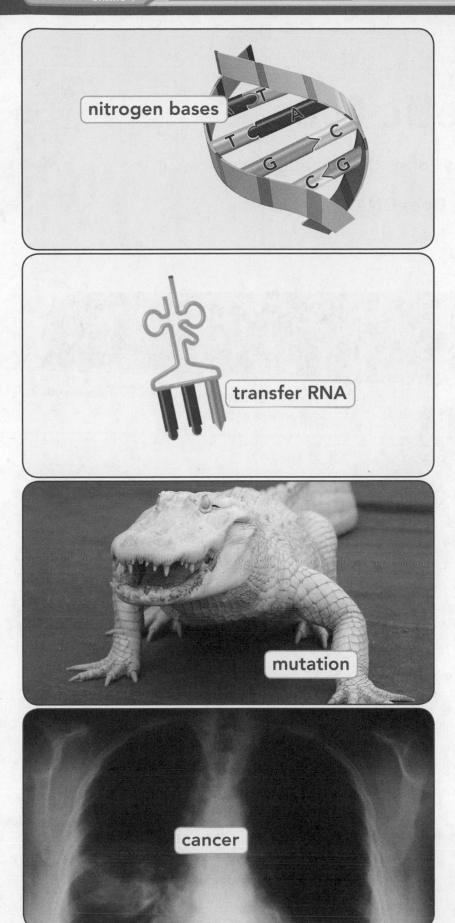

nitrogen bases

transfer RNA

mutation

cancer

Chapter Preview

LESSON 1
- nitrogen bases
- DNA replication
- 🔄 Identify the Main Idea
- △ Infer

LESSON 2
- messenger RNA
- transfer RNA
- 🔄 Summarize
- △ Design Experiments

LESSON 3
- mutation
- cancer
- tumor
- chemotherapy
- 🔄 Relate Cause and Effect
- △ Calculate

> VOCAB FLASH CARDS For extra help with vocabulary, visit **Vocab Flash Cards** and type in *DNA: The Code of Life.*

The Genetic Code

UNLOCK THE BIG ?

🔑 **What Forms the Genetic Code?**

🔑 **How Does DNA Copy Itself?**

MY PLANET DIARY

BIOGRAPHY

DNA Debut

In 1951, English scientist Rosalind Franklin discovered that DNA could exist in a dry form and a wet form. Franklin made an image of the wet form of DNA by exposing it to X-rays. The X-rays bounced off the atoms in the DNA to make the image. The image (see the background on the next journal page) was so clear that it helped scientists understand the structure of DNA for the first time. Her discovery was important for figuring out how genetic information is passed from parent to offspring. Franklin's contribution to science was not only in her research, but also in that she succeeded at a time when many people thought women shouldn't be scientists.

> PLANET DIARY Go to **Planet Diary** to learn more about the genetic code.

What does the X-ray of DNA look like to you? Write your answer below.

_____

_____

_____

_____

 Lab zone Do the Inquiry Warm-Up *Can You Crack the Code?*

Vocabulary
- nitrogen bases
- DNA replication

Skills
- ⟳ Reading: Identify the Main Idea
- △ Inquiry: Infer

1

What Forms the Genetic Code?

It took almost 100 years after the discovery of DNA for scientists to figure out that it looks like a twisted ladder. When James Watson and Francis Crick published the structure of DNA in 1953, they added another clue to how traits are passed from parent to offspring. DNA contains the genetic information for cells to make proteins. Proteins determine a variety of traits, from hair color to an organism's ability to digest food.

The Structure of DNA Parents pass traits to offspring through chromosomes. Chromosomes are made of DNA and proteins and are located in a cell's nucleus. Look at **Figure 1.** The twisted ladder structure of DNA is also known as a "double helix." The sides of the double helix are made up of sugar molecules called deoxyribose, alternating with phosphate molecules. The name DNA, or deoxyribonucleic acid (DEE ahk see ry boh noo klee ik), comes from this structure.

The rungs of DNA are made of nitrogen bases. **Nitrogen bases** are molecules that contain nitrogen and other elements. DNA has four kinds of nitrogen bases: adenine (AD uh neen), thymine (THY meen), guanine (GWAH neen), and cytosine (SY tuh seen). The capital letters *A, T, G,* and *C* are used to represent the bases.

FIGURE 1 ·····················
> ART IN MOTION **Genetic Structures**
Hummingbirds, like all organisms, contain all of the genetic structures below.
✎ **Sequence** Put the structures in order from largest to smallest by writing the numbers two through five in the blank circles.

DNA

Cell

Nitrogen bases

Chromosome

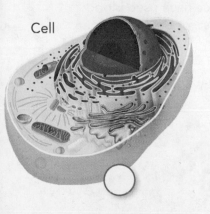

109

In **Figure 2**, you can see the relationship among chromosomes, genes, and DNA. A gene is a section of a DNA molecule that contains the information to code for one specific protein. A gene is made up of a series of bases in a row. The bases in a gene are arranged in a specific order—for example, ATGACGTAC. A single gene on a chromosome may contain anywhere from several hundred to a million or more of these bases. Each gene is located at a specific place on a chromosome.

Because there are so many possible combinations of bases and genes, each individual organism has a unique set of DNA. DNA can be found in all of the cells of your body except for red blood cells. DNA can be found in blood samples, however, because white blood cells do contain DNA.

Identify the Main Idea
Underline the sentence that explains the role of genes in making proteins.

FIGURE 2 ······················
Chromosomes and Genes
Humans have between 20,000 and 25,000 genes on their chromosomes. The corals that make up ocean reefs are thought to have as many as 25,000 genes too!

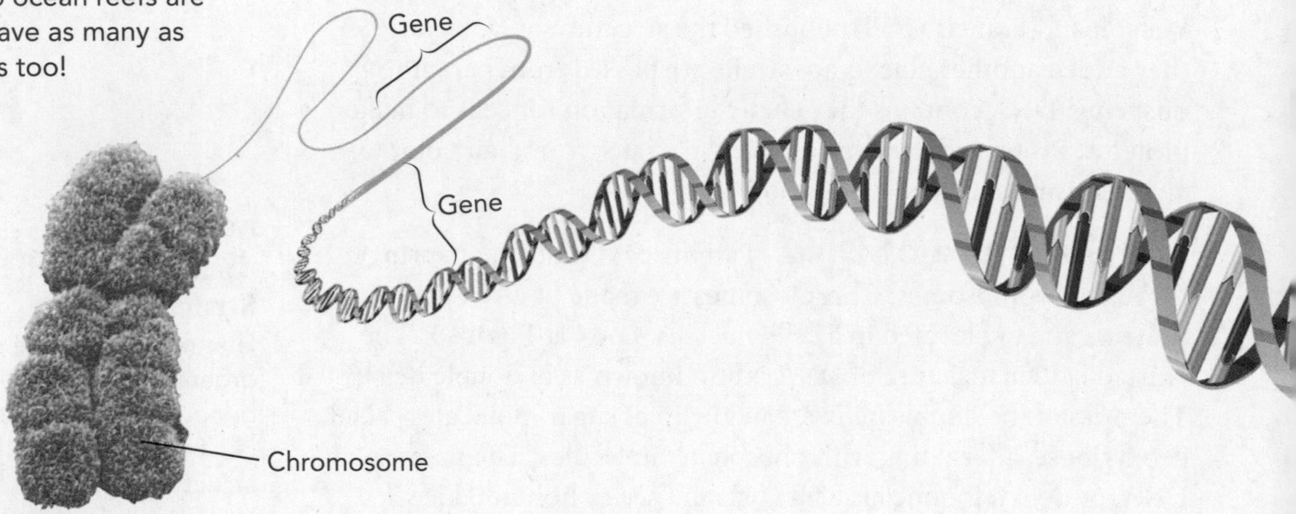

Gene

Gene

Chromosome

apply it!

Can you help solve the crime?

Someone robbed a jewelry store. The robber's DNA was extracted from skin cells found on the broken glass of a jewelry case. The police collected DNA samples from three suspects. The letters below represent the sequences of nitrogen bases in the DNA. Based on the DNA found at the crime scene, circle the DNA of the guilty suspect.

Robber: GACCAGTTAGCTAAGTCT

Suspect 1: TAGCTGA

Suspect 2: GACGAGT

Suspect 3: CTAAGTC

❶ **Explain** Why can you solve crimes using DNA?

_____
_____
_____

❷ **Infer** Could the police have used blood on the broken glass to test for DNA? Why or why not?

_____
_____
_____

Order of the Bases

A gene contains the code that determines the structure of a protein. **The order of the nitrogen bases along a gene forms a genetic code that specifies what type of protein will be produced.** Remember that proteins are long-chain molecules made of individual amino acids. In the genetic code, a group of three DNA bases codes for one specific amino acid. For example, the three-base sequence CGT (cytosine-guanine-thymine) always codes for the amino acid alanine. The order of the three-base code units determines the order in which amino acids are put together to form a protein.

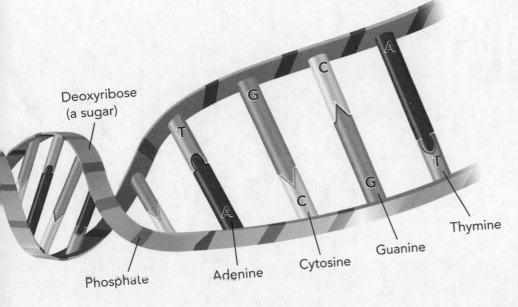

Deoxyribose (a sugar)

Phosphate

Adenine

Cytosine

Guanine

Thymine

FIGURE 3

DNA Bases

Notice the pattern in the DNA bases.

✏ **Interpret Diagrams**
Which base always pairs with cytosine?

_____

_____

Lab zone — Do the Lab Investigation *Guilty or Innocent?*

Assess Your Understanding

1a. Identify These letters represent the nitrogen bases on one strand of DNA: GGCTATCCA. What letters would form the other strand of the helix?

_____

b. Explain How can a parent pass a trait such as eye color to its offspring?

_____

_____

got it?

○ **I get it!** Now I know that the genetic code of nitrogen bases specifies_____

_____

○ **I need extra help with** _____

Go to MY SCIENCE ⓢ COACH *online for help with this subject.*

FIGURE 4 ••••••••••••••••••••••••••••••••••••••

> INTERACTIVE ART DNA Replication

Without DNA replication, daughter cells could not carry out their life functions.

✎ **Interpret Diagrams** Fill in the missing bases on the strands of DNA. Then complete the sentences below.

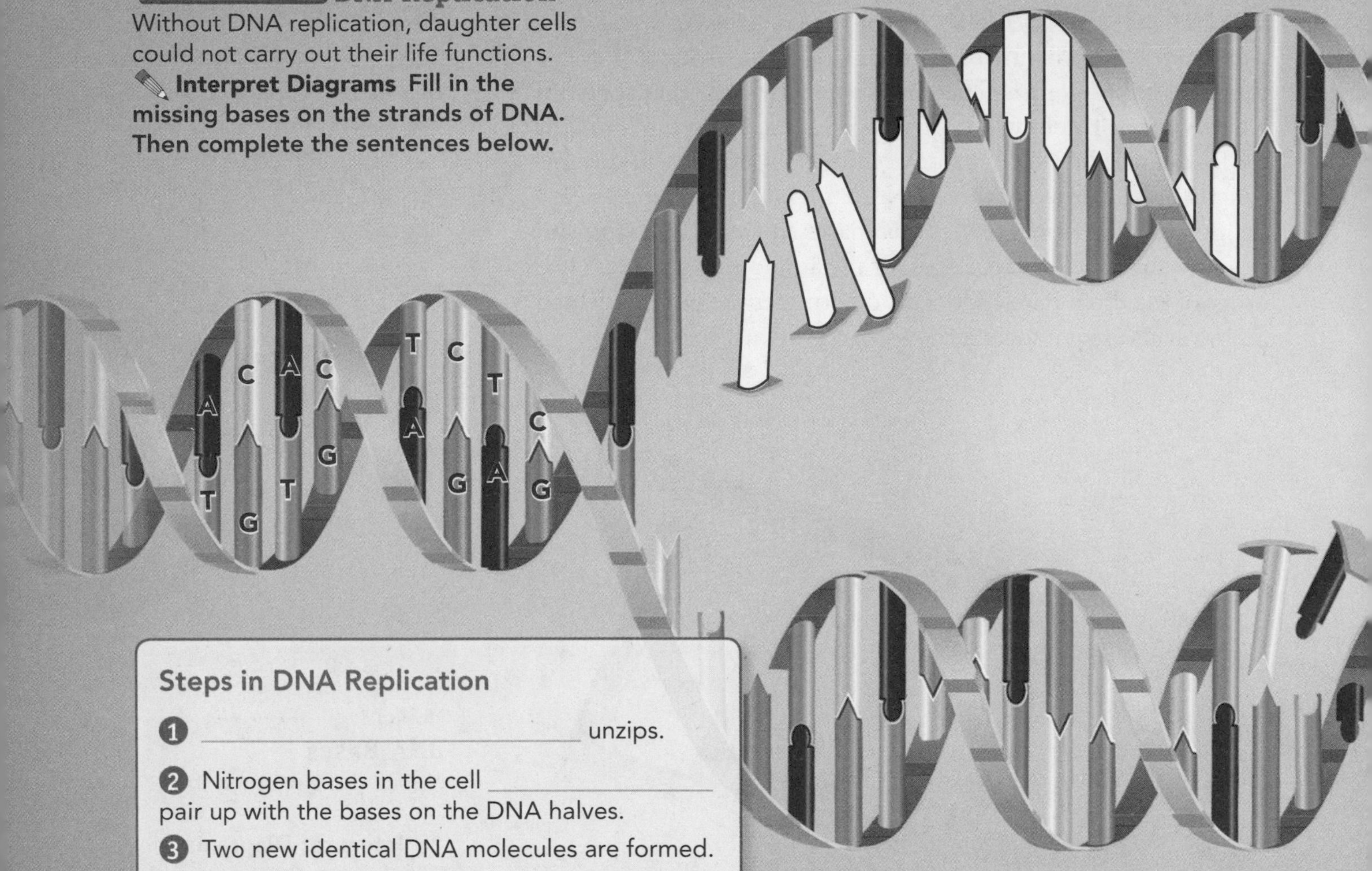

Steps in DNA Replication

❶ _____ unzips.

❷ Nitrogen bases in the cell _____ pair up with the bases on the DNA halves.

❸ Two new identical DNA molecules are formed.

How Does DNA Copy Itself?

Two new cells, or daughter cells, result when a cell divides. To ensure that each daughter cell has the genetic information it needs to carry out its activities, DNA copies itself. **DNA replication** is the process in which an identical copy of a DNA strand is formed for a new cell. Replication is very important, since daughter cells need a complete set of DNA to survive.

DNA replication begins when the two sides of a DNA molecule unwind and separate, like a zipper unzipping, between the nitrogen bases. Next, nitrogen bases in the nucleus pair up with the bases on each half of the DNA. 🔑 **Because of the way the nitrogen bases pair up, the order of the bases in each new DNA strand exactly matches the order in the original DNA strand.** This pattern is key to understanding how DNA replication occurs. Adenine always pairs with thymine, while guanine always pairs with cytosine. At the end of replication, two identical DNA molecules are formed.

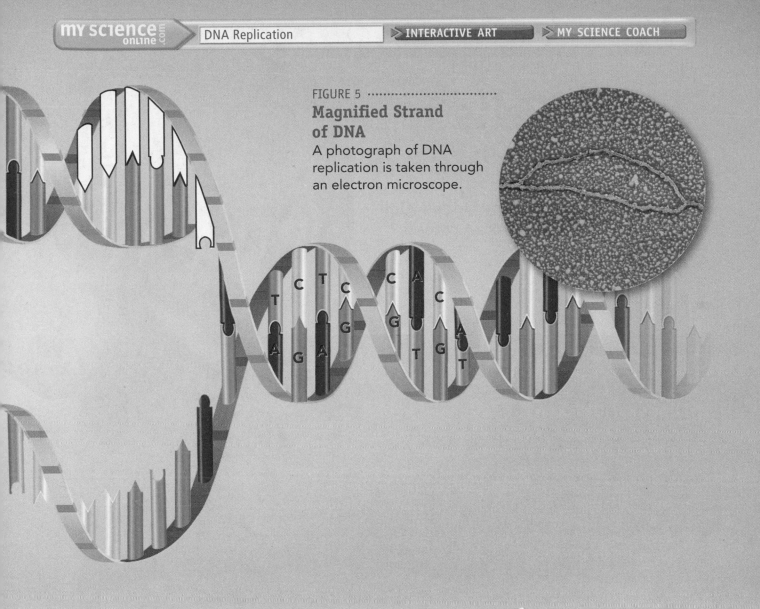

FIGURE 5 ·······················

Magnified Strand of DNA

A photograph of DNA replication is taken through an electron microscope.

 Do the Quick Lab *Modeling the Genetic Code.*

Assess Your Understanding

2a. Review The (nitrogen base pattern/ number of genes/size of DNA) determines how DNA is replicated.

b. Describe Where in the cell does DNA replication take place?

_____

_____

_____

c. CHALLENGE What do you think would happen if the DNA code in a daughter cell did not match the code in the parent cell?

_____

_____

_____

_____

got it? ···

○ I get it! Now I know that DNA replication is the process in which_____

○ I need extra help with _____

Go to MY SCIENCE ⑤ COACH online for help with this subject.

How Cells Make Proteins

UNLOCK THE BIG **?**

☞ **How Does a Cell Make Proteins?**

my planet Diary

DISCOVERY

Dinosaur Chicken?

In 2007, a 68-million-year-old dinosaur protein was discovered by Harvard scientists. The protein, called *collagen*, was extracted from the soft tissue of a *Tyrannosaurus rex* that died in Montana. Collagen is an important component of bone. The protein from the dinosaur is similar to protein found in modern-day chickens, supporting the connection between dinosaurs and birds. With this discovery, scientists have more evidence that these two species are related.

> **Communicate** Discuss the question with a group of classmates. Write your answer below.
>
> What other information about the two species would you want to
>
> compare? _____
>
> _____

> ▶ PLANET DIARY Go to **Planet Diary** to learn more about how cells make proteins.

Lab zone ® Do the Inquiry Warm-Up *What Is RNA?*

How Does a Cell Make Proteins?

The production of proteins in a cell is called protein synthesis. ☞ **During protein synthesis, the cell uses information from a gene on a chromosome to produce a specific protein.** Proteins help determine the size, shape, color, and other traits of an organism by triggering cellular processes. The protein code passes from parent to offspring through DNA, resulting in inherited traits.

Vocabulary
messenger RNA
transfer RNA

Skills
⊙ Reading: Summarize
△ Inquiry: Design Experiments

The Structure of Proteins Proteins are made up of molecules called amino acids, as shown in **Figure 1**. Although there are only 20 amino acids, cells can combine them in different ways to form thousands of different proteins. You can think of the 20 amino acids as being like the 26 letters of the alphabet. Those 26 letters can form thousands of words. The letters you use and their order determine the words you form. A change in just one letter, for example, from *rice* to *mice*, creates a new word. Similarly, a change in the type or order of amino acids can result in a different protein.

The Role of RNA Protein synthesis takes place in the cytoplasm outside the cell's nucleus. The chromosomes are found inside the nucleus, so a messenger must carry the genetic code from the DNA inside the nucleus to the cytoplasm. This genetic messenger is called RNA, or ribonucleic acid (ry boh noo KLEE ik).

Although both RNA and DNA are nucleic acids, they have some differences. RNA has only one strand and contains a different sugar molecule than DNA. Another difference is in the nitrogen bases. Like DNA, RNA contains adenine, guanine, and cytosine. However, instead of thymine, RNA contains uracil (YOOR uh sil).

Types of RNA Two types of RNA take part in protein synthesis. **Messenger RNA** (mRNA) copies the message from DNA in the nucleus and carries the message to the ribosome in the cytoplasm. **Transfer RNA** (tRNA) carries amino acids to the ribosome and adds them to the growing protein.

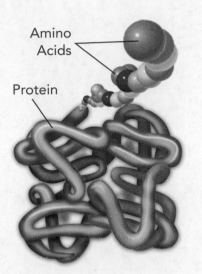

Amino Acids

Protein

FIGURE 1 ·····························
Proteins
Proteins help determine what you look like.
✏ **Interpret Diagrams**
**Complete the sentence.
Proteins are made of folded and bundled chains of**

_____

_____

apply it!

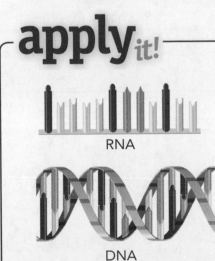

RNA

DNA

While working in the lab, your assistant accidentally mixes one beaker of DNA into a beaker containing RNA. You need to separate the molecules before doing your experiments.

△**Design Experiments** How could you test each molecule to determine if it was DNA or RNA? _____

_____

_____

_____

Protein Synthesis

What does DNA do?

FIGURE 2 ··

> **INTERACTIVE ART** The steps of protein synthesis are shown in the numbered boxes. Notice that the bases in the steps align with the bases in the summary chart on the far right.

mRNA

Nucleus

(1) mRNA Enters the Cytoplasm

DNA unzips between its base pairs. Then one of the strands of DNA directs the production of a strand of mRNA. To form the RNA strand, RNA bases pair up with the DNA bases. The process is similar to DNA replication. Cytosine always pairs with guanine. However, uracil, not thymine, pairs with adenine. The mRNA leaves the nucleus and enters the cytoplasm.

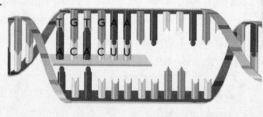

(2) Ribosomes Attach to mRNA

A ribosome attaches to mRNA in the cytoplasm. On the ribosome, the mRNA provides the code for the protein that will be made. In the cytoplasm, specific amino acids are attached to specific molecules of tRNA.

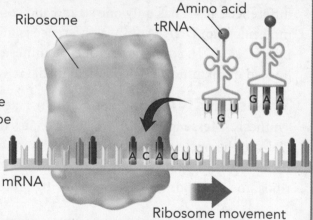

Ribosome

Amino acid

tRNA

mRNA

Ribosome movement

(3) tRNA Attaches to mRNA

Molecules of tRNA and their amino acids attach to the mRNA. The bases on tRNA "read" the message and pair with bases on mRNA.

4 Amino Acids Join in the Ribosome

Transfer molecules attach one at a time to the ribosome and continue to read the message. The amino acids are linked together and form a growing chain. The order of the amino acids is determined by the order of the three-base codes on the mRNA.

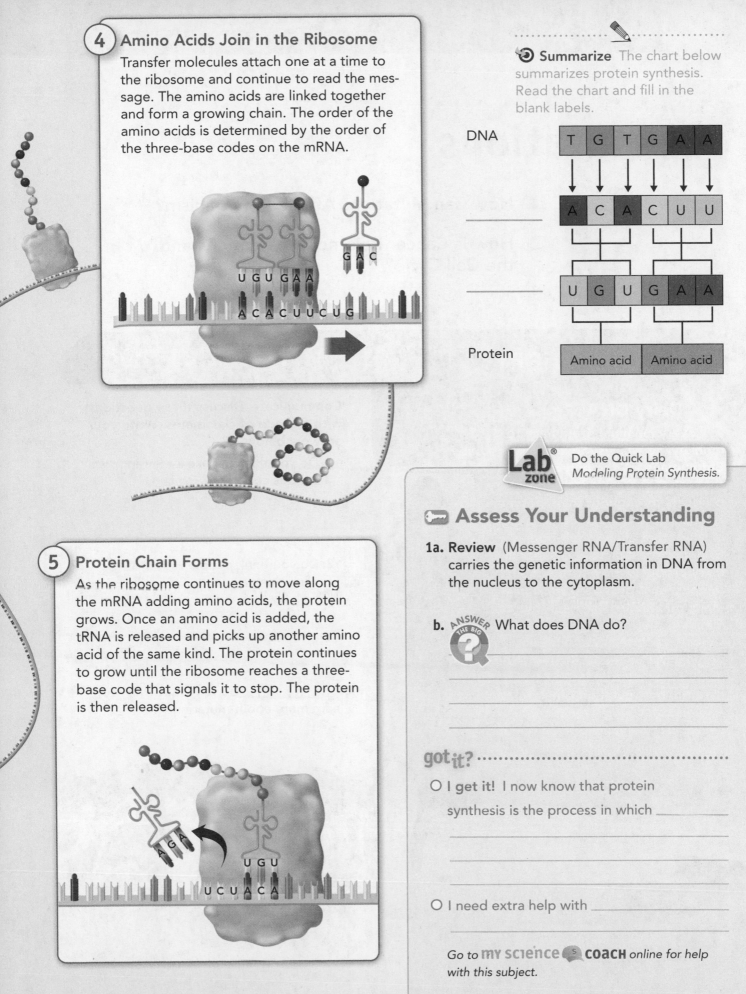

Do the Quick Lab Modeling Protein Synthesis.

Summarize The chart below summarizes protein synthesis. Read the chart and fill in the blank labels.

DNA   T | G | T | G | A | A

_____   A | C | A | C | U | U

_____   U | G | U | G | A | A

Protein   Amino acid | Amino acid

5 Protein Chain Forms

As the ribosome continues to move along the mRNA adding amino acids, the protein grows. Once an amino acid is added, the tRNA is released and picks up another amino acid of the same kind. The protein continues to grow until the ribosome reaches a three-base code that signals it to stop. The protein is then released.

Assess Your Understanding

1a. Review (Messenger RNA/Transfer RNA) carries the genetic information in DNA from the nucleus to the cytoplasm.

b. **ANSWER THE BIG ?** What does DNA do?

_____

_____

_____

got it?

○ I get it! I now know that protein synthesis is the process in which _____

_____

_____

○ I need extra help with _____

_____

Go to **MY SCIENCE COACH** online for help with this subject.

117

Mutations

🔑 **How Can Mutations Affect an Organism?**

🔑 **How Is Cancer Related to Mutations and the Cell Cycle?**

my planet Diary

Dairy DNA

Every mammal, from mice to monkeys to whales, drinks milk as a baby. But humans are the only mammals that can digest milk and other dairy products throughout their lifetime. Humans have a mutation (a change in DNA) that allows their bodies to break down lactose, a sugar in dairy products. However, not all people can digest dairy products. Many people are lactose intolerant, meaning their bodies cannot break down lactose. Lactose-intolerant people have the original DNA without the mutation. While many other mutations are considered harmful, this mutation is helpful to humans. And just think—ice cream might never have been invented if humans couldn't break down lactose!

MISCONCEPTION

Communicate Discuss these questions with a group of classmates. Write your answers below.

1. Do you think lactose intolerance is a serious condition? Explain.

_____

_____

2. Do you think people with this condition can *never* have milk?

_____

_____

_____

▶ PLANET DIARY Go to **Planet Diary** to learn more about mutations.

Lab zone® Do the Inquiry Warm-Up *Oops!*

Vocabulary
- mutation • cancer • tumor
- chemotherapy

Skills
↻ Reading: Relate Cause and Effect
△ Inquiry: Calculate

How Can Mutations Affect an Organism?

Some traits are not inherited from parent organisms. Traits can also be a result of a change in DNA. A **mutation** is any change in the DNA of a gene or chromosome. For example, instead of the base sequence AAG, the DNA might have the sequence ACG. 🔑 **Mutations can cause a cell to produce an incorrect protein during protein synthesis. As a result, the organism's trait may be different from what it normally would be.**

If a mutation occurs in a body cell, such as a skin cell, the mutation will not be passed on to the organism's offspring. But if a mutation occurs in a sex cell (egg or sperm), the mutation can be passed on to an offspring and affect the offspring's traits.

Types of Mutations Some mutations are the result of small changes in an organism's DNA. For example, a base pair may be added, a base pair may be substituted for another, or one or more bases may be deleted from a section of DNA. These types of mutations can occur during the DNA replication process. Other mutations may occur when chromosomes don't separate correctly during the formation of sex cells. When this type of mutation occurs, a cell can end up with too many or too few chromosomes. The cell can also end up with extra segments of chromosomes.

✏️ **Vocabulary** Latin Word Origins
Mutation comes from the Latin word *mutare*, meaning "to change." How can mutations change an organism's traits?

_____

_____

_____

_____

FIGURE 1 ....

Mutations
The types of mutations of DNA include deletion, addition, and substitution.
✏️ **Interpret Diagrams** Circle the added base pair on the third piece of DNA. Fill in the nitrogen bases on the fourth piece of DNA to illustrate a substitution.

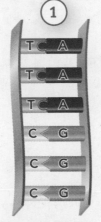

Original DNA sequence

One base pair is removed (deletion).

One base pair is added (addition).

One base pair is switched for another (substitution).

119

Effects of Mutations Mutations introduce changes in an organism. Mutations can be harmful, helpful, or neither harmful nor helpful. A mutation is harmful if it reduces the organism's chances for survival and reproduction.

Whether a mutation is harmful or not depends partly on the organism's environment. The mutation that led to this alligator's white color would probably be harmful to it in the wild. A white alligator is more visible to its prey. This alligator may find it difficult to catch prey and may not get enough food to survive. A white alligator in a zoo has the same chance for survival as a green alligator because it does not hunt. In a zoo, the mutation neither helps nor harms the alligator.

Helpful mutations increase an organism's ability to survive and reproduce. Mutations have allowed some bacteria that are harmful to humans to become resistant to drugs. The drugs do not kill the bacteria with the mutations, so they continue to survive and reproduce.

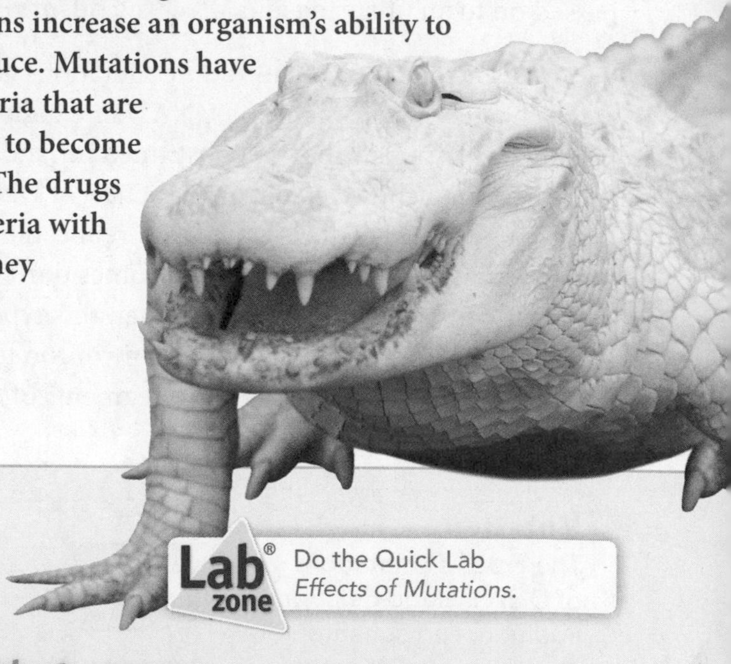

FIGURE 2 ·······································

✎ **Review** Check the phrase that best completes the sentence.

▶ **VIRTUAL LAB** Alligator Mutation

A white alligator does not blend into its natural habitat, but this color change may be a beneficial mutation for an organism if it

○ reduces its chances for survival.

○ increases its chances for survival.

○ decreases its chances for reproduction.

🔑 Assess Your Understanding

1a. Explain Mutations that occur in body cells (can/cannot) be passed on to offspring. Mutations that occur in sex cells (can/cannot) be passed on to offspring.

b. Apply Concepts Drug resistance in bacteria is a beneficial mutation for the bacteria, but how can it be harmful for humans?

_____

_____

_____

_____

Lab® **zone**
Do the Quick Lab
Effects of Mutations.

got it?

○ I get it! Now I know that mutations affect an organism's traits by _____

_____

○ I need extra help with _____

_____

Go to **MY SCIENCE** Ⓢ **COACH** online for help with this subject.

How Is Cancer Related to Mutations and the Cell Cycle?

Did you know cancer is not just one disease? There are more than 100 types of cancer, and they can occur in almost any part of the body. Cancer affects many people around the world, regardless of age, race, or gender. Cancers are often named for the place in the body where they begin. For example, lung cancer begins in lung tissues, as shown in **Figure 3**.

What Is Cancer? **Cancer** is a disease in which cells grow and divide uncontrollably, damaging the parts of the body around them. Cancer cells are like weeds in a garden. Weeds can overrun a garden by robbing plants of the space, sunlight, and water they need. Similarly, cancer cells can overrun normal cells.

Different factors work together in determining if a person gets cancer. Because of their inherited traits, some people are more likely than others to develop certain cancers. A woman with a mother or grandmother who had breast cancer has an increased chance of developing breast cancer herself. Some substances in the environment may also lead to cancer, like the tar in cigarettes or ultraviolet light from the sun or tanning beds. People who have a high-fat diet may also be more likely to develop cancer.

FIGURE 3 ·······································
Lung Tumor X-Ray
Tumors can be visible in X-rays.
✎ **Interpret Photos** Circle the tumor in the X-ray above.

do the math!

You may have noticed labels like SPF 15 on your sunscreen. *SPF* stands for "sun protection factor," and the number lets you know how long the sunscreen works. For example, a person who burns in the sun after 10 minutes could use sunscreen with an SPF of 15 and stay in the sun for as long as 150 minutes ($10 \times 15 = 150$). This time can vary greatly and sunscreen should be reapplied often to prevent damaging sunburns.

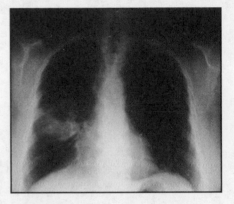

Sunscreen Strength Over Time

SPF	Time in the Sun
20	**a.** ___ h ___ min
30	**b.** ___ h ___ min
55	**c.** ___ h ___ min

1. Fill in the table with the length of time for sun protection each SPF rating offers for someone who burns in 10 minutes without sunscreen.

2. **Calculate** At the beach, you put on SPF 25 at 8:00 A.M. and your friend puts on SPF 15 at 9:00 A.M. You both would burn in 10 minutes without sunscreen. Who should reapply their sunscreen first? When?

Cancer cell

✐ Relate Cause and Effect
Underline a cause and circle the effect in each paragraph.

1 How Cancer Begins

Scientists think that cancer begins when something damages a portion of the DNA in a chromosome. The damage causes a mutation and the cells function abnormally. Normally, the cells in one part of the body live in harmony with the cells around them. Cells that go through the cell cycle divide in a controlled way. 🔑 **Cancer begins when mutations disrupt the normal cell cycle, causing cells to divide in an uncontrolled way.** Without the normal controls on the cell cycle, the cells may grow too large and divide too often.

Tumor

2 How a Tumor Forms

At first, one cell develops in an abnormal way. As the cell divides over and over, more and more abnormal cells are produced. In time, these cells form a tumor. A **tumor** is a mass of abnormal cells that develops when cells divide and grow uncontrollably.

3 How Cancer Spreads

Tumors often take years to grow to a noticeable size. During that time, the cells become more and more abnormal as they continue to divide. Some of the cancerous cells may break off from the tumor and enter the bloodstream. In this way, the cancer can spread to other areas of the body.

Bloodstream

How Cancer Is Treated

How Cancer Is Treated People with cancer can undergo a variety of treatments. Treatments include surgery, radiation, and drugs that destroy the cancer cells.

When cancer is detected before it has spread to other parts of the body, surgery is usually the best treatment. If doctors can completely remove a cancerous tumor, the person may be cured. If the cancer cells have spread or the tumor cannot be removed, doctors may use radiation. Radiation treatment uses beams of high-energy waves. The beams are more likely to destroy the fast-growing cancer cells than normal cells.

Chemotherapy is another treatment option. **Chemotherapy** is the use of drugs to treat a disease. Cancer-fighting drugs are carried throughout the body by the bloodstream. The drugs can kill cancer cells or slow their growth. Many of these drugs, however, destroy some normal cells as well, producing nausea and other side effects patients often experience with chemotherapy treatments.

Scientists are continuing to look for new ways to treat cancer. If scientists can better understand how the cell cycle is controlled, they may find ways to stop cancer cells from multiplying.

apply it!

Drugs are one cancer treatment option.

1 If you were a cancer researcher working on a cure, would you want to design a chemotherapy drug that would speed up the cell cycle or slow it down? Why?

_____

_____

_____

_____

2 [CHALLENGE] Based on what you have learned about cancer and chemotherapy, explain why you think cancer patients who are treated with chemotherapy drugs can lose their hair.

_____

_____

_____

_____

Lab zone® Do the Quick Lab *What Happens When There Are Too Many Cells?*

🗝 Assess Your Understanding

2a. List What are the options for treating cancer?

_____

_____

b. Draw Conclusions Based on the fact that people can get cancer regardless of their genetics, what are some things you can do to lower your risk of getting cancer?

_____

_____

_____

_____

got it?

○ **I get it!** Now I know that cancer is related to mutations and the cell cycle because _____

_____

_____

_____

○ **I need extra help with** _____

_____

Go to MY SCIENCE COACH *online for help with this subject.*

DNA passes information to _____ which passes the information to _____, the source of amino acids that make up _____.

LESSON 1 **The Genetic Code**

🔑 The order of the nitrogen bases along a gene forms a genetic code that specifies what type of protein will be produced.

🔑 Because of the way the nitrogen bases pair up, the order of the bases in each new DNA strand exactly matches the order in the original DNA strand.

Vocabulary
- nitrogen bases
- DNA replication

LESSON 2 **How Cells Make Proteins**

🔑 During protein synthesis, the cell uses information from a gene on a chromosome to produce a specific protein.

Vocabulary
- messenger RNA
- transfer RNA

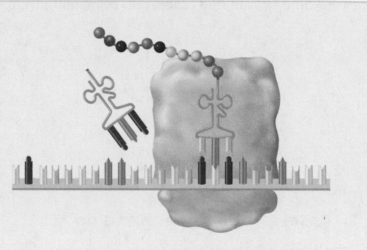

LESSON 3 **Mutations**

🔑 Mutations can cause a cell to produce an incorrect protein during protein synthesis. As a result, the organism's trait may be different from what it normally would be.

🔑 Cancer begins when mutations disrupt the normal cell cycle, causing cells to divide in an uncontrolled way.

Vocabulary
- mutation • cancer • tumor • chemotherapy

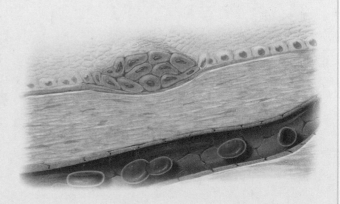

Review and Assessment

LESSON 1 The Genetic Code

1. DNA has four bases: A, C, G, and T. The base A always pairs with _____, and C always pairs with _____.

  a. A, C   **b.** C, G

  c. C, T   **d.** T, G

2. A _____ is a section of DNA within a chromosome that codes for a specific protein.

  a. double helix

  b. ribosome

  c. gene

  d. amino acid

3. Draw Conclusions How does the pairing of the nitrogen bases in a DNA molecule make sure that a replicated strand is exactly the same as the original strand?

_____

_____

_____

_____

4. Interpret Diagrams A DNA molecule is shaped like a double helix. Label the structures of the molecule. Draw in the missing bases and label each base with its code letter.

_____

_____

_____

LESSON 2 How Cells Make Proteins

5. Proteins are made up of molecules called

  a. RNA.   **b.** ribosomes.

  c. nitrogen bases.   **d.** amino acids.

6. _____ carries the information from the genetic code out of the nucleus and into the cytoplasm.

7. Form Operational Definitions During protein synthesis, what is the role of transfer RNA?

_____

_____

_____

8. Apply Concepts What is the relationship among a DNA molecule, messenger RNA, and a protein?

_____

_____

_____

_____

_____

9. **Write About It** Scientists can insert a gene for green fluorescent protein (GFP), which comes from jellyfish, into another organism, such as a flatworm. Explain the process that would then result in the flatworm producing GFP.

_____

_____

_____

_____

_____

_____

LESSON 3 **Mutations**

10. A mass of cancer cells is called a

   a. tumor.   **b.** chromosome.

   c. mutation.   **d.** phenotype.

11. A mutation is a change in _____.

12. Interpret Diagrams Circle the mutation shown in the illustration below.

   Original DNA   After mutation

13. Relate Cause and Effect What is the relationship between the cell cycle and cancer?

_____

_____

_____

14. Apply Concepts How can cancer spread from one part of the body to another?

_____

_____

_____

15. Infer Why does chemotherapy cause side effects such as nausea?

_____

_____

_____

 What does DNA do?

16. The ribosome in the diagram will start to build a protein by linking amino acids. Use what you know about how cells make proteins to fill in the missing letters of the bases in the messenger RNA strand. Then, on the blank strand below, write the DNA code that made the messenger RNA.

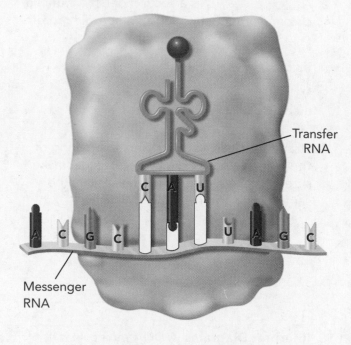

Transfer RNA

Messenger RNA

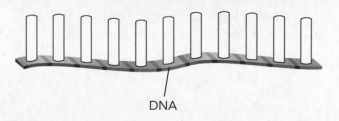

DNA

Standardized Test Prep

Multiple Choice

Circle the letter of the best answer.

1. Select the correct group of words to match the numbered circles in the image.

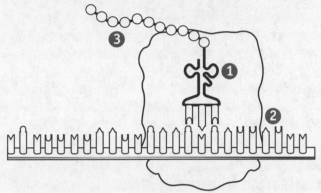

   A (1) tRNA, (2) mRNA, (3) amino acids

   B (1) mRNA, (2) protein, (3) DNA

   C (1) DNA, (2) tRNA , (3) amino acids

   D (1) protein, (2) mRNA, (3) tRNA

2. What is the main function of messenger RNA?

   A It adds amino acids to a growing protein chain.

   B It carries the information necessary for protein synthesis.

   C It carries the information necessary for DNA replication.

   D It carries information that causes deletions and other mutations.

3. What is the sequence of events that results in the growth of a tumor?

   A cancer, mutation, disrupted cell cycle, tumor

   B disrupted cell cycle, protein change, mutation, tumor

   C mutation, disrupted cell cycle, cancer, tumor

   D DNA, cancer, mutation, tumor

4. Imagine a new medication that slows the cell cycle. How would this medication likely affect cancer?

   A It might slow the rate of mutations.

   B It might slow blood flow to the tumor.

   C It might slow the division of cancerous cells.

   D It might slow the effectiveness of chemotherapy.

5. When DNA replicates, the new strand is _____ the original strand.

   A similar to

   B larger than

   C different from

   D identical to

Constructed Response

Use the diagram below and your knowledge of science to help you answer Question 6. Write your answer on a separate piece of paper.

6. The drawing below shows half of a DNA molecule. Write the letters of the bases that would form the other half. Then explain the relationship between DNA and your traits. What could happen if the base C were substituted for the first base T?

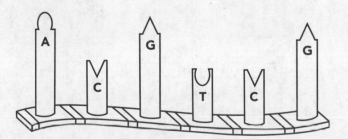

The Frozen ZOO

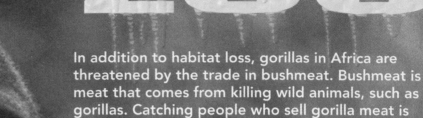

In addition to habitat loss, gorillas in Africa are threatened by the trade in bushmeat. Bushmeat is meat that comes from killing wild animals, such as gorillas. Catching people who sell gorilla meat is difficult because gorilla meat looks like other types of meat that are legal. Fortunately, researchers at the Frozen Zoo are developing genetic tools to catch people who sell gorilla meat.

The Frozen Zoo is a resource center that stores biological material to aid in the conservation of threatened and endangered animals. Researchers at the Frozen Zoo are building a database of genetic material from gorillas. They hope that this database will help conservation officers identify gorilla meat by using DNA barcoding. DNA barcoding is a method that uses a short DNA sequence, found in a cell's mitochondria, to identify an organism as belonging to a particular species.

Students at High Tech High in San Diego recently used DNA barcoding to identify samples of beef, ostrich meat, and turkey meat. Students in New York have also used this tool to identify the fish in their sushi. Now, researchers would like to teach this technique to conservation officers in Nigeria, where gorillas are severely threatened by the trade in bushmeat.

▲ Western Lowland Gorillas are one of the species that is most at risk from illegal hunting and the sale of bushmeat.

▼ Preserved DNA from many animals, including the Western Lowland Gorillas, is kept at the Frozen Zoo.

Research It Find out more about the Frozen Zoo. How do researchers use the biological material stored there? Create a concept map that shows the main ways that the Frozen Zoo aids in the conservation of threatened and endangered animals.

Fighting Cancer

The DNA mutations that cause cancer happen deep inside cells, where we can't see them, but that doesn't mean we are helpless. About one third of all cancer deaths in the United States are linked to poor diet and lack of exercise. A diet rich in fruits and vegetables reduces your cancer risk. So does regular exercise. Sunscreen or protective clothing can reduce the damage to DNA caused by sunlight when outdoors. And smoking is the largest cause of preventable cancer deaths in the world—by avoiding smoking and secondhand smoke, you are doing your cells a favor!

For existing cancer cases, scientists are using DNA studies to create treatments for specific types of cancers and even specific individuals! Scientists are also developing drugs that repair the damaged DNA.

Write About It Create a poster explaining one thing your classmates can do to reduce their risk of cancer. Use facts and other appropriate information to persuade your classmates.

There's Something Fishy About This Sushi!

Do restaurant menus always tell the truth? High school students Kate Stoeckle and Louisa Strauss asked themselves this question while eating sushi in New York City. They decided to identify the fish in their sushi. Kate and Louisa gathered 60 fish samples from local restaurants and grocery stores. They sent the samples to a lab that used DNA barcoding to test the samples.

The tests showed that 25 percent of the samples were mislabeled! Often, inexpensive fish was labeled as more expensive fish. For example, a sample labeled "red snapper" was actually Atlantic cod. Another sample was from an endangered fish.

In the future, DNA barcoding could be done by using a handheld device. Such a device might look similar to a supermarket barcode scanner. Then, anyone could quickly solve a DNA mystery at the dinner table or beyond!

Research It Find out more about DNA barcoding. Identify a question you could answer by using this technology. Describe how you could use DNA barcoding to answer your question.

HOW CAN SCIENTISTS IDENTIFY HUMAN REMAINS?

How can genetic information be used?

These forensic scientists are putting together the skeletons of war victims. They can determine the age, sex, height, and ancestry of each body by examining bones. But that does not identify who the person was. Other scientists work to determine the identities of the victims.

△ **Develop Hypotheses** How do you think a scientist might figure out a person's identity from bones?

_____
_____
_____
_____
_____
_____

▷ **UNTAMED SCIENCE** Watch the **Untamed Science** video to learn more about genetic technology.

Human Genetics and Genetic Technology

5 Getting Started

Check Your Understanding

1. **Background** Read the paragraph below and then answer the question.

Abdul has a white mouse named Pug. Both of Pug's parents had black fur, but they each had one **allele** for white fur and one allele for black fur. Because the **dominant allele** is for black fur, there was only a 25 percent **probability** that Pug would have white fur.

> An **allele** is a different form of a gene.
>
> The trait determined by a **dominant allele** always shows up in an organism if the allele is present.
>
> **Probability** is a number that describes how likely it is that an event will occur.

- What is the probability that Pug's parents would have an offspring with black fur? _____

> **MY READING WEB** If you had trouble completing the question above, visit **My Reading Web** and type in *Human Genetics and Genetic Technology.*

Vocabulary Skill

High-Use Academic Words High-use academic words are words that are used frequently in classrooms. Look for the words below as you read this chapter.

Word	Definition	Example
normal	*adj.* usual; typical, expected	It is *normal* to feel nervous about going to a new school.
resistant	*adj.* capable of preventing something from happening	The fabric stays clean easily because it is *resistant* to stains.

2. **Quick Check** Choose the word that best completes each sentence.

- Some bacteria are _____ to common antibiotic medicines, so they are not killed by them.

- A _____ body temperature in a human is about 37°C.

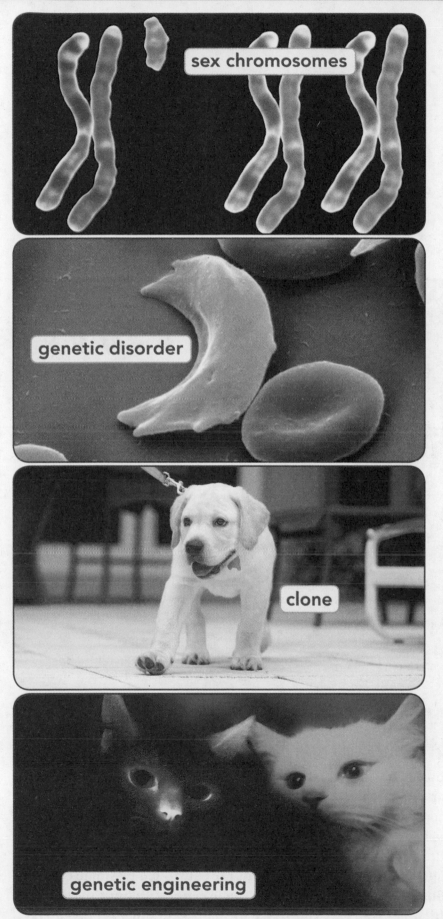

sex chromosomes

genetic disorder

clone

genetic engineering

Chapter Preview

LESSON 1
- sex chromosomes
- sex-linked gene
- carrier
- ↻ Relate Cause and Effect
- △ Infer

LESSON 2
- genetic disorder
- pedigree
- karyotype
- ↻ Outline
- △ Make Models

LESSON 3
- selective breeding
- inbreeding
- hybridization
- clone
- genetic engineering
- gene therapy
- ↻ Ask Questions
- △ Draw Conclusions

LESSON 4
- genome
- ethics
- ↻ Summarize
- △ Communicate

> **VOCAB FLASH CARDS** For extra help with vocabulary, visit **Vocab Flash Cards** and type in *Human Genetics and Genetic Technology.*

UNLOCK THE BIG Q?

🔑 **What Are Some Patterns of Human Inheritance?**

🔑 **What Are the Functions of the Sex Chromosomes?**

mY pLaNeT DiaRY

BLOG

Posted by: Hannah

Location: Old Tappan, New Jersey

I have many traits and characteristics that my parents have passed down to me. I have brown hair, like my mom's, but it's curly, like my dad's. I also have my dad's dark brown eyes, while my mom has blue. Both my parents have fair skin tone, but I have an olive complexion like my grandfather. I'm an interesting mix of all my relatives.

Write your answer below.

What characteristics do you have that resemble those of your relatives?

_____

_____

_____

_____

_____

▶ **PLANET DIARY** Go to **Planet Diary** to learn more about human inheritance.

Lab zone® Do the Inquiry Warm-Up *How Tall Is Tall?*

What Are Some Patterns of Human Inheritance?

Look at the other students in your classroom. Some people have curly hair; others have straight hair. Some people are tall, some are short, and many others are in between. You'll probably see eyes of many different colors, ranging from pale blue to dark brown. The different traits you see are determined by a variety of inheritance patterns. 🔑 **Some human traits are controlled by single genes with two alleles, and others by single genes with multiple alleles. Still other traits are controlled by many genes that act together.**

Vocabulary
- sex chromosomes • sex-linked gene • carrier

Skills
- ↻ Reading: Relate Cause and Effect
- △ Inquiry: Infer

Single Genes With Two Alleles A number of human traits, such as a dimpled chin or a widow's peak, are controlled by a single gene with either a dominant or a recessive allele. These traits have two distinctly different physical appearances, or phenotypes.

Single Genes With Multiple Alleles Some human traits are controlled by a single gene that has more than two alleles. Such a gene is said to have multiple alleles—three or more forms of a gene that code for a single trait. Even though a gene may have multiple alleles, a person can carry only two of those alleles. This is because chromosomes exist in pairs. Each chromosome in a pair carries only one allele for each gene. Recall that an organism's genetic makeup is its genotype. The physical characteristics that result are called the organism's phenotype.

Human blood type is controlled by a gene with multiple alleles. There are four main blood types—A, B, AB, and O. Three alleles control the inheritance of blood types. The allele for blood type A is written as I^A. The allele for blood type B is written as I^B. The allele for blood type A and the allele for blood type B are codominant. This means that both alleles for the gene are expressed equally. A person who inherits an I^A allele from one parent and an I^B allele from the other parent will have type AB blood. The allele for blood type O—written as i—is recessive. **Figure 1** shows the different allele combinations that result in each blood type.

FIGURE 1 ··

Inheritance of Blood Type
The table below shows which combinations of alleles result in each human blood type.

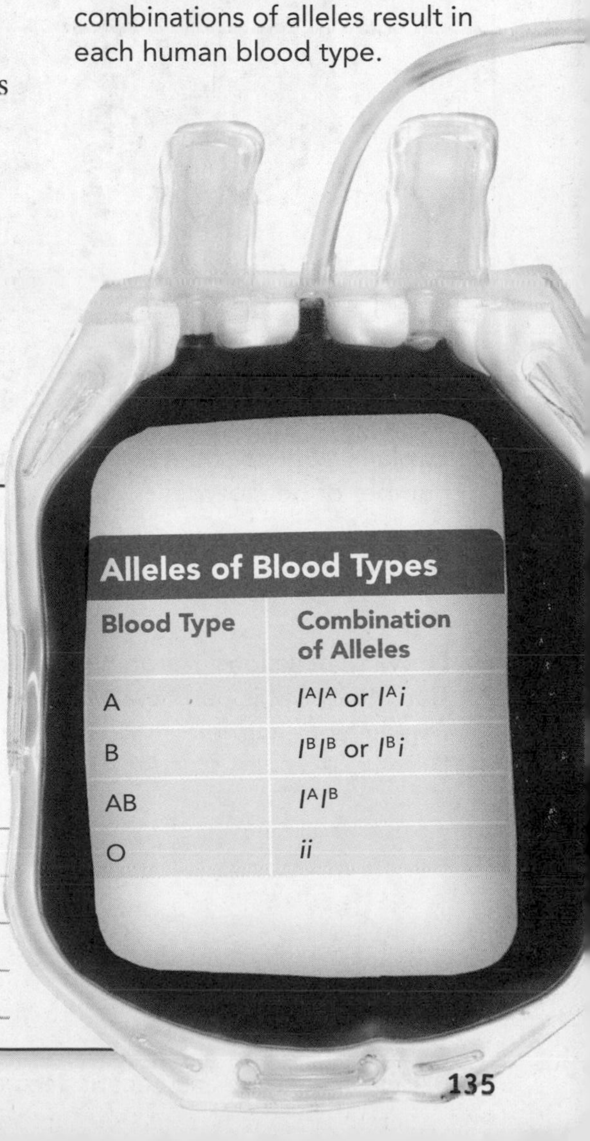

Alleles of Blood Types	
Blood Type	**Combination of Alleles**
A	$I^A I^A$ or $I^A i$
B	$I^B I^B$ or $I^B i$
AB	$I^A I^B$
O	ii

apply it!

Use what you have learned about blood types and **Figure 1** to answer the following questions.

1 **Interpret Tables** Genotypes are listed in the (left/right) column of the table, while phenotypes are on the (left/right).

2 △ **Infer** Why are there more genotypes than phenotypes for blood types?

_____

_____

_____

_____

250 cm
225 cm
200 cm
175 cm
150 cm
125 cm
100 cm
75 cm
50 cm
25 cm
0 cm

Traits Controlled by Many Genes
If you look around your classroom, you'll see that height in humans has more than two distinct phenotypes. In fact, there is an enormous variety of phenotypes for height. Some human traits show a large number of phenotypes because the traits are controlled by many genes. The alleles of the different genes act together as a group to produce a single trait. At least four genes control height in humans. You can see the extreme range of heights in **Figure 2.** Skin color is another human trait that is controlled by many genes.

FIGURE 2 ··

Extreme Heights
Human heights are known to range from the tall Bao Xishun, at 236 cm, to the short He Pingping, at 76 cm.

✎ **On the scale, mark your height and the heights of Bao Xishun and He Pingping.**

1. Calculate How many times taller are you than He Pingping?

_____

2. Predict Do you think Bao Xishun's parents are also tall? Why?

_____

_____

Lab ® **Do the Quick Lab**
zone *The Eyes Have It.*

⚷ Assess Your Understanding

1a. Explain Why do some traits exhibit a large number of phenotypes?

_____

_____

b. Draw Conclusions Aaron has blood type O. Can either of his parents have blood type AB? Explain your answer.

_____

_____

_____

_____

_____

got it?

○ **I get it!** Now I know that some human traits are controlled by _____

_____

_____

_____

○ **I need extra help with** _____

_____

Go to MY SCIENCE 💬 COACH *online for help with this subject.*

What Are the Functions of the Sex Chromosomes?

The body cells of humans contain 23 chromosome pairs, or 46 chromosomes. The **sex chromosomes** are one of the 23 pairs of chromosomes in each body cell. **The sex chromosomes carry genes that determine a person's sex as being either male or female. They also carry genes that determine other traits.**

Girl or Boy? The sex chromosomes are the only chromosome pair that do not always match. Girls have two sex chromosomes that match. The two chromosomes are called X chromosomes. Boys have two sex chromosomes that do not match. They have an X chromosome and a Y chromosome. The Y chromosome is much smaller than the X chromosome. To show the size difference, the sex chromosomes in **Figure 3** have been stained and magnified.

Sex Chromosomes and Fertilization When egg cells and sperm cells form, what happens to the sex chromosomes? Since both of a female's sex chromosomes are X chromosomes, all eggs carry one X chromosome. Males, however, have two different sex chromosomes. Therefore, half of a male's sperm cells carry an X chromosome, while half carry a Y chromosome.

When a sperm cell with an X chromosome fertilizes an egg, the egg has two X chromosomes. The fertilized egg will develop into a girl. When a sperm with a Y chromosome fertilizes an egg, the egg has one X chromosome and one Y chromosome. The fertilized egg will develop into a boy.

X Chromosome

Y Chromosome

X Chromosomes

FIGURE 3 ·······················
Male or Female?
The father's chromosome determines the sex of his child.

✎ **Using the genotypes given for the mother and father, complete the Punnett square to show their child's genotype and phenotype.**

1. **Calculate** What is the probability that the child will be a girl? A boy?

_____

_____

2. **Interpret Diagrams** What sex will the child be if a sperm with a Y chromosome fertilizes an egg? _____

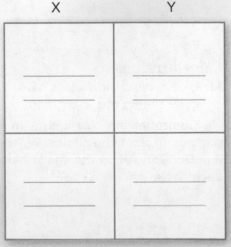

X   Y

X

X

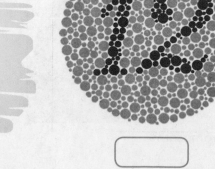

Relate Cause and Effect
Underline the cause of sex-linked traits in males and circle the effect of the traits.

Sex-Linked Genes The genes for some human traits are carried on the sex chromosomes. Genes found on the X and Y chromosomes are often called **sex-linked genes** because their alleles are passed from parent to child on a sex chromosome. Traits controlled by sex-linked genes are called sex-linked traits. One sex-linked trait is red-green colorblindness. A person with this trait cannot see the difference between red and green. Normal vision is dominant, while colorblindness is recessive.

FIGURE 4 ·······················

▶ **VIRTUAL LAB** **X and Y Chromosomes**
The human X chromosome is larger and carries more genes than the human Y chromosome.

Y Chromosome

Recall that a Y chromosome is smaller than an X chromosome. Females have two X chromosomes, but males have one X chromosome and one Y chromosome. These chromosomes have different genes.

X Chromosome

Most of the genes on the X chromosome are not on the Y chromosome. So an allele on an X chromosome may have no corresponding allele on a Y chromosome.

Like other genes, sex-linked genes can have dominant and recessive alleles. In females, a dominant allele on an X chromosome will mask a recessive allele on the other X chromosome. But in males, there is usually no matching allele on the Y chromosome to mask the allele on the X chromosome. As a result, any allele on the X chromosome—even a recessive allele—will produce the trait in a male who inherits it. This means that males are more likely than females to express a sex-linked trait that is controlled by a recessive allele. Individuals with colorblindness may have difficulty seeing the numbers in **Figure 5.** Test your vision below.

FIGURE 5 ·······················

Colorblindness
Most colorblind individuals have difficulty seeing red and green.

✎ **Communicate** Working with a partner, look at the circles. Write the number you see in the space below each circle.

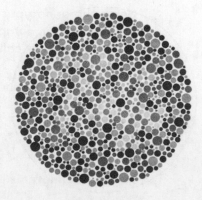

Inheritance of Colorblindness

Colorblindness is a trait controlled by a recessive allele on the X chromosome. Many more males than females have red-green colorblindness. You can understand why this is the case by examining the Punnett square in **Figure 6**. Both parents have normal color vision. Notice that the mother carries the dominant allele for normal vision (X^C) and the recessive allele for colorblindness (X^c). A **carrier** is a person who has one recessive allele for a trait and one dominant allele. A carrier of a trait controlled by a recessive allele does not express the trait. However, the carrier can pass the recessive allele on to his or her offspring. In the case of sex-linked traits, only females can be carriers because they are the only ones who can carry two alleles for the trait.

FIGURE 6 ·

Colorblindness Punnett Square

Red-green colorblindess is a sex-linked trait.

✎ **Using the parents' information and the key, complete the Punnett square.**

1. **Identify** Complete the Punnett square by filling in the child's genotype, sex, and phenotype. For each child, draw the correct shape, and color it in to match the key.

2. **Calculate** What is the probability that this couple will have a colorblind child?

   _____

3. **Apply Concepts** What allele combination would a daughter need to inherit to be colorblind?

   _____

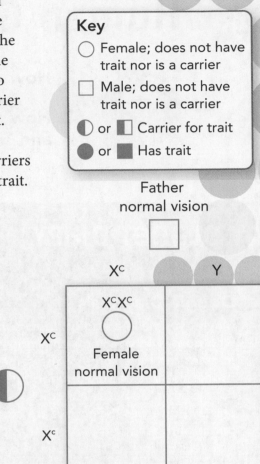

Key
- ○ Female; does not have trait nor is a carrier
- □ Male; does not have trait nor is a carrier
- ◖ or ◧ Carrier for trait
- ● or ■ Has trait

Father
normal vision

	X^C	Y
X^C	$X^C X^C$ ○ Female normal vision	
X^c		

Mother carrier

Do the Lab Investigation
How Are Genes on the Sex Chromosomes Inherited?

🔑 Assess Your Understanding

2a. Review What is the sex of a person who is a carrier for colorblindness? _____

b. [CHALLENGE] Mary and her mother are both colorblind. Is Mary's father colorblind, too? How do you know?

_____

_____

_____

_____

got it?

○ I get it! Now I know that the functions of the sex chromosomes are _____

_____

_____

○ I need extra help with _____

_____

Go to MY SCIENCE ⓢ COACH *online for help with this subject.*

Human Genetic Disorders

🔑 **How Are Genetic Disorders Inherited in Humans?**

🔑 **How Are Genetic Disorders Traced, Diagnosed, and Treated?**

MY PLANET DiARY

Doggie Diagnosis

Maybe you have a dog or know someone who does. Did you know that dogs and humans can have some of the same health problems? It is not uncommon for dogs to have cancer, diabetes, allergies, epilepsy, and eye diseases. Scientists are studying the genes and genetic mutations that cause diseases in dogs in the hopes of better understanding human diseases. Most diseases in dogs are caused by a mutation on one gene. In humans, the mutations can be on multiple genes. The genes that cause diseases in dogs are much easier to find than those in humans. So far, scientists are looking into the genes that cause blindness, cancer, and spinal cord disorders in dogs.

German shepherds can have a form of cancer similar to breast cancer in humans.

Dachshunds and humans can both suffer from blindness.

DISCOVERY

Communicate Discuss the questions with a classmate. Then write your answers.

1. Why are scientists studying dog genes to understand human diseases?

_____

_____

_____

_____

2. In what other ways could studying dog diseases be beneficial?

_____

_____

_____

_____

_____

▷ **PLANET DIARY** Go to **Planet Diary** to learn more about human genetic disorders.

Golden retrievers can have cancer that affects the blood vessels.

Lab zone® Do the Inquiry Warm-Up *How Many Chromosomes?*

Vocabulary
- genetic disorder   • pedigree
- karyotype

Skills
- Reading: Outline
- Inquiry: Make Models

How Are Genetic Disorders Inherited in Humans?

Many of the athletes who compete in the Special Olympics have disabilities that result from genetic disorders. A **genetic disorder** is an abnormal condition that a person inherits through genes or chromosomes. **Some genetic disorders are caused by mutations in the DNA of genes. Other disorders are caused by changes in the overall structure or number of chromosomes.** In this lesson, you will learn about some common genetic disorders.

Cystic Fibrosis   Cystic fibrosis is a genetic disorder in which the body produces abnormally thick mucus in the lungs and intestines. The thick mucus fills the lungs, making it hard for the affected person to breathe. Cystic fibrosis occurs when two mutated alleles are inherited, one from each parent. The mutation causes three bases to be removed from a DNA molecule.

Sickle-Cell Disease   Sickle-cell disease is caused by a mutation that affects hemoglobin. Hemoglobin is a protein in red blood cells that carries oxygen. The red blood cells of people with the disease have a sickle, or crescent, shape. Sickle-shaped red blood cells cannot carry as much oxygen as normal cells and also clog blood vessels. The allele for the sickle-cell trait (*S*) is codominant with the normal allele (*A*). A person with one normal allele and one sickle-cell allele (*AS*) will produce both normal hemoglobin and abnormal hemoglobin. This person usually does not have symptoms of the disease. He or she has enough normal hemoglobin to carry oxygen to cells. A person with two sickle-cell alleles (*SS*) will have the disease.

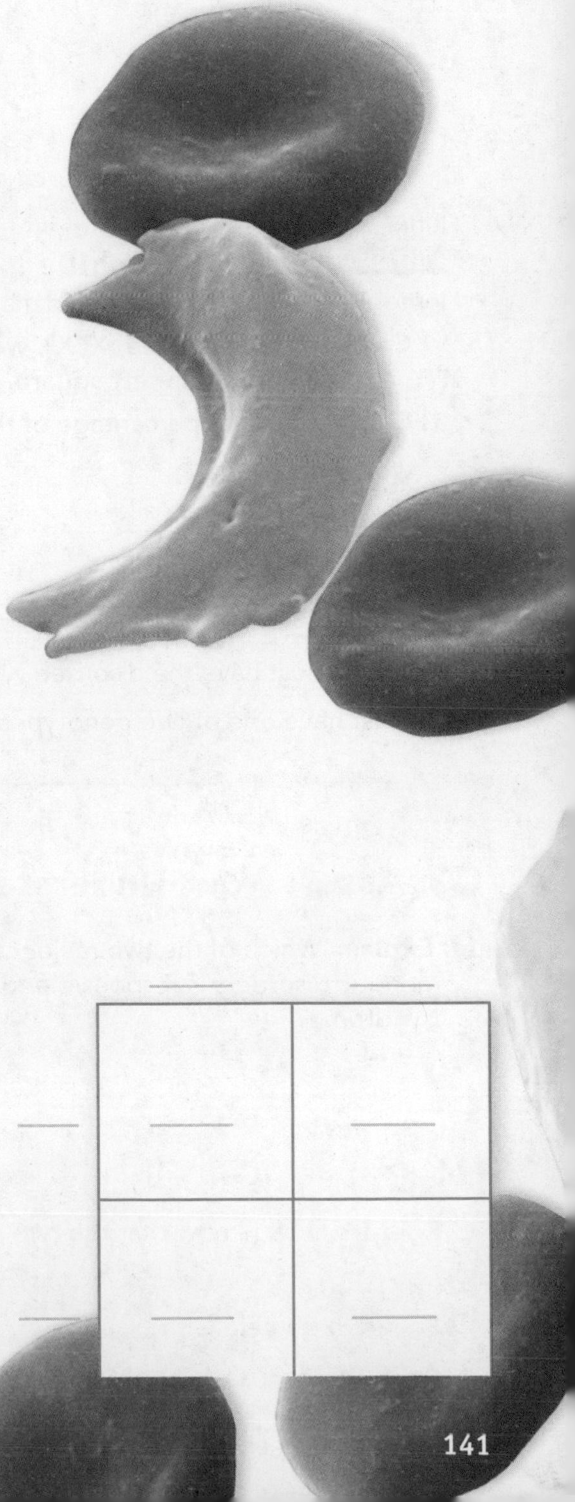

FIGURE 1 ·········
Sickle-Cell Disease
In a person with sickle-cell disease, red blood cells can become sickle-shaped instead of round.

✏ **Predict** A man has sickle-cell disease. His wife does not have the disease, but is heterozygous for the sickle-cell trait. Use the parents' information to fill in the Punnett square. What is the probability that their child will have sickle-cell disease?

....

Outline After you read this section, make an outline on a separate sheet of paper that includes the different types of genetic disorders. Use the red headings to help you organize your outline.

Hemophilia Hemophilia is a genetic disorder in which a person's blood clots very slowly or not at all. People with the disorder do not produce enough of one of the proteins needed for normal blood clotting. The danger of internal bleeding from small bumps and bruises is very high. Hemophilia is caused by a recessive allele on the X chromosome. Because hemophilia is a sex-linked disorder, it occurs more frequently in males than in females.

Down Syndrome In Down syndrome, a person's cells have an extra copy of chromosome 21. Instead of a pair of chromosomes, a person with Down syndrome has three copies. Down syndrome most often occurs when chromosomes fail to separate properly during meiosis, when sex cells (egg and sperm) form. People with Down syndrome have some degree of intellectual disability. Heart defects are also common, but can be treated.

FIGURE 2 ································

> **INTERACTIVE ART** **Hemophilia**

Hemophilia occurs more often in males than in females.

✎ **Cross a carrier female, $X^H X^h$, with a healthy male, $X^H Y$, and fill in the Punnett square.**

1. **Calculate** What percentage of the offspring

   would be normal?_____

   would be carriers? _____

   would have hemophilia? _____

2. **CHALLENGE** To have a daughter with hemophilia, the father must have the disorder ($X^h Y$) and the mother must have one of two genotypes. What are they?

   _____

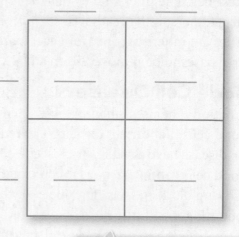

Lab ® Do the Quick Lab
zone *What Went Wrong?*

🔑 **Assess Your Understanding**

1a. Explain Which of the two major causes of genetic disorders is responsible for Down syndrome?

_____

_____

b. Infer Why is hemophilia more common in males?

_____

_____

_____

got it? ··

○ **I get it!** Now I know that the two major causes of genetic disorders are _____

_____

○ **I need extra help with** _____

Go to **MY SCIENCE ⓢ COACH** *online for help with this subject.*

How Are Genetic Disorders Traced, Diagnosed, and Treated?

Years ago, only Punnett squares were used to predict whether a child might have a genetic disorder. **Today, doctors use tools such as pedigrees, karyotypes, and genetic testing to trace and diagnose genetic disorders. People with genetic disorders are helped through medical care, education, and job training.**

Pedigrees Suppose that you are interested in tracing the occurrence of a trait through several generations of a family. What would you do? A **pedigree** is a chart or "family tree" that tracks which members of a family have a particular trait. The trait in a pedigree can be an ordinary trait, such as eye color, or a genetic disorder. The pedigree shown below is for albinism, a condition in which a person's skin, hair, and eyes lack normal coloring.

apply it!

This pedigree shows the inheritance of the allele for albinism in three generations of a family.

❶ Interpret Diagrams Circle the place in the pedigree that shows an albino male.

Key
- ◯ Female; does not have trait nor is a carrier
- ☐ Male; does not have trait nor is a carrier
- ◐ or ◖ Carrier for trait
- ● or ◼ Has trait

A horizontal line connecting a male and a female represents a marriage.

A vertical line and a bracket connect the parents to their children.

❷ Make Models Using what you have learned about pedigrees and pedigree symbols, construct a two-generation pedigree for sickle-cell disease, starting with parents who are both carriers, *AS × AS*. (*Hint:* Construct Punnett squares on a separate sheet of paper to determine the possible genotypes of the offspring.)

Karyotypes To detect a chromosomal disorder such as Down syndrome, doctors examine karyotypes. A **karyotype** (KA ree uh typ) is a picture of all the chromosomes in a person's cell. Look at **Figure 3.** As you can see, the chromosomes in a karyotype are arranged in pairs. A karyotype can reveal whether a person has the correct number of chromosomes in his or her cells.

FIGURE 3 ···

Karyotypes

Look at the karyotypes below. One is a normal karyotype and the other is an abnormal karyotype.

✎ **Working with a classmate, compare the two karyotypes.**

1. **Interpret Photos** What numbered set of chromosomes are the most different between the karyotypes? _____

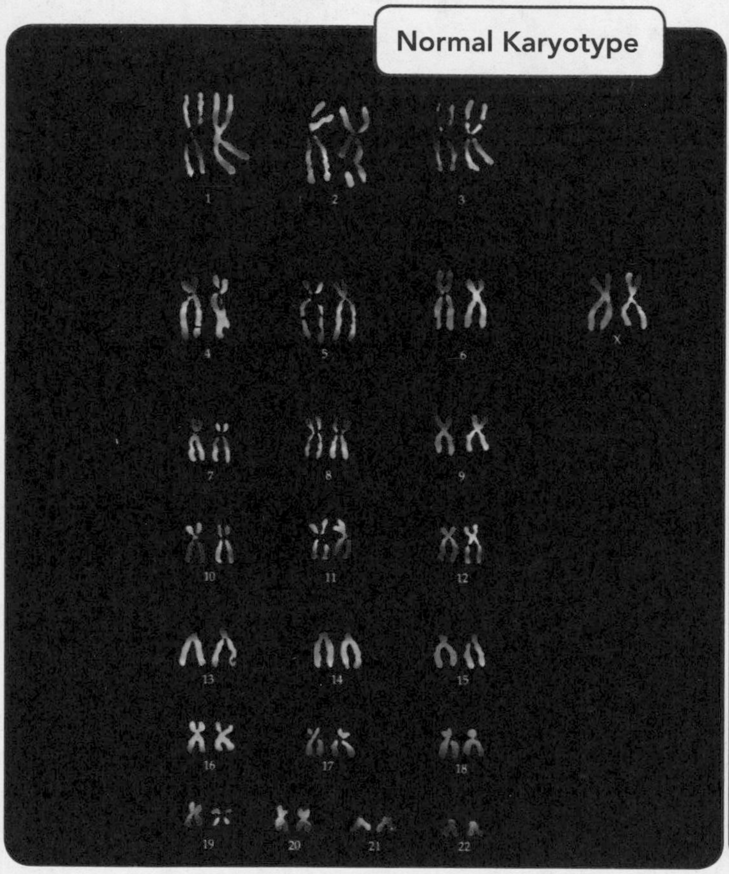

Normal Karyotype

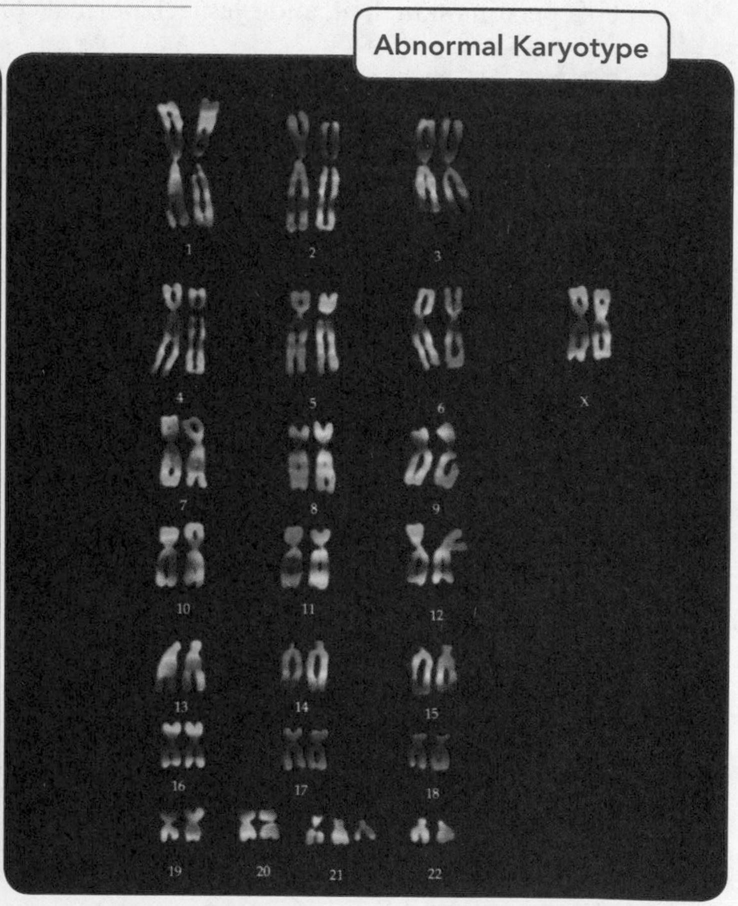

Abnormal Karyotype

2. **Draw Conclusions** What can you conclude about the individual with the abnormal karyotype? Use evidence to support your answer.

_____

_____

_____

_____

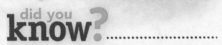

Genetic Counseling

Genetic Counseling A couple that has a family history of a genetic disorder may turn to a genetic counselor for advice. Genetic counselors help couples understand their chances of having a child with a particular genetic disorder. Genetic counselors also help couples prepare for having children with a disorder. Karyotypes, pedigree charts, and Punnett squares assist genetic counselors in their work.

With advances in technology, new tests have been developed to screen for genetic disorders. Genetic tests examine genes, DNA, enzymes, and proteins to see if an individual has a genetic disorder or carries a gene for a genetic disorder. Whether or not the person develops the disease also depends on many other genetic factors, environmental conditions, and lifestyle.

Dealing With Genetic Disorders

Dealing With Genetic Disorders People with genetic disorders face serious challenges, but they can be helped. Medical treatments help people with the symptoms of some disorders. For example, physical therapy helps remove mucus from the lungs of people with cystic fibrosis. People with sickle-cell disease take folic acid, a vitamin, to help their bodies manufacture red blood cells. Because of education and job training programs, adults with Down syndrome can find work in banks, restaurants, and other places. Most genetic disorders do not prevent people from living active, productive lives.

did you know?

Malaria is an infectious disease that kills more than a million people a year. This disease is transmitted to people when they are bitten by an infected mosquito. However, people who have the gene that causes sickle-cell disease are less likely to develop malaria.

FIGURE 4 ·······

Genetic Disorders

These athletes have Down syndrome, a genetic disorder.

✎ **List** Name two types of programs that benefit individuals with Down syndrome.

_____

_____

_____

 Lab zone Do the Quick Lab *Family Puzzle.*

🔖 Assess Your Understanding

got it? ···

○ **I get it!** Now I know that genetic disorders are traced, diagnosed, and treated by _____

_____

○ **I need extra help with** _____

Go to MY SCIENCE ⬤ COACH online for help with this subject.

Advances in Genetics

How Can Organisms Be Produced With Desired Traits?

my planet Diary

Zorses and Zedonks

Most people can tell the difference between a zebra and a horse. But would you be able to tell the difference between a zorse and a zedonk? Both types of animals are zebroids, or zebra hybrids. These animals result when a zebra mates with a horse or a donkey. Zebroids do not usually occur in nature. They generally result when people cross them on purpose. People may have first crossed zebras and horses in an effort to develop disease-resistant transportation animals for use in Africa. Zebras are resistant to African sleeping sickness. It was hoped that zorses, the offspring of zebras and horses, would have this resistance.

Communicate Discuss these questions with a classmate. Write your answers below.

1. Why may zebras and horses have been first crossed by people?

_____

_____

2. If zebras and horses do not usually mate in nature, should people intentionally cross them? Why or why not?

_____

_____

_____

_____

> PLANET DIARY Go to **Planet Diary** to learn more about advances in genetics.

Lab zone® Do the Inquiry Warm-Up *What Do Fingerprints Reveal?*

Vocabulary

- selective breeding
- inbreeding
- hybridization
- clone
- genetic engineering
- gene therapy

Skills

- Reading: Ask Questions
- Inquiry: Draw Conclusions

How Can Organisms Be Produced With Desired Traits?

Unless you are an identical twin, your DNA is different from everyone else's. Because of advances in genetics, DNA evidence can show many things, such as family relationships or the ability to produce organisms with desirable traits. **Selective breeding, cloning, and genetic engineering are three different methods for developing organisms with desired traits.**

Selective Breeding The process of selecting organisms with desired traits to be parents of the next generation is called **selective breeding.** Thousands of years ago, in what is now Mexico, the food that we call corn was developed in this way. Every year, farmers saved seeds from the healthiest plants that produced the best food. In the spring, they planted only those seeds. This process was repeated over and over. In time, farmers developed plants that produced better corn. People have used selective breeding with many types of plants and animals. Two techniques for selective breeding are inbreeding and hybridization.

Ask Questions Before you read this lesson, preview the red headings. In the graphic organizer below, ask a question for each heading. As you read, write answers to your questions.

Question	Answer
What is selective breeding?	Selective breeding is

Vocabulary High-Use Academic Words Use the word *resistant* to explain how hybridization can be useful.

_____

_____

_____

_____

_____

_____

Inbreeding The technique of **inbreeding** involves crossing two individuals that have similar desirable characteristics. Suppose a male and a female golden retriever are both friendly and have the same coloring. Their offspring will probably also have those qualities. Inbreeding produces organisms that are genetically very similar. When inbred organisms are mated, the chance of their offspring inheriting two recessive alleles increases. This can lead to genetic disorders. For example, inherited hip problems are common in golden retrievers and other types of inbred dogs.

Hybridization In **hybridization** (hy brid ih ZAY shun), breeders cross two genetically different individuals. Recall that a hybrid organism has two different alleles for a trait. The hybrid organism that results is bred to have the best traits from both parents. For example, a farmer might cross corn that produces many kernels with corn that is resistant to disease. The farmer is hoping to produce a hybrid corn plant with both of the desired traits. Roses and other types of flowers are also commonly crossed.

apply it!

Since the late eighteenth century, gardeners and plant breeders have used hybridization to develop roses with certain characteristics.

1 Observe Look at each rose below. One characteristic for each flower is given to you. List any other observable characteristics you see.

2 Draw Conclusions Based on the characteristics of the two roses, draw with colored pencils or describe what you think the hybrid offspring will look like. Name the flower and list its characteristics.

Parent A

fragrant

_____

_____

Parent B

survives cold temperatures

_____

_____

Hybrid name:_____

_____

_____

_____

do the math!

Year	Yield
1965	2.04
1970	2.38
1975	2.52
1980	2.75
1985	3.26
1990	3.53
1995	3.66
2000	3.89
2005	4.09

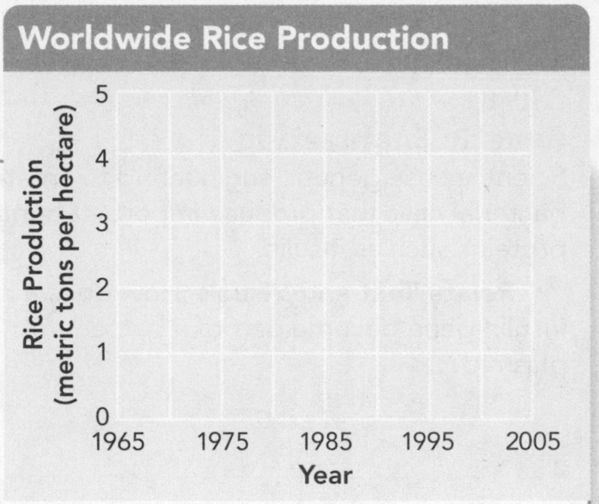

Changing Rice Production

This data table shows how worldwide rice production changed between 1965 and 2005. New hybrid varieties of rice plants are one factor that has affected the amount of rice produced.

Worldwide Rice Production

1 Graph Plot the data from the table and draw a line graph.

2 Interpret Data What is the approximate difference between rice production in 1965 and 2005? _____

3 CHALLENGE What other factors might help account for the difference in rice production between 1965 and 2005?

_____

_____

_____

Cloning

For some organisms, such as the dog shown in **Figure 1,** a technique called cloning can be used to produce offspring with desired traits. A **clone** is an organism that has exactly the same genes as the organism from which it was produced. It isn't hard to clone some kinds of plants such as African violets. Just cut a stem from one plant and put the stem in soil. Water it, and soon you will have a whole new plant. The new plant is genetically identical to the plant from which the stem was cut.

Genetic Engineering

Geneticists have developed another powerful technique for producing organisms with desired traits. In this process, called **genetic engineering,** genes from one organism are transferred into the DNA of another organism. Genetic engineering can produce medicines and improve food crops.

FIGURE 1 ···

Cloning

This puppy, Lancelot Encore, is thought to be the first commercially cloned puppy in the United States. His owners paid $150,000 to have him cloned in South Korea.

✎ **Make Judgments** Would you pay $150,000 to clone a pet? Why or why not?

_____

_____

FIGURE 2

Genetic Engineering

Scientists use genetic engineering to create bacterial cells that produce important human proteins such as insulin.

✎ **Relate Text and Visuals** How does a human insulin gene become part of a bacterium's plasmid?

_____

_____

_____

_____

_____

_____

_____

Genetic Engineering in Bacteria One type of bacterium is genetically engineered to produce a human protein called insulin. Many people with diabetes need insulin injections. Bacteria have a single DNA molecule in the cytoplasm. Some bacterial cells also contain small circular pieces of DNA called plasmids. You can see how scientists insert the DNA for the human insulin gene into the plasmid of a bacterium in **Figure 2.** Once the gene is inserted into the plasmid, the bacterial cell and all of its offspring will contain this human gene. As a result, the bacteria produce the protein that the human gene codes for—in this case, insulin. Because bacteria can reproduce quickly, large amounts of insulin can be produced in a short time.

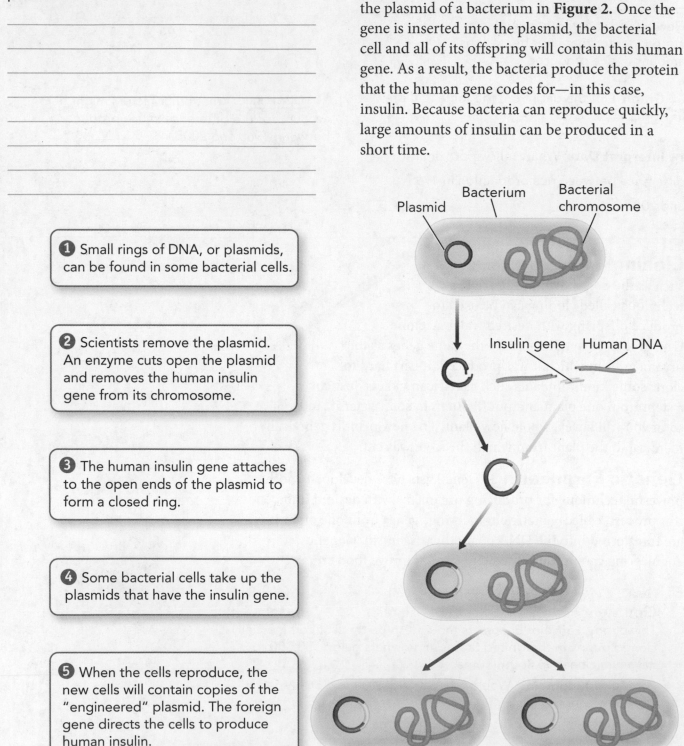

❶ Small rings of DNA, or plasmids, can be found in some bacterial cells.

❷ Scientists remove the plasmid. An enzyme cuts open the plasmid and removes the human insulin gene from its chromosome.

❸ The human insulin gene attaches to the open ends of the plasmid to form a closed ring.

❹ Some bacterial cells take up the plasmids that have the insulin gene.

❺ When the cells reproduce, the new cells will contain copies of the "engineered" plasmid. The foreign gene directs the cells to produce human insulin.

Genetic Engineering in Other Organisms

Scientists can also use genetic engineering techniques to insert genes into animals. For example, human genes can be inserted into the cells of cows. The cows then produce milk containing the human protein coded by the gene. Scientists have used this technique to produce the blood-clotting protein needed by people with hemophilia.

Genes have also been inserted into the cells of plants, such as tomatoes and rice. Some of the genes enable the plants to survive in cold temperatures or in poor soil. Other genetically engineered crops can resist insect pests or contain more nutrients.

Gene Therapy Someday it may be possible to use genetic engineering to correct some genetic disorders in humans. This process, called gene therapy, will involve inserting copies of a gene directly into a person's cells. For example, doctors may be able to treat hemophilia by replacing the defective allele on the X chromosome. The inserted gene would provide the body the correct instructions to clot blood normally.

Concerns About Genetic Engineering

Some people are concerned about the long-term effects of genetic engineering. For example, some people think that genetically engineered crops may not be entirely safe. People fear that these crops may harm the environment or cause health problems in humans. To address such concerns, scientists are studying the effects of genetic engineering.

FIGURE 3 ·······················

▶ ART IN MOTION **Glow Cats**
A fluorescent protein was added to the cells of the cat below. This protein allows the cat to glow red when exposed to ultraviolet light. The cat above lacks this protein.

Lab® zone Do the Quick Lab
Selective Breeding.

Assess Your Understanding

1a. Identify The technique of crossing two individuals with similar characteristics is (inbreeding/hybridization).

b. Explain Why are identical twins not clones according to the text definition?

_____

_____

c. Apply Concepts Lupita has a houseplant. Which method would be the best way of producing a similar plant for a friend? Explain your answer.

_____

_____

_____

_____

got it? ·································

O **I get it!** Now I know that the three ways of producing organisms with desired traits are

_____

_____

O **I need extra help with** _____

_____

Go to **MY SCIENCE** 🔊 **COACH** *online for help with this subject.*

Using Genetic Information

🔑 **What Are Some Uses of Genetic Information?**

my planet Diary

TECHNOLOGY

Freedom Fighters

DNA technology saves lives, and not just through medicine. Since 1992, hundreds of innocent people have been freed from prison—some from death row—thanks to DNA testing. The Innocence Project is an organization that uses DNA testing to free prisoners who were wrongfully convicted. First, a sample of DNA is obtained from evidence saved from the crime scene. Then, a sample is taken from the prisoner. Laboratory procedures allow scientists to compare the two samples. If the prisoner's DNA is different from the DNA at the crime scene, the evidence may help free the prisoner.

Infer If the DNA from the crime scene matches the DNA from the prisoner, what might that suggest?

_____

_____

_____

_____

_____

_____

▶ **PLANET DIARY** Go to **Planet Diary** to learn more about using genetic information.

Lab zone® Do the Inquiry Warm-Up *Using Genetic Information.*

What Are Some Uses of Genetic Information?

Each person's genes contain unique information about that particular person's growth and development. If we could "read" those genes, think of all we could learn! 🔑 **Genetic information can be used positively to identify individuals and to learn about health and disease, or negatively to discriminate against people.**

Vocabulary
- genome
- ethics

Skills
- ⊙ Reading: Summarize
- △ Inquiry: Communicate

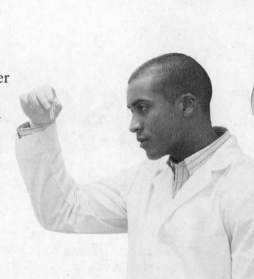

Human Genome Project
Imagine trying to crack a code that is six billion letters long. That's exactly what scientists working on the Human Genome Project did. An organism's full set of DNA is called its **genome.** The main goal of the Human Genome Project was to identify the DNA sequence of the entire human genome. In 2003, the project was completed. Scientists continue to research the functions of the tens of thousands of human genes.

DNA Fingerprinting
DNA technology used in the Human Genome Project can also identify people and show whether people are related. DNA from a person's cells is broken down into small pieces, or fragments. Selected fragments are used to produce a pattern called a DNA fingerprint. Except for identical twins, no two people have exactly the same DNA fingerprint.

Genetic "fingerprints" can tie a person to the scene of a crime or prevent the wrong person from going to jail. They also can be used to identify skeletal remains. Today, soldiers and sailors give blood and saliva samples so their DNA fingerprints can be saved. DNA records can be used to identify the bodies of unknown soldiers or civilians.

apply it!

DNA fingerprints are stored in national DNA databases such as the Combined DNA Index System (CODIS). Databases contain the genetic information from crime scenes, convicted offenders, and missing persons. Law enforcement uses these databases to see if the DNA they have collected matches a known sample.

△ **Communicate** Discuss the following statement with a partner. Identify the pros and cons related to the statement.
Each citizen of the United States should have his or her DNA fingerprint added to the national databases.

Pros: _____

_____

Cons: _____

_____

Summarize What is the main purpose of the Genetic Information Nondiscrimination Act?

_____

_____

_____

_____

Genetic Discrimination

As it becomes easier to obtain genetic information, there are concerns about who can access that information. There are concerns about how it can be used, too. For example, soldiers provide the government with a DNA sample for identification. It could be possible for the government to use their DNA in other ways such as in criminal cases or paternity suits. **Ethics** is the study of principles about what is right and wrong, fair and unfair. Using genetic information in an ethical way means using it in a way that is fair and just.

The Genetic Information Nondiscrimination Act (GINA) was signed into law in 2008. This act makes it illegal for health insurance companies and employers to discriminate against individuals based on genetic information. It also makes it illegal for insurance companies and employers to ask or tell individuals that they must have a genetic test done.

We Are Family!

EXPLORE THE BIG **?**

How can genetic information be used?

FIGURE 1 ....

> INTERACTIVE ART You have been assigned to develop a family pedigree. Several members of this family have a hairline that comes to a point on their forehead. This characteristic, called a widow's peak, is a dominant trait.

Complete these tasks.

1. **Make Models** Draw and label this family's pedigree that shows how children may have inherited a widow's peak from their parents.

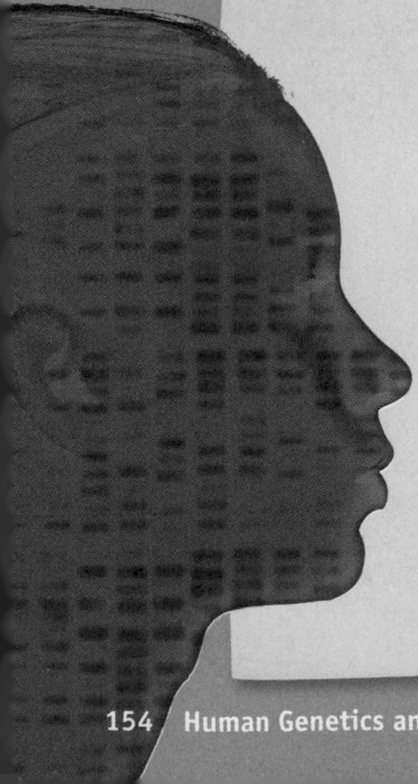

Genetic Privacy Doctors are expected to protect patients' privacy by not revealing their medical information. Patients' medical records may include information such as their medical history and their family's medical history. This information could indicate if a patient is at risk for developing a disease or mental illness. Details about a person's lifestyle may also be included in medical records. Doctors may record if a person drinks alcohol, smokes, or participates in sports that are dangerous.

If a patient has a genetic condition, the patient's relatives are likely at risk, too. Should other family members have the right to know? Or should a patient's medical records be kept private?

2. ⟳ **Summarize** What tools and techniques would you use if you wanted to know what your chances were of inheriting a genetic disease from a family member?

_____

_____

_____

_____

_____

3. **Evaluate the Impact on Society** If you learn that you have inherited a particular trait or genetic disease, who would you want to know? For each group of people listed, mark whether or not you think they should have the right to access your personal genetic information. Then explain why in the space below.

Immediate family members   Yes / No

_____

_____

Your principal and teachers   Yes / No

_____

_____

_____

 **Do the Quick Lab** *Extraction in Action.*

⌬ **Assess Your Understanding**

1a. Define What is a genome?

_____

_____

b. [CHALLENGE] Do you think it is ethical for doctors to share a patient's medical records? Explain.

_____

_____

_____

_____

_____

_____

c. ANSWER THE BIG ? How can genetic information be used?

_____

_____

_____

_____

_____

_____

got it? ··

○ **I get it!** Now I know that there are positive and negative ways of using genetic information such as _____

_____

_____

○ **I need extra help with** _____

Go to MY SCIENCE ⓢ COACH *online for help with this subject.*

155

5 Study Guide

Genetic information can be used to _____,
_____, and _____.

LESSON 1 Human Inheritance

🔑 Some human traits are controlled by single genes with two alleles, and others by single genes with multiple alleles. Still other traits are controlled by many genes that act together.

🔑 The sex chromosomes carry genes that determine whether a person is male or female. They also carry genes that determine other traits.

Vocabulary
• sex chromosomes • sex-linked gene • carrier

LESSON 2 Human Genetic Disorders

🔑 Some genetic disorders are caused by mutations in the DNA of genes. Other disorders are caused by changes in the overall structure or number of chromosomes.

🔑 Today, doctors use tools such as pedigrees, karyotypes, and genetic testing to help trace and diagnose genetic disorders. People with genetic disorders are helped through medical care, education, and job training.

Vocabulary
• genetic disorder • pedigree • karyotype

LESSON 3 Advances in Genetics

🔑 Selective breeding, cloning, and genetic engineering are three methods for developing organisms with desired traits.

Vocabulary
• selective breeding
• inbreeding
• hybridization
• clone
• genetic engineering
• gene therapy

LESSON 4 Using Genetic Information

🔑 Genetic information can be used positively to identify individuals and to learn about health and disease, or negatively to discriminate against people.

Vocabulary
• genome • ethics

Review and Assessment

LESSON 1 Human Inheritance

1. Which human trait is controlled by a single gene with multiple alleles?

   a. height   **b.** dimples

   c. skin color   **d.** blood type

2. Colorblindness is carried on the

X chromosome and is more common in males

than in females because it is a _____

_____

3. Compare and Contrast Describe the main differences between the inheritance patterns for a dimpled chin and for height.

_____

_____

_____

_____

_____

_____

_____

4. Interpret Data Complete the Punnett square below to show the possible genotypes for the offspring of a colorblind mother and a father with normal vision. Circle the genotypes that would produce colorblind offspring.

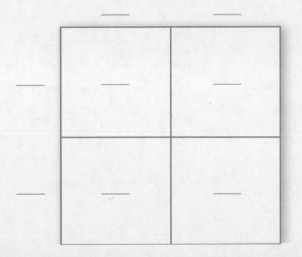

LESSON 2 Human Genetic Disorders

5. Which of the following would most likely be used to diagnose Down syndrome?

   a. a pedigree   **b.** a karyotype

   c. a Punnett square **d.** a blood-clotting test

6. Cystic fibrosis and hemophilia are two

examples of _____

7. Make Generalizations What information is shown by a karyotype?

_____

_____

8. Relate Cause and Effect How does the cause of cystic fibrosis differ from the cause of Down syndrome?

_____

_____

_____

_____

_____

9. Interpret Diagrams The pedigree chart below shows the inheritance of sickle-cell disease. Circle all the individuals on the chart who have the disease. Draw a square around individuals who are carriers.

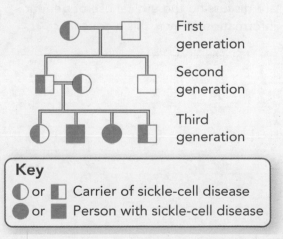

First generation

Second generation

Third generation

Key

◑ or ▢ Carrier of sickle-cell disease

● or ■ Person with sickle-cell disease

5 Review and Assessment

LESSON 3 Advances in Genetics

10. An organism that has the same genes as the organism that produced it is called a

    a. clone.   **b.** hybrid.

    c. genome.   **d.** pedigree.

11. Inbreeding and hybridization are two different

types of _____

12. **Write About It** Suppose that you are giving a presentation about genetic engineering to a group of people who are not familiar with the topic. Write a short speech that includes a definition of genetic engineering, a description of how it is used, and an explanation of some of the concerns about its use.

LESSON 4 Using Genetic Information

13. Genetic fingerprinting is a tool that is used in

    a. hybridization.   **b.** selective breeding.

    c. cloning.   **d.** identification.

14. An organism's _____ is its full

set of DNA.

15. **Apply Concepts** Around the globe, people are discussing the ethical use of genetic information. Why is this a concern?

_____

_____

_____

_____

_____

_____

APPLY THE BIG How can genetic information be used?

16. Genetic information can be applied in healthcare, agriculture, forensics, and many other fields. Using at least three vocabulary terms from this chapter, describe a situation in which genetic information such as this karyotype could have either a positive or negative impact on your daily life. Explain your reasoning.

_____

_____

_____

_____

_____

_____

_____

_____

_____

_____

_____

_____

_____

Standardized Test Prep

Multiple Choice

Circle the letter of the best answer.

1. This Punnett square shows the possible genotypes for the offspring of a colorblind father and a mother who is a carrier. If this couple has a daughter, what is the probability that she will be colorblind?

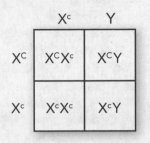

	X^c	Y
X^c	$X^c X^c$	$X^c Y$
X^c	$X^c X^c$	$X^c Y$

   A   0 percent   B   25 percent
   C   50 percent   D   100 percent

2. Inserting a human gene into a bacterial plasmid is an example of

   A   inbreeding.
   B   selective breeding.
   C   DNA fingerprinting.
   D   genetic engineering.

3. What was the main goal of the Human Genome Project?

   A   to clone a human
   B   to identify the sequence of the human genome
   C   to protect the genetic privacy of individuals
   D   to collect the genetic fingerprints of all humans

4. Which of the following is a selective breeding technique?

   A   cloning   B   forensics
   C   inbreeding   D   gene therapy

5. How is human blood type inherited?

   A   through a sex-linked gene
   B   through a single gene with multiple alleles
   C   through many genes, which produce many possible combinations of genes and alleles
   D   through a single gene with two alleles, one that is dominant and one that is recessive

Constructed Response

Use the key below and your knowledge of science to help you answer Question 6. Write your answer on a separate piece of paper.

6. Sasha's mother has sickle-cell disease. Her father does not have the disease and is not a carrier. Sasha has one brother and one sister. Using the key below, draw a pedigree chart that shows the genotypes of each person in Sasha's family.

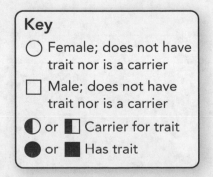

Key
○ Female; does not have trait nor is a carrier
□ Male; does not have trait nor is a carrier
◐ or ▨ Carrier for trait
● or ■ Has trait

159

TECH & DESIGN

Museum of Science

MINI BUT MIGHTY

On TV crime shows, cases are solved in one hour. In real life, lab results may take weeks or months. Who knows how many more criminals could be caught if the lab techniques could be improved?

Scientists have recently developed technology that can run the same genetic tests that a lab can. "Lab-on-a-chip" devices are small and portable. They can usually produce results within an hour, right where the sample is taken. Scientists hope that one day, the units will be as small as a USB flash drive and affordable for everyone. Doctors could then diagnose and treat patients more quickly. Scientists at a crime scene could also get the answers they need almost immediately!

Analyze It Can you imagine any risks of a lab-on-a-chip? Do research about this new technology with its costs and benefits in mind. Make a presentation to your class on the impacts this device may have.

Museum of Science

CODIS:
THE DNA DATABASE

Genetic evidence is one of the most powerful tools that investigators can use to solve a crime. A genetic fingerprint is the unique information stored in a piece of each person's DNA. Forensic investigators use a computer program called the Combined DNA Index System (CODIS) to identify suspects by using their DNA fingerprint. CODIS compares DNA fingerprints that are stored in databases across the country. These DNA fingerprints can be used to link different crime scenes or to identify a suspect. CODIS has also been used to prove that convicted criminals are innocent.

CODIS has been used in more than 79,000 criminal investigations. However, the system is limited by the amount of information in the databases. Many law enforcement agencies do not have enough people to analyze all of the genetic samples gathered from crime scenes. As a result, the CODIS system is incomplete. As more information is added to the system, the technology will become more and more useful.

Write About It Find out more about how genetic evidence is used to investigate crimes. Then, write a short detective story to explain how a forensic investigator uses genetic technologies to solve a burglary.

▲ DNA samples can be collected at a crime scene and analyzed at a lab. Then, the analysis can be entered into a database to make the information available to CODIS.

The DNA from a human hair, like the one shown in this photomicrograph, can be used as evidence in criminal cases.

DOES THIS FISH HAVE LEGS?

How do life forms change over time?

This is not your average fish. Besides having bright red lips, the rosy-lipped batfish is a poor swimmer. Instead of using its pectoral fins for swimming, the batfish uses them to crawl along the seafloor.

△ **Develop Hypotheses** How do you think the batfish's leglike fins help it survive?

_____

_____

_____

_____

_____

▷ **UNTAMED SCIENCE** Watch the **Untamed Science** video to learn more about adaptations.

Change Over Time

6 Getting Started

Check Your Understanding

1. Background Read the paragraph below and then answer the question.

Last fall, Jerome collected more than 100 seeds from a single sunflower in his garden. In the spring, he planted all the seeds. He was not surprised that the new plants all varied in many **traits.** Jerome knows that, because of **sexual reproduction,** each plant's **DNA** is different.

A **trait** is a characteristic that an organism passes to offspring through its genes.

Sexual reproduction results in offspring that are genetically different from each parent.

DNA is genetic material that carries information about an organism and is passed from parent to offspring.

• How are the plants' different traits related to sexual reproduction?

_____

_____

▶ MY READING WEB If you had trouble completing the question above, visit **My Reading Web** and type in *Change Over Time.*

Vocabulary Skill

Identify Multiple Meanings Familiar words may mean something else in science. Look at the different meanings of the words below.

Word	Everyday Meaning	Scientific Meaning
theory	*n.* a guess **Example:** Sue has a theory that soccer is harder to play than basketball.	*n.* a well-tested concept that explains a wide range of observations **Example:** The cell theory says that all organisms are made of cells.
adaptation	*n.* a change in an individual's behavior **Example:** Talia's adaptation to her new school was hard, but she did it.	*n.* a trait that helps an individual survive and reproduce **Example:** Fur is an adaptation to cold.

2. Quick Check Circle the sentence that uses the scientific meaning of the word *theory.*

• Evolutionary *theory* describes change over time.

• Do you have a *theory* about why Sarah is a vegetarian?

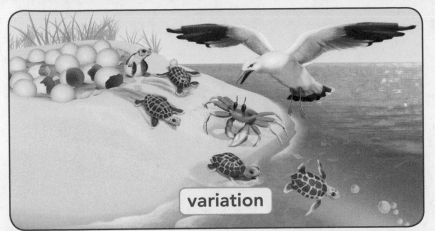
variation

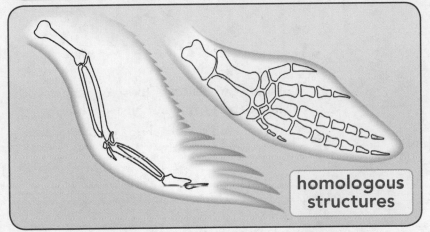
homologous structures

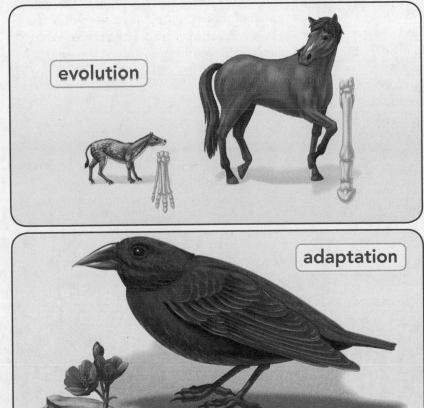
evolution

adaptation

Chapter Preview

LESSON 1
- species
- fossil
- adaptation
- evolution
- scientific theory
- natural selection
- variation

↻ **Relate Cause and Effect**
△ **Develop Hypotheses**

LESSON 2
- homologous structures

↻ **Identify the Main Idea**
△ **Communicate**

LESSON 3
- gradualism
- punctuated equilibrium

↻ **Compare and Contrast**
△ **Make Models**

> **VOCAB FLASH CARDS** For extra help with vocabulary, visit **Vocab Flash Cards** and type in *Change Over Time.*

165

UNLOCK THE BIG ?

🔑 **What Was Darwin's Hypothesis?**

🔑 **What Is Natural Selection?**

my planet Diary

Charles Darwin

In 1839, Charles Darwin published his book *The Voyage of the Beagle*. Read the following excerpt about an animal Darwin encountered while in the Galápagos Islands.

The inhabitants believe that these animals are absolutely deaf; certainly they do not overhear a person walking close behind them. I was always amused when overtaking one of these great monsters, as it was quietly pacing along, to see how suddenly, the instant I passed, it would draw in its head and legs, and uttering a deep hiss fall to the ground with a heavy sound, as if struck dead. I frequently got on their backs, and then giving a few raps on the hinder part of their shells, they would rise up and walk away; — but I found it very difficult to keep my balance.

VOICES FROM HISTORY

Communicate Discuss these questions with a classmate. Write your answers below.

1. What kind of animal do you think Darwin was describing?

   _____

   _____

2. Describe your reaction to an unusual animal that you may have seen at a zoo, at an aquarium, or in a pet store. What was your first impression of the animal?

   _____

   _____

   _____

▷ **PLANET DIARY** Go to **Planet Diary** for more information about Charles Darwin.

Lab zone® Do the Inquiry Warm-Up *How Do Living Things Vary?*

Vocabulary

- species
- fossil
- adaptation
- evolution
- scientific theory
- natural selection
- variation

Skills

- Reading: Relate Cause and Effect
- Inquiry: Develop Hypotheses

What Was Darwin's Hypothesis?

In 1831, the British ship HMS *Beagle* set sail from England on a five-year trip around the world. Charles Darwin was on board. Darwin was a naturalist—a person who observes and studies the natural world.

Diversity Darwin was amazed by the diversity of living things that he saw during the voyage. He wondered why they were so different from those in England. Darwin saw insects that looked like flowers. He also observed sloths, slow-moving animals that spent much of their time hanging in trees. Today, scientists know that organisms are even more diverse than Darwin thought. In fact, scientists have identified more than 1.6 million species of organisms on Earth. A **species** is a group of similar organisms that can mate with each other and produce fertile offspring. The exact number of species is unknown because many areas of Earth have not yet been studied.

Fossils Darwin saw fossils of animals that had died long ago. A **fossil** is the preserved remains or traces of an organism that lived in the past. Darwin was puzzled by some of the fossils he observed. For example, he saw fossils that resembled the bones of living sloths but were much larger in size. He wondered what had happened to the ancient, giant ground sloths. See **Figure 1.**

FIGURE 1 ·······················
Sloth Similarities

Darwin thought that the fossil bones of the giant ground sloths (left) resembled the bones of modern-day sloths (above).

✎ **Observe** List two similarities that you notice between the two sloths.

Similarities
_____
_____
_____
_____

Galápagos Organisms

The *Beagle* made many stops along the Atlantic and Pacific coasts of South America. From the Pacific coast, the ship traveled west to the Galápagos Islands. Darwin observed many unusual life forms there. He compared organisms from the Galápagos Islands to organisms that lived elsewhere. He also compared organisms living on the different islands.

Comparisons to South American Organisms Darwin discovered many similarities between Galápagos organisms and those found in South America. Many of the birds and plants on the islands resembled those on the mainland. However, he also noted important differences between the organisms. For instance, you can see differences between island and mainland iguanas in **Figure 2**.

Darwin became convinced that species do not always stay the same. Instead, he thought species could change and even produce new species over time. Darwin began to think that maybe the island species were somehow related to South American species. Perhaps, he thought, the island species had become different from their mainland relatives over time.

FIGURE 2

Comparing Iguanas

The iguanas on the Galápagos Islands have large claws that allow them to grip slippery rocks so they can feed on seaweed.

The iguanas on the mainland have smaller claws that allow them to climb trees so they can eat leaves.

✏️ **Infer** The color of each iguana is an adaptation to its

○ food.   ○ habitat.
○ predators.   ○ climate.

Explain your answer.

_____

_____

_____

Berries

Insects

Vegetarian
tree finch

Hard seeds
and nuts

Cactus
ground
finch

Medium
ground
finch

Cactus

Small tree
finch

FIGURE 3 ·········

> INTERACTIVE ART **Galápagos Finches**

The structure of each bird's beak is an adaptation to the type of food the bird eats. Birds with long, pointed, sharp beaks pick at cacti. Those with short, thick beaks crush seeds.

Birds with narrow, pointed beaks grasp insects. Those with short, hooked beaks tear open fruit.

✎ **Interpret Diagrams** Look at the different beak structures. Draw a line from each finch to the type of food you think it eats.

Comparisons Among the Islands Darwin also discovered many differences among organisms on the different Galápagos Islands. For example, the tortoises on one island had dome-shaped shells. Those on another island had saddle-shaped shells. A government official in the islands told Darwin that he could tell which island a tortoise came from just by looking at its shell.

Adaptations Birds were also different from one island to the next. Look at **Figure 3.** When Darwin returned to England, he learned that the different birds were all finches. Darwin concluded that the finch species were all related to a single ancestor species that came from the mainland. Over time, different finches developed different beak shapes and sizes that were well suited to the food that they ate. Beak shape is an example of an **adaptation,** a trait that increases an organism's ability to survive and reproduce.

✎
Vocabulary Identify Multiple Meanings Write a sentence using the everyday meaning of the word *adapt.*

_____

_____

_____

_____

_____

Darwin's Hypothesis Darwin thought about what he had seen during his voyage on the *Beagle*. By this time, Darwin was convinced that organisms change over time. The process of change over time is called **evolution.** Darwin, however, wanted to know *how* organisms change. Over the next 20 years, he consulted with other scientists and gathered more information. Based on his observations, Darwin reasoned that plants or animals that arrived on the Galápagos Islands faced conditions that were different from those on the nearby mainland. 🔑 **Darwin hypothesized that species change over many generations and become better adapted to new conditions**.

Darwin's ideas are often referred to as a theory of evolution. A **scientific theory** is a well-tested concept that explains a wide range of observations. From the evidence he collected, Darwin concluded that organisms on the Galápagos Islands had changed over time.

apply *it!*

The first labradoodle dog was bred in 1989. A labradoodle is a cross between a standard poodle and a Labrador retriever. The poodle is very smart and has fur that sheds very little. The poodle may be less irritating for people allergic to dogs. Labradors are gentle, easily trained, and shed seasonally.

Standard poodle   Labrador retriever   Labradoodle

❶ **Make Generalizations** Why do you think people breed these two dogs together?

_____

_____

❷ ⚠️ **Develop Hypotheses** Would you expect the first labradoodle puppies to be the same as puppies produced several generations later? Explain.

_____

_____

Artificial Selection Darwin studied the offspring of domesticated animals that were produced by artificial selection in an effort to understand how evolution might occur. In artificial selection, only the organisms with a desired characteristic, such as color, are bred. Darwin himself had bred pigeons with large, fan-shaped tails. By repeatedly allowing only those pigeons with many tail feathers to mate, Darwin produced pigeons with two or three times the usual number of tail feathers. Darwin thought that a process similar to artificial selection might happen in nature. But he wondered what natural process selected certain traits.

FIGURE 4 ·····································
Artificial Selection
The pigeons that Darwin bred were all descended from the rock dove (left). Pigeons can be bred for characteristics such as color, beak shape, wingspan, and feather patterns.

✏ **Describe** If you were to breed an animal, what would it be and what traits would you want it to have?

_____
_____
_____

 Do the Quick Lab
Bird Beak Adaptations.

🔑 **Assess Your Understanding**

1a. List Make a list of three observations that Darwin made during the *Beagle's* voyage.

_____
_____
_____

b. Describe An adaptation is a trait that

increases an organism's ability to _____

and _____

c. Develop Hypotheses How does artificial selection support Darwin's hypothesis?

_____
_____
_____
_____

got**it?** ···

○ **I get it!** Now I know that Darwin's hypothesis was _____

_____

○ **I need extra help with** _____

Go to **MY SCIENCE ⓢ COACH** online for help with this subject.

171

What Is Natural Selection?

In 1858, Darwin and Alfred Russel Wallace, another British biologist, both proposed the same explanation for how evolution occurs. The next year, Darwin described his explanation in his book *The Origin of Species*. In this book, Darwin proposed that evolution occurs by means of natural selection. **Natural selection** is the process by which individuals that are better adapted to their environment are more likely to survive and reproduce more than other members of the same species. Darwin identified factors that affect the process of natural selection: overproduction, variation, and competition. **Figure 5** shows how natural selection might happen in a group of sea turtles.

Overproduction Darwin knew that most species produce far more offspring than can possibly survive. In many species, so many offspring are produced that there are not enough resources—food, water, and living space—for all of them.

Factors That Affect Natural Selection
How do life forms change over time?

FIGURE 5 ···

▶ **REAL-WORLD INQUIRY** Overproduction, variation, and competition are factors that affect the process of natural selection.

✎ **Summarize** Examine the sequence below that shows how natural selection could affect a group of sea turtles over time. Label each factor in the illustration and write a brief caption explaining what is occurring.

Variation Members of a species differ from one another in many of their traits. Any difference between individuals of the same species is called a **variation.** For example, sea turtles may differ in color, size, the ability to swim quickly, and shell hardness.

Competition Since food, space, and other resources are limited, the members of a species must compete with one another to survive. Competition does not always involve physical fights between members of a species. Instead, competition is usually indirect. For example, some turtles may not find enough to eat. A slower turtle may be caught by a predator, while a faster turtle may escape. Only a few turtles will survive to reproduce.

Selection Darwin observed that some variations make individuals better adapted to their environment. Those individuals are more likely to survive and reproduce. Their offspring may inherit the helpful characteristic. The offspring, in turn, will be more likely to survive and reproduce, and pass the characteristic to their offspring. After many generations, more members of the species will have the helpful characteristic.

In effect, the environment selects organisms with helpful traits to become parents of the next generation. **Darwin proposed that, over a long time, natural selection can lead to change. Helpful variations may accumulate in a species, while unfavorable ones may disappear.**

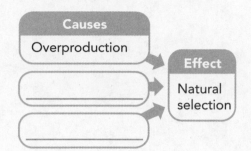

Relate Cause and Effect
Fill in the graphic organizer to identify the factors that cause natural selection.

Causes
Overproduction

Effect

Natural selection

Environmental Change A change in the environment can affect an organism's ability to survive and therefore lead to natural selection. For example, monkey flowers are plants that do not normally grow in soil that has a high concentration of copper. However, because of genetic variation, some varieties of monkey flower now grow near copper mines. In **Figure 6** you can see how natural selection might have resulted in monkey flowers that can grow in copper-contaminated soil.

Genes and Natural Selection Without variations, all the members of a species would have the same traits and the same chance of surviving and reproducing. But where do variations come from? How are they passed on from parents to offspring?

Darwin could not explain what caused variations or how they were passed on. As scientists later learned, variations can result from changes in genes and the shuffling of different forms of genes when egg and sperm join. Genes, such as those for hair color and height, are passed from parents to their offspring. Only traits that are inherited, or controlled by genes that are passed on to offspring, can be acted upon by natural selection.

do the math!

The typical clutch size, or number of eggs, a loggerhead sea turtle can lay at once is around 113. Even with producing so many offspring, the loggerhead sea turtle is endangered in many areas. Suppose that scientists counted the number of eggs laid at seven different nesting sites along the southeast coast of the United States. The following year, scientists check the nesting sites to see how many offspring survived and returned.

Loggerhead Sea Turtle Data

Site	A	B	C	D	E	F	G
Clutch Size	114	103	121	118	107	103	104
Returning Turtles	45	35	55	53	40	66	38

1 Calculate Determine the mean for the clutch sizes of the seven nesting sites in the table. _____ How does the mean compare to the typical clutch size for loggerheads? _____

_____

_____

2 Interpret Data Do you think clutch size influences the survival rates of the offspring? Use the data to support your answer.

_____

_____

_____

_____

3 CHALLENGE Hypothesize why Site F had the largest number of returning turtles.

_____

_____

_____

_____

Monkey flowers grow successfully in healthy, unpolluted soil.

Copper seeps into the soil around the copper mine. Most monkey flowers cannot grow in this polluted soil, and they begin to die.

Some monkey flowers have genetic variations that allow them to survive and reproduce in copper-contaminated soil.

_____
_____
_____
_____

FIGURE 6 ···

Environmental Change

When copper contaminated the soil surrounding the monkey flowers, the environment changed. Due to a genetic variation, some varieties of monkey flower are now able to survive in that soil.

✎ **Draw Conclusions** In the last circle, draw what you think the area will look like in ten years' time. Write a caption describing what has taken place.

Lab ® **zone**   Do the Lab Investigation *Nature at Work.*

🔑 Assess Your Understanding

2a. Define A variation is any (similarity/difference) between individuals of the same species.

b. How do life forms change over time?

_____
_____
_____

c. 🔄 Relate Cause and Effect Explain how unfavorable traits can disappear in a species.

_____
_____
_____
_____
_____

got it? ···

○ I get it! Now I know that natural selection occurs _____
_____
_____

○ I need extra help with _____

Go to **MY SCIENCE** 🔵ˢ **COACH** online for help with this subject.

Evidence of Evolution

UNLOCK
THE BIG
?

🔑 **What Evidence Supports Evolution?**

my PLANeT DiaRY

DISCOVERY

Moving On Up

In 2004, researchers on Ellesmere Island, Nunavut, in the Canadian Arctic, found a fossil that provides information about when fish first came onto land. The fossil, called *Tiktaalik*, is 375 million years old. *Tiktaalik* has characteristics of both fish and four-legged animals. Like other fish, it has fins. However, the fins have interior bones that helped push the animal up in the shallow waters close to shore to find food. The discovery of *Tiktaalik* has provided new fossil evidence to help scientists understand the relationship between marine vertebrates and land vertebrates.

Researcher from
Ellesmere Island

Communicate Discuss these questions with a partner. Write your answers below.

1. Do you think the discovery of *Tiktaalik* is important to understanding evolution? Why?

_____

_____

_____

2. Do you think *Tiktaalik* spent most of its time on land or in water? Why?

_____

_____

_____

> **PLANET DIARY** Go to **Planet Diary** to learn more about fossil evidence.

This illustration of *Tiktaalik* shows what it may have looked like 375 million years ago.

Lab ® Do the Inquiry Warm-Up
zone *How Can You Classify a Species?*

Vocabulary
• homologous structures

Skills
↻ Reading: Identify the Main Idea
△ Inquiry: Communicate

What Evidence Supports Evolution?

Since Darwin's time, scientists have found a great deal of evidence that supports the theory of evolution. 🔑 **Fossils, patterns of early development, similar body structures, and similarities in DNA and protein structures all provide evidence that organisms have changed over time.**

Fossils By examining fossils, scientists can infer the structures of ancient organisms. Fossils show that, in many cases, organisms that lived in the past were very different from organisms alive today. The millions of fossils that scientists have collected are called the fossil record. The fossil record provides clues about how and when new species evolved and how organisms are related.

Similarities in Early Development Scientists also infer evolutionary relationships by comparing the early development of different organisms. For example, the organisms in **Figure 1** look similar during the early stages of development. All four organisms have a tail. They also have a row of tiny slits along their throats. The similarities suggest that these vertebrate species are related and share a common ancestor.

FIGURE 1 ·······························

Similarities in Development

These four organisms all look similar during their early development.

✎ **Complete each task.**

1. **Observe** Circle at least two similarities shared by all four organisms.

2. **Describe** What are some differences between the organisms?

_____

_____

_____

_____

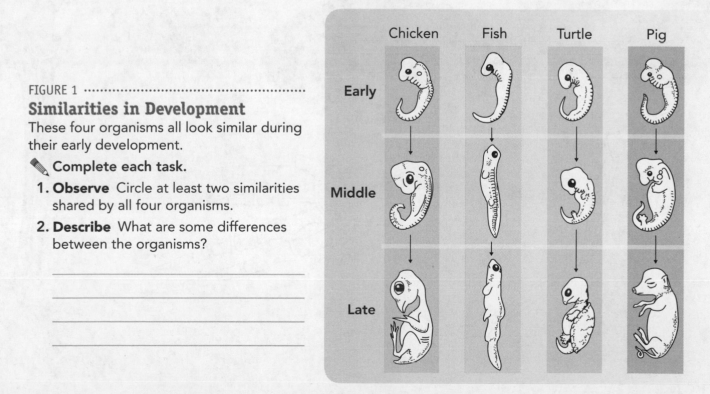

Chicken   Fish   Turtle   Pig

Early

Middle

Late

Similarities in Body Structure An organism's body structure is its basic body plan, which in vertebrates includes how its bones are arranged. Fishes, amphibians, reptiles, birds, and mammals all have an internal skeleton with a backbone. This similarity provides evidence that these animal groups all evolved from a common ancestor.

Similar structures that related species have inherited from a common ancestor are known as **homologous structures** (hoh MAHL uh gus). In **Figure 2,** you can see some examples of homologous structures. These include a bird's wing, a dolphin's flipper, and a dog's leg.

Sometimes fossils show structures that are homologous with structures in living species. For example, scientists have recently found fossils of ancient whalelike creatures. The fossils show that the ancestors of today's whales had legs and walked on land. This evidence supports other evidence that whales and other vertebrates share a common ancestor that had a skeleton with a backbone.

Identify the Main Idea Describe the main idea on this page.

____

____

____

____

____

____

FIGURE 2

INTERACTIVE ART **Homologous Structures**

The bones in a bird's wing, a dolphin's flipper, and a dog's leg have similar structures.

Interpret Diagrams Use the drawing of the dog's leg as a guide. Color in the matching bones in the bird's wing and the dolphin's flipper with the appropriate colors.

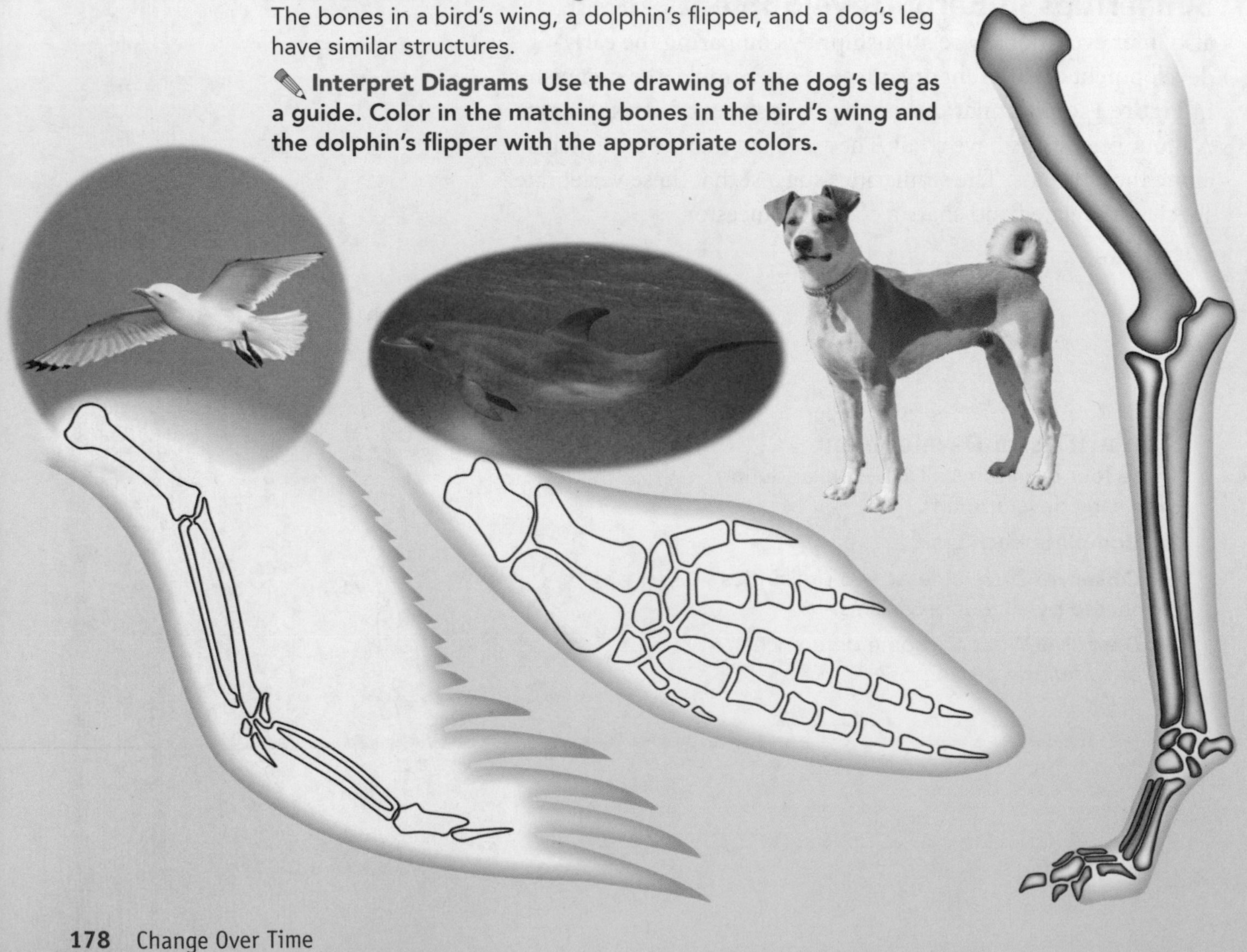

Similarities in DNA and Protein Structure

Why do some species have similar body structures and development patterns? Scientists infer that the species inherited many of the same genes from a common ancestor.

Recall that genes are segments of DNA. Scientists compare the sequence of nitrogen bases in the DNA of different species to infer how closely related the two species are. The more similar the DNA sequences, the more closely related the species are. The DNA bases along a gene specify what type of protein will be produced. Therefore, scientists can also compare the order of amino acids in a protein to see how closely related two species are.

In most cases, evidence from DNA and protein structure has confirmed conclusions based on fossils, embryos, and body structure. For example, DNA comparisons show that dogs are more similar to wolves than to coyotes. Scientists had already reached this conclusion based on similarities in the structure and development of these three species.

apply it!

The table shows the sequence of amino acids in one region of a protein, cytochrome c, for five different animals. Each letter corresponds to a different amino acid in the protein.

Section of Cytochrome c Protein in Animals

Animal	Amino Acid Position in the Sequence											
	39	40	41	42	43	44	45	46	47	48	49	50
Horse	N	L	H	G	L	F	G	R	K	T	G	Q
Donkey	N	L	H	G	L	F	G	R	K	T	G	Q
Rabbit	N	L	H	G	L	F	G	R	K	T	G	Q
Snake	N	L	H	G	L	F	G	R	K	T	G	Q
Turtle	N	L	N	G	L	I	G	R	K	T	G	Q

1 **Interpret Tables** Which species is most distantly related to the horse? _____

2 **Communicate** Explain how amino acid sequences provide information about evolutionary relationships among organisms.

_____

_____

_____

_____

_____

_____

Lab zone Do the Quick Lab *Finding Proof.*

Assess Your Understanding

1a. Define _____ structures are structurally similar body parts in related species.

b. CHALLENGE Insects and birds both have wings. What kinds of evidence might show whether or not insects and birds are closely related? Explain.

_____

_____

_____

_____

got it?

○ **I get it!** Now I know that the theory of evolution is supported by evidence that includes _____

_____

_____

○ **I need extra help with** _____

Go to MY SCIENCE COACH online for help with this subject.

179

Rate of Change

UNLOCK THE BIG Q?

🔑 How Do New Species Form?

🔑 What Patterns Describe the Rate of Evolution?

my planet diary

Crickets, Maggots, and Flies, Oh My!

A male cricket chirps to attract a mate. Unfortunately, chirping also attracts a parasitic fly. Parasitic flies listen for chirping crickets. When a cricket is located, a female fly deposits larvae onto the cricket's back. The larvae, or maggots, burrow into the cricket. The maggots come out seven days later, killing the cricket in the process. Parasitic flies reduced the cricket population on the Hawaiian island of Kauai between 1991 and 2001. By 2003, the cricket population on Kauai had increased. The male crickets were silent! In about 20 cricket generations, the crickets had evolved into an almost silent population.

Lab® zone Do the Inquiry Warm-Up *Making a Timeline.*

FUN FACT

Communicate Discuss these questions with a classmate. Write your answers below.

1. Why do you think the crickets on Kauai evolved so quickly?

_____

_____

_____

2. If most of the male crickets can no longer chirp, how do you think it might affect the size of the cricket population?

_____

_____

_____

_____

▶ **PLANET DIARY** Go to **Planet Diary** to learn more about evolution.

How Do New Species Form?

Natural selection explains how variations can lead to changes in a species. But how could an entirely new species form? 🔑 **A new species can form when a group of individuals remains isolated from the rest of its species long enough to evolve different traits that prevent reproduction.** Isolation, or complete separation, occurs when some members of a species become cut off from the rest of the species. One way this can happen is when a natural barrier, such as a river, separates group members.

Vocabulary
- gradualism
- punctuated equilibrium

Skills
- ⟳ Reading: Compare and Contrast
- △ Inquiry: Make Models

FIGURE 1

Kaibab and Abert's Squirrels

The Kaibab squirrel (left) and the Abert's squirrel (right) have been isolated from each other for a long time. Eventually, this isolation may result in two different species.

✎ **Identify** What conditions might differ from one side of the Grand Canyon to the other that would cause the squirrels to be different colors?

_____

_____

_____

Key

| | Range of Kaibab squirrel | | Range of Abert's squirrel |

As you can see in **Figure 1,** the populations of Kaibab and Abert's squirrels are separated by the Grand Canyon. The two kinds of squirrels are the same species, but they have slightly different characteristics. For example, the Kaibab squirrel has a black belly, while Abert's squirrel has a white belly. It is possible that one day these squirrels will become so different that they will no longer be able to mate with each other and will become separate species.

 Do the Quick Lab
Large-Scale Isolation.

🔑 Assess Your Understanding

got it? ....

○ I get it! Now I know that new species form when _____

_____

○ I need extra help with _____

Go to MY SCIENCE ⑤ COACH *online for help with this subject.*

What Patterns Describe the Rate of Evolution?

The fossil record has provided scientists with a lot of important information about past life on Earth. For example, scientists have found many examples of the appearance of new species as older species vanish. Sometimes the new species appear rapidly, and at other times they are the result of more gradual change. 🔑 **Scientists have developed two patterns to describe the pace of evolution: gradualism and punctuated equilibrium.**

Gradual Change Some species in the fossil record seem to change gradually over time. **Gradualism** involves small changes that add up to major changes over a long period of time. Since the time scale of the fossil record involves hundreds, thousands, or even millions of years, there is plenty of time for gradual changes to produce new species. The fossil record contains many examples of species that are intermediate between two others. One example is the horse relative, *Merychippus*, shown in **Figure 2**. Many such intermediate forms seem to be the result of gradual change.

✏️ **Compare and Contrast**
Identify the similarity and the key differences between gradualism and punctuated equilibrium.

• Both describe the

_____

• Gradualism states that evolution occurs (quickly/slowly) and (steadily/in short bursts).

• Punctuated equilibrium states that evolution occurs (quickly/slowly) over_____ periods of time.

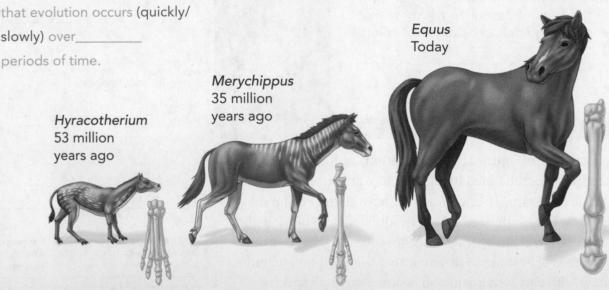

Equus
Today

Merychippus
35 million
years ago

Hyracotherium
53 million
years ago

FIGURE 2 •••••••••••••••••••••••••••••••
▶ ART IN MOTION **Horse Evolution**
Horses left a rich and detailed fossil record of their evolution. Many intermediate forms have been found between modern horses and their four-toed ancestors. *Merychippus* is shown here.

✏️ **Answer these questions.**

1. List Name two differences between the horses.

_____
_____

2. CHALLENGE How could the evolution of the shape of the leg and the number of toes have benefited *Equus*?

_____
_____
_____
_____

Rapid Change Scientists have also found that many species remain almost unchanged during their existence. Then, shortly after they become extinct, related species often appear in the fossil record. This pattern, in which species evolve during short periods of rapid change and then don't change much, is called **punctuated equilibrium.** Today most scientists think that evolution can occur rapidly at some times, and more gradually at others.

apply it!

Two patterns that describe the rate of evolution are modeled at the right.

△ **Make Models** Look at the shells in the key. For each pattern, decide if—and at what point—each shell belongs on the timelines. Using colored pencils, draw and color in the shells at their correct locations to show how they have evolved over time.

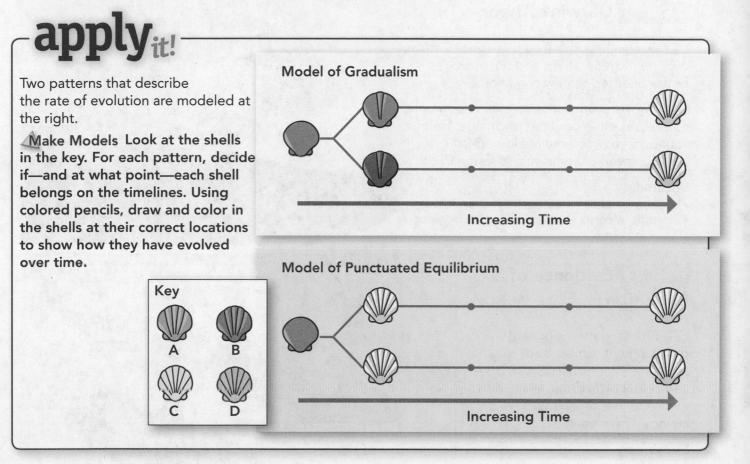

Model of Gradualism

Increasing Time

Model of Punctuated Equilibrium

Increasing Time

Key

A   B

C   D

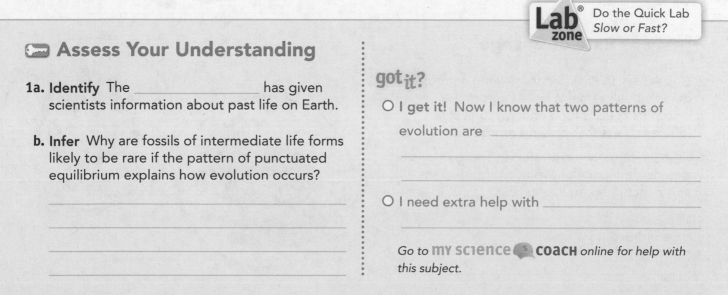

Lab zone® Do the Quick Lab Slow or Fast?

🔲 Assess Your Understanding

1a. Identify The _____ has given scientists information about past life on Earth.

b. Infer Why are fossils of intermediate life forms likely to be rare if the pattern of punctuated equilibrium explains how evolution occurs?

_____

_____

_____

got it?

○ **I get it!** Now I know that two patterns of evolution are _____

_____

○ **I need extra help with** _____

_____

Go to my science ⑤ coach *online for help with this subject.*

Living things change over time, or _____, through a process
called _____

Darwin's Theory

🔑 Darwin hypothesized that species change over many generations and become better adapted to new conditions.

🔑 Darwin proposed that, over a long time, natural selection can lead to change. Helpful variations may accumulate in a species, while unfavorable ones may disappear.

Vocabulary
- species • fossil • adaptation • evolution
- scientific theory • natural selection • variation

Evidence of Evolution

🔑 Fossils, patterns of early development, similar body structures, and similarities in DNA and protein structures all provide evidence that organisms have changed over time.

Vocabulary
- homologous structures

Rate of Change

🔑 A new species can form when a group of individuals remains isolated from the rest of its species long enough to evolve different traits that prevent reproduction.

🔑 Scientists have developed two patterns to describe the pace of evolution: gradualism and punctuated equilibrium.

Vocabulary
- gradualism
- punctuated equilibrium

Review and Assessment

LESSON 1 Darwin's Theory

1. A trait that helps an organism to survive and reproduce is called a(n)

  a. variation.   **b.** adaptation.

  c. species.   **d.** selection.

2. Two organisms that can mate and produce fertile offspring are members of the same

_____

3. Infer Why are Darwin's ideas classified as a scientific theory?

_____

_____

_____

_____

4. Apply Concepts What is one factor that affects natural selection? Give an example.

_____

_____

_____

_____

5. Compare and Contrast Identify one similarity and one difference between natural selection and artificial selection.

_____

_____

_____

_____

_____

6. Write About It You are a reporter in the 1800s interviewing Charles Darwin about his theory of evolution. Write three questions you would ask him. Then write answers that Darwin might have given.

LESSON 2 Evidence of Evolution

7. Similar structures that related species have inherited from a common ancestor are called

  a. adaptations.

  b. fossils.

  c. ancestral structures.

  d. homologous structures.

8. The more _____ the DNA sequences between two organisms are, the more closely related the two species are.

9. Draw Conclusions Look at the drawing, at the right, of the bones in a crocodile's leg. Do you think that crocodiles share a common ancestor with birds, dolphins, and dogs? Support your answer with evidence.

Crocodile

_____

_____

_____

_____

10. Make Judgments What type of evidence is the best indicator of how closely two species are related? Explain your answer.

_____

_____

_____

_____

_____

_____

_____

185

6 Review and Assessment

Rate of Change

11. The pattern of evolution that involves short periods of rapid change is called

   a. adaptation.

   b. gradualism.

   c. isolation.

   d. punctuated equilibrium.

12. _____ involves tiny changes in a species that slowly add up to major changes over time.

13. Apply Concepts A population of deer lives in a forest. Draw a picture that illustrates how a geographic feature could isolate this deer population into two separate groups. Label the geographic feature.

14. Develop Hypotheses Describe the conditions that could cause these two groups of deer to become separate species over time.

_____

_____

_____

_____

_____

_____

_____

APPLY THE BIG Q

How do life forms change over time?

15. Suppose that over several years, the climate in an area becomes much drier than it was before. How would plants, like the ones shown below, be affected? Using the terms *variation* and *natural selection*, predict what changes you might observe in the plants as a result of this environmental change.

_____

_____

_____

_____

_____

_____

_____

_____

_____

_____

_____

_____

_____

_____

Standardized Test Prep

Multiple Choice

Circle the letter of the best answer.

1. The illustration below has no title. Which of the following titles would best describe the concept shown in this drawing?

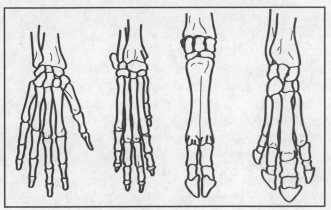

   A Wrist Bone Adaptations
   B Similarities in Wrist Bone Development
   C Evolutionary Change Through Gradualism
   D Homologous Structures in Four Animals

2. The process by which individuals that are better adapted to their environment are more likely to survive and reproduce than other members of the same species is called

   A natural selection.
   B evolution.
   C competition.
   D overproduction.

3. Which of the following is the best example of an adaptation that helps organisms survive in their environment?

   A green coloring in lizards living on gray rocks
   B a thick coat of fur on animals that live in the desert
   C an extensive root system in desert plants
   D thin, delicate leaves on plants in a cold climate

4. Which of the following sets of factors did Darwin identify as affecting natural selection?

   A adaptations, gradualism, and evolution
   B overproduction, variation, and competition
   C adaptations, traits, and variations
   D predation, competition, and mutualism

5. Evolution that occurs slowly is described by the pattern of _____, while rapid changes are described by

   _____.

   A gradualism; natural selection
   B homologous structures; fossils
   C gradualism; punctuated equilibrium
   D natural selection; punctuated equilibrium

Constructed Response

Use the diagram below and your knowledge of science to help you answer Question 6. Write your answer on a separate piece of paper.

6. This drawing shows variations in wing size within a species of fly. Describe a situation in which natural selection might favor flies with the smallest wings.

Science and Society

THE INCREDIBLE SHRINKING FISH

For years, fishers have followed a simple rule: keep the big fish and release the small fish. This practice aims to keep fish populations stable by allowing young fish to reach reproductive age. However, a scientist named David Conover thinks that this practice of throwing back small fish might be affecting the evolution of fish species.

Not all small fish are young. Like humans, adult fish come in different sizes. Conover hypothesized that removing the largest fish from fish populations might result in populations of smaller fish because smaller adult fish would survive to reproduce more often than larger adult fish. To test this hypothesis, Conover's team divided a population of 6,000 fish into different groups. Over four generations, the scientists selectively removed 90 percent of the fish in each group before they could reproduce.

The results showed that over just a few generations, selection pressures can influence not only the size of fish, but also the health of fish populations. Currently, Conover is researching ways to change fishing regulations so fish populations can recover.

▲ The practice of commercial fishing may be leading to populations of smaller and smaller fish.

This diagram shows how Dr. Conover and his team set up and performed their experiment. It also shows the results. ▶

Design It If current policies are causing the average size of fish to decrease, what is the best way to help fish populations recover? Design an experiment that would test your method for helping fish populations recover.

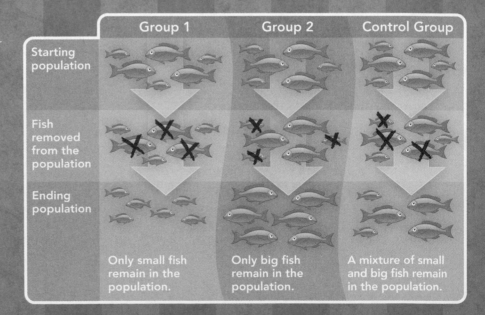

	Group 1	Group 2	Control Group
Starting population			
Fish removed from the population			
Ending population			
	Only small fish remain in the population.	Only big fish remain in the population.	A mixture of small and big fish remain in the population.

WALKING WHALES?

Over 50 million years, whales evolved from a species of doglike land mammals to the aquatic giants we know today.

If you could visit Earth 50 million years ago, you would see many amazing sights. One of the strangest things you might see is the ancestor of modern whales—walking on land!

For years, scientists have thought that whales evolved from land-dwelling mammals. About 50 million years ago, the ancestors of modern whales had four legs and were similar to large dogs. Over 50 million years, whales evolved to become the giant marine mammals we recognize today. However, scientists have had difficulty finding fossils of whales that show how this dramatic change occurred. These missing links could reveal how whales lost their legs.

Now, several new discoveries are helping scientists fill in the blanks in the evolutionary history of whales. A fossil whale skeleton discovered in Washington State has a pelvis with large cuplike sockets. These sockets likely held short legs that enabled the whale to move on land. Other whale fossils, found in Alabama, include large hind limbs that probably helped the animals swim. Researchers have also discovered the gene mutation that could have been responsible for whales losing their legs about 35 million years ago.

Design It Find out more about the evolutionary history of whales. How is a whale flipper similar to a bat wing and a human hand? Design a poster that shows the evolutionary history of whales.

Mesonychids

Ambulocetus

Dalanistes

Takracetus

Dorudon

Blue Whale

APPENDIX A

Using a Microscope

The microscope is an essential tool in the study of life science. It allows you to see things that are too small to be seen with the unaided eye.

You will probably use a compound microscope like the one you see here. The compound microscope has more than one lens that magnifies the object you view.

Typically, a compound microscope has one lens in the eyepiece, the part you look through. The eyepiece lens usually magnifies 10×. Any object you view through this lens would appear 10 times larger than it is.

A compound microscope may contain one or two other lenses called objective lenses. If there are

two, they are called the low-power and high-power objective lenses. The low-power objective lens usually magnifies 10×. The high-power objective lens usually magnifies 40×.

To calculate the total magnification with which you are viewing an object, multiply the magnification of the eyepiece lens by the magnification of the objective lens you are using. For example, the eyepiece's magnification of 10× multiplied by the low-power objective's magnification of 10× equals a total magnification of 100×.

Use the photo of the compound microscope to become familiar with the parts of the microscope and their functions.

The Parts of a Microscope

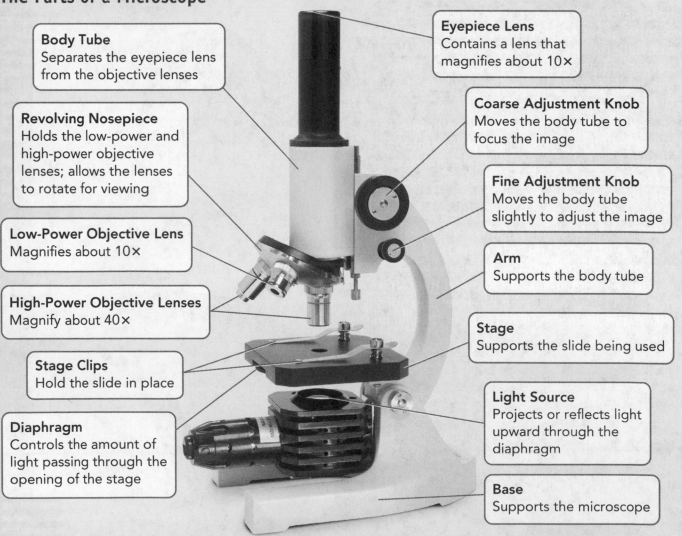

Body Tube
Separates the eyepiece lens from the objective lenses

Revolving Nosepiece
Holds the low-power and high-power objective lenses; allows the lenses to rotate for viewing

Low-Power Objective Lens
Magnifies about 10×

High-Power Objective Lenses
Magnify about 40×

Stage Clips
Hold the slide in place

Diaphragm
Controls the amount of light passing through the opening of the stage

Eyepiece Lens
Contains a lens that magnifies about 10×

Coarse Adjustment Knob
Moves the body tube to focus the image

Fine Adjustment Knob
Moves the body tube slightly to adjust the image

Arm
Supports the body tube

Stage
Supports the slide being used

Light Source
Projects or reflects light upward through the diaphragm

Base
Supports the microscope

Using the Microscope

Use the following procedures when you are working with a microscope.

1. To carry the microscope, grasp the microscope's arm with one hand. Place your other hand under the base.
2. Place the microscope on a table with the arm toward you.
3. Turn the coarse adjustment knob to raise the body tube.
4. Revolve the nosepiece until the low-power objective lens clicks into place.
5. Adjust the diaphragm. While looking through the eyepiece, also adjust the mirror until you see a bright white circle of light. **CAUTION:** *Never use direct sunlight as a light source.*
6. Place a slide on the stage. Center the specimen over the opening on the stage. Use the stage clips to hold the slide in place. **CAUTION:** *Glass slides are fragile.*
7. Look at the stage from the side. Carefully turn the coarse adjustment knob to lower the body tube until the low-power objective almost touches the slide.
8. Looking through the eyepiece, very slowly turn the coarse adjustment knob until the specimen comes into focus.
9. To switch to the high-power objective lens, look at the microscope from the side. Carefully revolve the nosepiece until the high-power objective lens clicks into place. Make sure the lens does not hit the slide.
10. Looking through the eyepiece, turn the fine adjustment knob until the specimen comes into focus.

Making a Wet-Mount Slide

Use the following procedures to make a wet-mount slide of a specimen.

1. Obtain a clean microscope slide and a coverslip. **CAUTION:** *Glass slides and coverslips are fragile.*
2. Place the specimen on the center of the slide. The specimen must be thin enough for light to pass through it.
3. Using a plastic dropper, place a drop of water on the specimen.
4. Gently place one edge of the coverslip against the slide so that it touches the edge of the water drop at a 45° angle. Slowly lower the coverslip over the specimen. If you see air bubbles trapped beneath the coverslip, tap the coverslip gently with the eraser end of a pencil.
5. Remove any excess water at the edge of the coverslip with a paper towel.

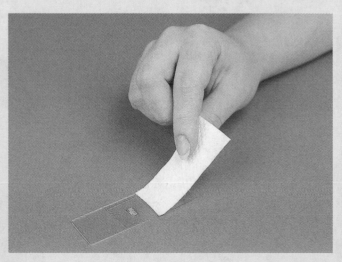

Using a Laboratory Balance

The laboratory balance is an important tool in scientific investigations. You can use a balance to determine the masses of materials that you study or experiment with in the laboratory.

Different kinds of balances are used in the laboratory. One kind of balance is the triple-beam balance. The balance that you may use in your science class is probably similar to the balance illustrated in this Appendix. **To use the balance properly, you should learn the name, location, and function of each part of the balance you are using. What kind of balance do you have in your science class?**

The Triple-Beam Balance

The triple-beam balance is a single-pan balance with three beams calibrated in grams. The back, or 100-gram, beam is divided into ten units of 10 grams each. The middle, or 500-gram, beam is divided into five units of 100 grams each. The front, or 10-gram, beam is divided into ten units of 1 gram each. Each of the units on the front beam is further divided into units of 0.1 gram. What is the largest mass you could find with a triple-beam balance?

The following procedure can be used to find the mass of an object with a triple-beam balance:
1. Place the object on the pan.
2. Move the rider on the middle beam notch by notch until the horizontal pointer on the right drops below zero. Move the rider back one notch.
3. Move the rider on the back beam notch by notch until the pointer again drops below zero. Move the rider back one notch.
4. Slowly slide the rider along the front beam until the pointer stops at the zero point.
5. The mass of the object is equal to the sum of the readings on the three beams.

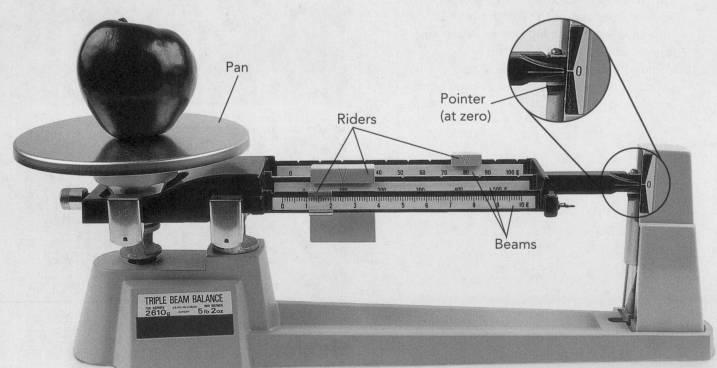

Pan

Riders

Pointer (at zero)

Beams

TRIPLE BEAM BALANCE
700 SERIES   800 SERIES
2610g   CAPACITY   5 lb 2 oz

List of Chemical Elements

Name	Symbol	Atomic Number	Atomic Mass†
Actinium	Ac	89	(227)
Aluminum	Al	13	26.982
Americium	Am	95	(243)
Antimony	Sb	51	121.75
Argon	Ar	18	39.948
Arsenic	As	33	74.922
Astatine	At	85	(210)
Barium	Ba	56	137.33
Berkelium	Bk	97	(247)
Beryllium	Be	4	9.0122
Bismuth	Bi	83	208.98
Bohrium	Bh	107	(264)
Boron	B	5	10.81
Bromine	Br	35	79.904
Cadmium	Cd	48	112.41
Calcium	Ca	20	40.08
Californium	Cf	98	(251)
Carbon	C	6	12.011
Cerium	Ce	58	140.12
Cesium	Cs	55	132.91
Chlorine	Cl	17	35.453
Chromium	Cr	24	51.996
Cobalt	Co	27	58.933
Copernicium	Cn	112	(277)
Copper	Cu	29	63.546
Curium	Cm	96	(247)
Darmstadtium	Ds	110	(269)
Dubnium	Db	105	(262)
Dysprosium	Dy	66	162.50
Einsteinium	Es	99	(252)
Erbium	Er	68	167.26
Europium	Eu	63	151.96
Fermium	Fm	100	(257)
Fluorine	F	9	18.998
Francium	Fr	87	(223)
Gadolinium	Gd	64	157.25
Gallium	Ga	31	69.72
Germanium	Ge	32	72.59
Gold	Au	79	196.97
Hafnium	Hf	72	178.49
Hassium	Hs	108	(265)
Helium	He	2	4.0026
Holmium	Ho	67	164.93
Hydrogen	H	1	1.0079
Indium	In	49	114.82
Iodine	I	53	126.90
Iridium	Ir	77	192.22
Iron	Fe	26	55.847
Krypton	Kr	36	83.80
Lanthanum	La	57	138.91
Lawrencium	Lr	103	(262)
Lead	Pb	82	207.2
Lithium	Li	3	6.941
Lutetium	Lu	71	174.97
Magnesium	Mg	12	24.305
Manganese	Mn	25	54.938

Name	Symbol	Atomic Number	Atomic Mass†
Meitnerium	Mt	109	(268)
Mendelevium	Md	101	(258)
Mercury	Hg	80	200.59
Molybdenum	Mo	42	95.94
Neodymium	Nd	60	144.24
Neon	Ne	10	20.179
Neptunium	Np	93	(237)
Nickel	Ni	28	58.71
Niobium	Nb	41	92.906
Nitrogen	N	7	14.007
Nobelium	No	102	(259)
Osmium	Os	76	190.2
Oxygen	O	8	15.999
Palladium	Pd	46	106.4
Phosphorus	P	15	30.974
Platinum	Pt	78	195.09
Plutonium	Pu	94	(244)
Polonium	Po	84	(209)
Potassium	K	19	39.098
Praseodymium	Pr	59	140.91
Promethium	Pm	61	(145)
Protactinium	Pa	91	231.04
Radium	Ra	88	(226)
Radon	Rn	86	(222)
Rhenium	Re	75	186.21
Rhodium	Rh	45	102.91
Roentgenium	Rg	111	(272)
Rubidium	Rb	37	85.468
Ruthenium	Ru	44	101.07
Rutherfordium	Rf	104	(261)
Samarium	Sm	62	150.4
Scandium	Sc	21	44.956
Seaborgium	Sg	106	(263)
Selenium	Se	34	78.96
Silicon	Si	14	28.086
Silver	Ag	47	107.87
Sodium	Na	11	22.990
Strontium	Sr	38	87.62
Sulfur	S	16	32.06
Tantalum	Ta	73	180.95
Technetium	Tc	43	(98)
Tellurium	Te	52	127.60
Terbium	Tb	65	158.93
Thallium	Tl	81	204.37
Thorium	Th	90	232.04
Thulium	Tm	69	168.93
Tin	Sn	50	118.69
Titanium	Ti	22	47.90
Tungsten	W	74	183.85
Uranium	U	92	238.03
Vanadium	V	23	50.941
Xenon	Xe	54	131.30
Ytterbium	Yb	70	173.04
Yttrium	Y	39	88.906
Zinc	Zn	30	65.38
Zirconium	Zr	40	91.22

†Numbers in parentheses give the mass number of the most stable isotope.

APPENDIX D

Periodic Table of the Elements

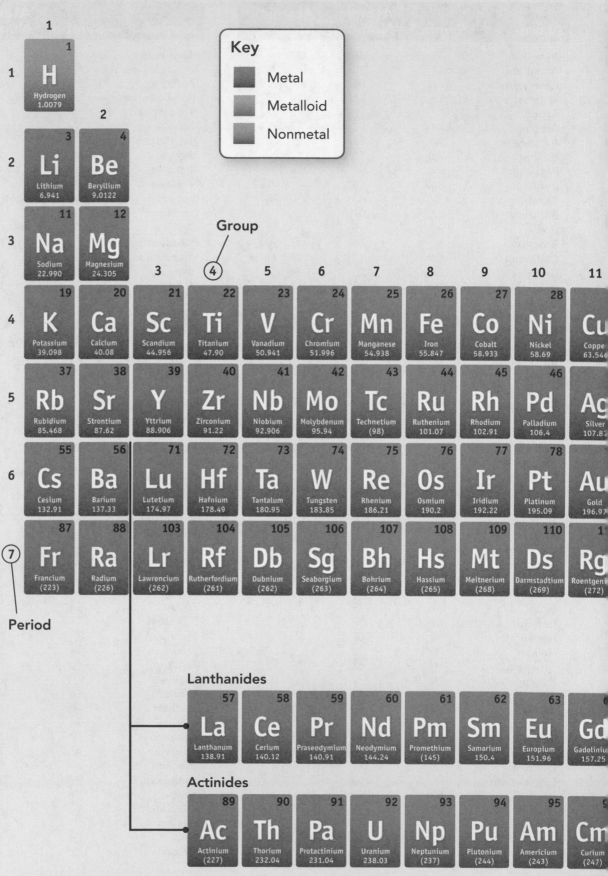

Key
- Metal
- Metalloid
- Nonmetal

Group

Period

1											
1 H Hydrogen 1.0079											

2

3 Li Lithium 6.941	4 Be Beryllium 9.0122

11 Na Sodium 22.990	12 Mg Magnesium 24.305

| | | 3 | 4 | 5 | 6 | 7 | 8 | 9 | 10 | 11 |

19 K Potassium 39.098	20 Ca Calcium 40.08	21 Sc Scandium 44.956	22 Ti Titanium 47.90	23 V Vanadium 50.941	24 Cr Chromium 51.996	25 Mn Manganese 54.938	26 Fe Iron 55.847	27 Co Cobalt 58.933	28 Ni Nickel 58.69	29 Cu Coppe 63.546

| 37 Rb Rubidium 85.468 | 38 Sr Strontium 87.62 | 39 Y Yttrium 88.906 | 40 Zr Zirconium 91.22 | 41 Nb Niobium 92.906 | 42 Mo Molybdenum 95.94 | 43 Tc Technetium (98) | 44 Ru Ruthenium 101.07 | 45 Rh Rhodium 102.91 | 46 Pd Palladium 106.4 | 47 Ag Silver 107.87 |

| 55 Cs Cesium 132.91 | 56 Ba Barium 137.33 | 71 Lu Lutetium 174.97 | 72 Hf Hafnium 178.49 | 73 Ta Tantalum 180.95 | 74 W Tungsten 183.85 | 75 Re Rhenium 186.21 | 76 Os Osmium 190.2 | 77 Ir Iridium 192.22 | 78 Pt Platinum 195.09 | 79 Au Gold 196.97 |

| 87 Fr Francium (223) | 88 Ra Radium (226) | 103 Lr Lawrencium (262) | 104 Rf Rutherfordium (261) | 105 Db Dubnium (262) | 106 Sg Seaborgium (263) | 107 Bh Bohrium (264) | 108 Hs Hassium (265) | 109 Mt Meitnerium (268) | 110 Ds Darmstadtium (269) | 111 Rg Roentgeni (272) |

Lanthanides

57 La Lanthanum 138.91	58 Ce Cerium 140.12	59 Pr Praseodymium 140.91	60 Nd Neodymium 144.24	61 Pm Promethium (145)	62 Sm Samarium 150.4	63 Eu Europium 151.96	64 Gd Gadolinium 157.25

Actinides

| 89 Ac Actinium (227) | 90 Th Thorium 232.04 | 91 Pa Protactinium 231.04 | 92 U Uranium 238.03 | 93 Np Neptunium (237) | 94 Pu Plutonium (244) | 95 Am Americium (243) | 96 Cm Curium (247) |

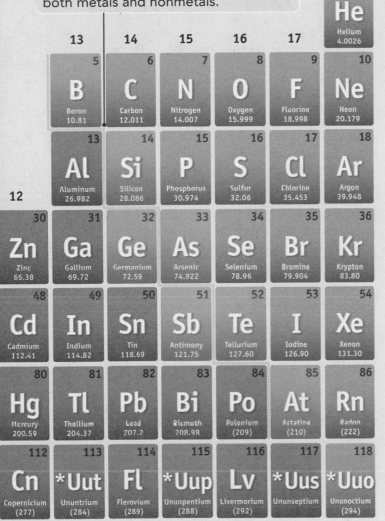

Many periodic tables include a zigzag line that separates the metals from the nonmetals. Metalloids, found on either side of the line, share properties of both metals and nonmetals.

*The discoveries of elements 113, 115, 117, and 118 have not yet been officially confirmed.

Atomic masses in parentheses are those of the most stable isotopes.

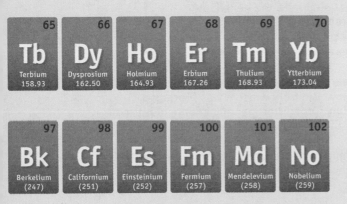

GLOSSARY

A

active transport The movement of materials across a cell membrane using cellular energy. (32)
transporte activo Proceso que usa la energía celular para mover materiales a través de la membrana celular.

adaptation An inherited behavior or physical characteristic that helps an organism survive and reproduce in its environment. (169)
adaptación Comportamiento o característica física hereditaria que le permite a un organismo sobrevivir y reproducirse en un ambiente.

alleles The different forms of a gene. (77)
alelos Diferentes formas de un gen.

autotroph An organism that is able to capture energy from sunlight or chemicals and use it to produce its own food. (46)
autótrofo Organismo que capta energía de la luz del Sol o de sustancias químicas y la usa para producir sus propios alimentos.

C

cancer A disease in which some body cells grow and divide uncontrollably, damaging the parts of the body around them. (121)
cáncer Enfermedad en la que algunas células del cuerpo crecen y se dividen sin control, y así afectan negativamente las partes del cuerpo que las rodean.

carbohydrate An energy-rich organic compound, such as a sugar or a starch, that is made of the elements carbon, hydrogen, and oxygen. (24)
carbohidrato Compuesto orgánico rico en energía, como un azúcar o almidón, formado por los elementos carbono, hidrógeno y oxígeno.

carrier A person who has one recessive allele and one dominant allele for a trait. (139)
portador Persona que tiene un alelo recesivo y un alelo dominante para un rasgo.

cell The basic unit of structure and function in living things. (4)
célula Unidad básica de la estructura y función de todos los seres vivos.

cell cycle The series of events in which a cell grows, prepares for division, and divides to form two daughter cells. (58)
ciclo celular Serie de sucesos en los que una célula crece, se prepara para dividirse y se divide para formar dos células hijas.

cell membrane A thin, flexible barrier that surrounds a cell and controls which substances pass into and out of a cell. (13)
membrana celular Barrera delgada y flexible alrededor de la célula que controla lo que entra y sale de la célula.

cell theory A widely accepted explanation of the relationship between cells and living things. (6)
teoría celular Explicación ampliamente aceptada sobre la relación entre las células y los seres vivos.

cell wall A rigid supporting layer that surrounds the cells of plants and some other organisms. (13)
pared celular Capa fuerte de apoyo alrededor de las células de las plantas y algunos otros organismos.

cellular respiration The process in which oxygen and glucose undergo a complex series of chemical reactions inside cells, releasing energy. (51)
respiración celular Proceso en el cual el oxígeno y la glucosa pasan por una serie compleja de reacciones químicas dentro de las células y así liberan energía.

chemotherapy The use of drugs to treat diseases such as cancer. (123)
quimioterapia Uso de medicamentos para tratar enfermedades como el cáncer.

chlorophyll A green photosynthetic pigment found in the chloroplasts of plants, algae, and some bacteria. (47)
clorofila Pigmento verde fotosintético de los cloroplastos de las plantas, algas y algunas bacterias.

chloroplast An organelle in the cells of plants and some other organisms that captures energy from sunlight and changes it to an energy form that cells can use in making food. (19)
cloroplasto Orgánulo de las células de las plantas y algunos otros organismos que atrapa la energía de la luz del Sol y la convierte en energía que las células pueden usar para fabricar alimentos.

chromosome A threadlike structure within a cell's nucleus that contains DNA that is passed from one generation to the next. (58)
cromosoma Estructura filamentosa en el núcleo celular que contiene el ADN que se transmite de una generación a la siguiente.

clone An organism that is genetically identical to the organism from which it was produced. (149)
clon Organismo genéticamente idéntico al organismo del que proviene.

codominance A situation in which both alleles for a gene are expressed equally. (87)

codominancia Situación en la que ambos alelos de un gen se manifiestan de igual manera.

compound A substance made of two or more elements chemically combined in a specific ratio, or proportion. (23)
compuesto Sustancia compuesta de dos o más elementos combinados químicamente en una razón o proporción específica.

cytokinesis The final stage of the cell cycle, in which the cell's cytoplasm divides, distributing the organelles into each of the two new daughter cells. (62)
citocinesis Última etapa del ciclo celular en la que se divide el citoplasma y se reparten los orgánulos entre las dos células hijas nuevas.

cytoplasm The thick fluid region of a cell located inside the cell membrane (in prokaryotes) or between the cell membrane and nucleus (in eukaryotes). (15)
citoplasma Región de fluido espeso de la célula dentro de la membrana celular (en los procariotas) o entre la membrana celular y el núcleo (en los eucariotas).

D

diffusion The process by which molecules move from an area of higher concentration to an area of lower concentration. (30)
difusión Proceso en el que las moléculas se mueven de un área de mayor concentración a otra de menor concentración.

DNA Deoxyribonucleic acid; the genetic material that carries information about an organism and is passed from parent to offspring. (26)
ADN Ácido desoxirribonucleico; material genético que lleva información sobre un organismo y que se transmite de padres a hijos.

DNA replication Before a cell divides, the process in which DNA copies itself. (112)
replicación del ADN Proceso en el que el ADN se duplica, antes de que la célula se divida.

dominant allele An allele whose trait always shows up in the organism when the allele is present. (77)
alelo dominante Alelo cuyo rasgo siempre se manifiesta en el organismo, cuando el alelo está presente.

double helix The shape of a DNA molecule. (26)
doble hélice Forma de una molécula de ADN.

E

element A pure substance that cannot be broken down into other substances by chemical or physical means. (22)
elemento Sustancia pura que no se puede separar en otras sustancias por medios químicos o físicos.

endocytosis The process by which the cell membrane takes particles into the cell by changing shape and engulfing the particles. (33)
endocitosis Proceso en el que la membrana celular absorbe partículas al cambiar de forma y envolver las partículas.

endoplasmic reticulum An organelle that forms a maze of passageways in which proteins and other materials are carried from one part of the cell to another. (15)
retículo endoplasmático Orgánulo que forma un laberinto de conductos que llevan proteínas y otros materiales de una parte de la célula a otra.

enzyme 1. A type of protein that speeds up a chemical reaction in a living thing. (25) **2.** A biological catalyst that lowers the activation energy or reactions in cells.
enzima 1. Tipo de proteína que acelera una reacción química en un ser vivo. **2.** Catalizador biológico que reduce la energía de activación o la reacción de las células.

ethics The study of principles about what is right and wrong, fair and unfair. (154)
ética Estudio de los principios de qué es lo bueno y lo malo, lo justo y lo injusto.

evolution Change over time; the process by which modern organisms have descended from ancient organisms. (170)
evolución Cambio con el tiempo; proceso por el cual los organismos modernos se originaron a partir de organismos antiguos.

exocytosis The process by which the vacuole surrounding particles fuses with the cell membrane, forcing the contents out of the cell. (33)
exocitosis Proceso en el que la vacuola que envuelve partículas se funde con la membrana celular, expulsando así el contenido al exterior de la célula.

F

fermentation The process by which cells release energy by breaking down food molecules without using oxygen. (54)
fermentación Proceso en el que las células liberan energía al descomponer las moléculas de alimento sin usar oxígeno.

fertilization The process in sexual reproduction in which an egg cell and a sperm cell join to form a new cell. (75)
fertilización Proceso de la reproducción sexual en el que una célula huevo y una célula esperma se unen y forman una célula nueva.

fossil The preserved remains or traces of an organism that lived in the past. (167)
fósil Restos o huellas preservados de un organismo que vivió en el pasado.

G

gene A sequence of DNA that determines a trait and is passed from parent to offspring. (77)
gen Secuencia de ADN que determina un rasgo y que se pasa de los progenitores a los hijos.

gene therapy The process of changing a gene to treat a medical disease or disorder. An absent or faulty gene is replaced by a normal working gene. (151)
terapia genética Proceso que consiste en cambiar un gen para tratar una enfermedad o un trastorno médico. El gen ausente o defectuoso se cambia por un gen con función normal.

genetic disorder An abnormal condition that a person inherits through genes or chromosomes. (141)
desorden genético Condición anormal que hereda una persona a través de los genes o cromosomas.

genetic engineering The transfer of a gene from the DNA of one organism into another organism, in order to produce an organism with desired traits. (149)
ingeniería genética Transferencia de un gen desde el ADN de un organismo a otro, para producir un organismo con los rasgos deseados.

genetics The scientific study of heredity. (75)
genética Ciencia que estudia la herencia.

genome A complete set of genetic information that an organism carries in its DNA. (153)
genoma Toda la información genética que un organismo lleva en su ADN.

genotype An organism's genetic makeup, or allele combinations. (84)
genotipo Composición genética de un organismo, es decir, las combinaciones de los alelos.

Golgi apparatus An organelle in a cell that receives proteins and other newly formed materials from the endoplasmic reticulum, packages them, and distributes them to other parts of the cell. (18)
aparato de Golgi Orgánulo de la célula que recibe, empaqueta y distribuye a otras partes de la célula las proteínas y otros materiales que se forman en el retículo endoplasmático.

gradualism Pattern of evolution characterized by the slow and steady accumulation of small genetic changes over long periods of time. (182)
gradualismo Evolución de una especie por medio de la acumulación lenta pero continua de cambios genéticos a través de largos períodos de tiempo.

H

heredity The passing of traits from parents to offspring. (74)
herencia Transmisión de rasgos de padres a hijos.

heterotroph An organism that cannot make its own food and gets food by consuming other living things. (46)
heterótrofo Organismo que no puede producir sus propios alimentos y que se alimenta al consumir otros seres vivos.

heterozygous Having two different alleles for a particular gene. (84)
heterocigoto Que tiene dos alelos distintos para un gen particular.

homologous structures Structures that are similar in different species and that have been inherited from a common ancestor. (178)
estructuras homólogas Estructuras parecidas de especies distintas y que se han heredado de un antepasado común.

homozygous Having two identical alleles for a particular gene. (84)
homocigoto Que tiene dos alelos idénticos para un gen particular.

hybrid An offspring of crosses that has two different alleles for a trait. (78)
híbrido Descendiente de cruces que tiene dos alelos distintos para un rasgo.

hybridization A selective breeding method that involves crossing different individuals to bring together the best traits from both parents. (148)
hibridación Técnica reproductiva en la que se cruzan individuos distintos para reunir los mejores rasgos de ambos progenitores.

I

---

inbreeding A selective breeding method in which two individuals with similar sets of alleles are crossed. (148)
endogamia Técnica reproductiva en la que se cruzan dos individuos con conjuntos de alelos parecidos.

incomplete dominance A situation in which one allele is not completely dominant over another allele. (87)
dominancia incompleta Situación en la que un alelo no es completamente dominante sobre el otro.

interphase The first stage of the cell cycle that takes place before cell division occurs, during which a cell grows and makes a copy of its DNA. (58)
interfase Primera etapa del ciclo celular que ocurre antes de la división celular y durante la cual la célula crece y duplica su ADN.

K

---

karyotype A picture of all the human chromosomes in a cell grouped together in pairs and arranged in order of decreasing size. (144)
cariotipo Fotografía de todos los cromosomas humanos en una célula agrupados en pares y ordenados de los más grandes a los más pequeños.

L

---

lipid An energy-rich organic compound, such as a fat, oil, or wax, that is made of carbon, hydrogen, and oxygen. (25)
lípido Compuesto orgánico rico en energía, como una grasa, aceite o cera, formado por los elementos carbono, hidrógeno y oxígeno.

lysosome A cell organelle which contains chemicals that break down large food particles into smaller ones and that can be used by the rest of the cell. (19)
lisosoma Orgánulo de una célula, que tiene sustancias químicas que convierten partículas grandes de alimentos en partículas más pequeñas que el resto de la célula puede utilizar.

M

---

meiosis The process that occurs in the formation of sex cells (sperm and egg) by which the number of chromosomes is reduced by half. (96)
meiosis Proceso durante la formación de las células sexuales (espermatozoide y óvulo) por el cual el número de cromosomas se reduce a la mitad.

messenger RNA Type of RNA that carries copies of instructions for the assembly of amino acids into proteins from DNA to ribosomes in the cytoplasm. (115)
ARN mensajero Tipo de ARN que lleva, del ADN a los ribosomas del citoplasma, copias de instrucciones para sintetizar a los aminoácidos en proteínas.

microscope An instrument that makes small objects look larger. (6)
microscopio Instrumento que permite que los objetos pequeños se vean más grandes.

mitochondria Rod-shaped organelles that convert energy in food molecules to energy the cell can use to carry out its functions. (15)
mitocondria Estructura celular con forma de bastón que transforma la energía de las moléculas de alimentos en energía que la célula puede usar para llevar a cabo sus funciones.

mitosis The second stage of the cell cycle during which the cell's nucleus divides into two new nuclei and one set of DNA is distributed into each daughter cell. (59)
mitosis Segunda etapa del ciclo celular, durante la cual se divide el núcleo de la célula en dos núcleos nuevos y el conjunto del ADN se reparte entre cada célula hija.

multicellular Consisting of many cells. (20)
multicelular Compuesto por muchas células.

multiple alleles Three or more possible alleles of a gene that determine a trait. (88)
alelo múltiple Tres o más alelos posibles del gen que determina un rasgo.

mutation Any change in the DNA of a gene or a chromosome. (119)
mutación Cualquier cambio del ADN de un gen o cromosoma.

N

---

natural selection The process by which organisms that are best adapted to their environment are most likely to survive and reproduce. (172)

GLOSSARY

selección natural Proceso por el que los organismos que se adaptan mejor a su ambiente tienen mayor probabilidad de sobrevivir y reproducirse.

nitrogen bases Molecules that contain nitrogen and other elements. (109)
bases nitrogenadas Moléculas que contienen nitrógeno y otros elementos.

nucleic acid A very large organic molecule made of carbon, oxygen, hydrogen, nitrogen, and phosphorus, that contains the instructions cells need to carry out all the functions of life. (26)
ácido nucleico Molécula muy grande formada por carbono, oxígeno, hidrógeno, nitrógeno y fósforo, que porta las instrucciones necesarias para que las células realicen todas las funciones vitales.

nucleus 1. In cells, a large oval organelle that contains the cell's genetic material in the form of DNA and controls many of the cell's activities. (14) **2.** The central core of an atom which contains protons and neutrons. **3.** The solid inner core of a comet.
núcleo 1. En las células, orgánulo grande y ovalado que contiene el material genético de la célula en forma de ADN y que controla muchas actividades celulares. **2.** Centro del átomo que contiene los protones y neutrones. **3.** Centro sólido de un cometa.

O

organ A body structure that is composed of different kinds of tissues that work together. (21)
órgano Estructura corporal compuesta de distintos tipos de tejidos que trabajan juntos.

organ system A group of organs that work together to perform a major function. (21)
sistema de órganos Grupo de órganos que trabajan juntos para realizar una función importante.

organelle A tiny cell structure that carries out a specific function within the cell. (14)
orgánulo Estructura celular diminuta que realiza una función específica dentro de la célula.

osmosis The diffusion of water molecules across a selectively permeable membrane. (31)
ósmosis Difusión de moléculas de agua a través de una membrana permeable selectiva.

P

passive transport The movement of dissolved materials across a cell membrane without using cellular energy. (30)
transporte pasivo Movimiento de materiales a través de una membrana celular sin usar energía celular.

pedigree A chart that shows the presence or absence of a trait according to the relationships within a family across several generations. (143)
genealogía Diagrama que muestra la presencia o ausencia de un rasgo según las relaciones familiares a través de varias generaciones.

phenotype An organism's physical appearance, or visible traits. (84)
fenotipo Apariencia física, o rasgos visibles, de un organismo.

photosynthesis The process by which plants and other autotrophs capture and use light energy to make food from carbon dioxide and water. (46)
fotosíntesis Proceso en el que las plantas y otros autótrofos capturan y usan energía luminosa para convertir el dióxido de carbono y el agua en alimentos.

polygenic inheritance The inheritance of traits that are controlled by two or more genes, such as height in humans. (88)
herencia poligénica Herencia de los rasgos controlados por dos o más genes, como la altura en los seres humanos.

probability A number that describes how likely it is that a particular event will occur. (81)
probabilidad Número que describe cuán probable es que ocurra un suceso.

protein Large organic molecule made of carbon, hydrogen, oxygen, nitrogen, and sometimes sulfur. (25)
proteína Molécula orgánica grande compuesta de carbono, hidrógeno, oxígeno, nitrógeno y, a veces, azufre.

punctuated equilibrium Pattern of evolution in which long stable periods are interrupted by brief periods of more rapid change. (183)
equilibrio puntual Patrón de la evolución en el que los períodos largos estables son interrumpidos por breves períodos de cambio rápido.

Punnett square A chart that shows all the possible combinations of alleles that can result from a genetic cross. (82)

cuadrado de Punnett Tabla que muestra todas las combinaciones posibles de los alelos que se pueden derivar de un cruce genético.

purebred An offspring of many generations that has the same form of a trait. (75)
raza pura Descendiente de varias generaciones que tienen los mismos rasgos.

R

recessive allele An allele that is hidden whenever the dominant allele is present. (77)
alelo recesivo Alelo que se no manifiesta cuando el alelo dominante está presente.

replication The process by which a cell makes a copy of the DNA in its nucleus before cell division. (58)
replicación Proceso en el que la célula copia el ADN de su núcleo antes de la división celular.

ribosome A small grain-shaped organelle in the cytoplasm of a cell that produces proteins. (14)
ribosoma Orgánulo pequeño con forma de grano en el citoplasma de una célula que produce proteínas.

S

scientific theory A well-tested explanation for a wide range of observations or experimental results. (170)
teoría científica Explicación comprobada de una gran variedad de observaciones o resultados de experimentos.

selective breeding Method of breeding that allows only those organisms with desired traits to produce the next generation. (147)
cruce selectivo Técnica reproductiva por medio de la cual sólo los organismos con rasgos deseados producen la próxima generación.

selectively permeable A property of cell membranes that allows some substances to pass across it, while others cannot. (29)
permeabilidad selectiva Propiedad de las membranas celulares que permite el paso de algunas sustancias y no de otras.

sex chromosomes A pair of chromosomes carrying genes that determine whether a person is male or female. (137)
cromosomas sexuales Par de cromosomas portadores de genes que determinan el sexo (masculino o femenino) de una persona.

sex-linked gene A gene that is carried on a sex (X or Y) chromosome. (138)
gen ligado al sexo Gen de un cromosoma sexual (X o Y).

species A group of similar organisms that can mate with each other and produce offspring that can also mate and reproduce. (167)
especie Grupo de organismos semejantes que pueden cruzarse y producir descendencia fértil.

T

tissue A group of similar cells that perform a specific function. (21)
tejido Grupo de células semejantes que realizan una función específica.

trait A specific characteristic that an organism can pass to its offspring through its genes. (74)
rasgo Característica específica que un organismo puede transmitir a sus descendientes a través de los genes.

transfer RNA Type of RNA in the cytoplasm that carries an amino acid to the ribosome during protein synthesis. (115)
ARN de transferencia Tipo de ARN del citoplasma que lleva un aminoácido al ribosoma durante la síntesis de proteínas.

tumor A mass of rapidly dividing cells that can damage surrounding tissue. (122)
tumor Masa de células que se dividen rápidamente y que puede dañar los tejidos que la rodean.

U

unicellular Made of a single cell. (20)
unicelular Compuesto por una sola célula.

V

vacuole A sac-like organelle that stores water, food, and other materials. (18)
vacuola Orgánulo con forma de saco que almacena agua, alimento y otros materiales.

variation Any difference between individuals of the same species. (173)
variación Cualquier diferencia entre individuos de la misma especie.

INDEX

Page numbers for key terms are printed in **boldface** type.

A

Acquired traits, 89–91
Active transport, 32
Adaptation, 169
Alcoholic fermentation, 54
Alleles, 77–79
  of blood type, 135
  dominant and recessive, **77,** 103, 135, 139
  and genotype, 84
  human, 134–136
  incomplete dominance and codominance, 87
  multiple, **88,** 135
  and polygenic inheritance, 88
  and range of phenotypes, 136
  symbols for, 78
  See also Genetics
Amino acids, 115–117
Animals
  cytokinesis in, 62
  function of cells in, 4–5, 20–21
  structure of cells in, 13–19
Application of skills
  Apply It!, 10, 18, 31, 46, 54, 59, 79, 85, 88, 93, 110, 115, 123, 135, 143, 148, 153, 170, 179, 183
  Do the Math!, 36, 99
    calculate, 81, 121, 174
    draw conclusions, 26
    graph, 149
    interpret data, 63, 149, 174
    read graphs, 26, 62
  Interactivities, 7, 13, 14, 17, 24, 25, 27, 30, 31, 32, 46, 48, 51, 60, 76, 82, 109, 112, 117, 119, 121, 139, 141, 142, 143, 144, 154, 169, 172, 173, 175, 177, 178, 186
  Science Matters
    Athletic Trainer, 68
    Codis: The DNA Database, 161
    Electron Eyes, 38
    Fighting Cancer, 129
    Frozen Zoo, 128
    Genographic Project, 39
    Incredible Shrinking Fish, 188
    Mini But Mighty, 160
    Nature *vs.* Nurture, 102
    Seeing Spots, 103
    There's Something Fishy About This Sushi, 129
    Walking Whales?, 189
    Why Hearts Don't Get Cancer, 69
Apply It! *See* Application of skills

Artificial selection, 171
Assessment
  Assess Your Understanding, 5, 7, 11, 19, 21, 23, 27, 33, 46, 49, 53, 55, 57, 63, 76, 79, 83, 85, 88, 91, 95, 97, 111, 113, 117, 120, 123, 136, 139, 142, 145, 151, 155, 171, 175, 179, 181, 183
  Review and Assessment, 35–36, 65–66, 99–100, 125–126, 157–158, 185–186
  Standardized Test Prep, 37, 67, 101, 127, 159, 187
  Study Guide, 34, 64, 98, 124, 156, 184
Athletic trainers, 68
Atom, 22
Autotroph, 46

B

Bacteria and gene therapy, 150
Big Idea, xx–xxi
Big Question
  Answer the Big Question, 19, 55, 91, 117, 155, 175
  Apply the Big Question, 36, 66, 100, 126, 158, 186
  chapter opener, 1, 41, 71, 105, 131, 163
  Explore the Big Question, 16, 55, 90, 116, 154, 172
  Review the Big Question, 34, 64, 98, 124, 156, 184
  Unlock the Big Question, 4, 12, 22, 28, 44, 50, 56, 74, 80, 86, 92, 108, 114, 118, 134, 140, 146, 152, 166, 176, 180
Breathing, 51

C

Cancer, 121
  and cell division, 69
  and mutation, 121–122
  prevention, 129
  treatment, 123
Carbohydrates, 24
  and cell transport, 29
Carbon dioxide
  and cell transport, 32
  and cellular respiration, 52–53
  in photosynthesis, 48–49
Carrier, 139

Cell, 4
  cell cycle, **58**–63
    and cancer mutation, 121–122
    function of, 56–57
    interphase, mitosis, and cytokinesis, 58–62
    length of, 56, 63
  cell division, 56–57, 69
  cell membrane, **13,** 16–17, 29
    selectively permeable, **29**
  cell theory, **6**–7
  cell wall, **13,** 16–17
  cellular respiration, 50, **51**–53
  chemical compounds in, 22–27
  and energy, 22, 24–26, 45–55
  function of, 5, 13–19
  genetics. *See* Genetics
  meiosis, 96–97
  and movement of materials, 28–33
  and mutation, 118–122, 129, 141
  and protein synthesis, 114–117
  role of
    in fermentation, 54–55
    in organisms, 4–5
    in photosynthesis, 44–49
  seeing through microscopes, 6–12
  specialized cells, 20
  structure of, 4, 13–19
Chemotherapy, 123
Chlorophyll, 47
Chloroplasts, 16–17, **19,** 47
Chromatin, 14
Chromosomes, 58
  and meiosis, 96–97
  sex chromosomes, 93–95, 137–139
Clone, 149
Codominance, 87
Colorblindness, 139
Competition, 173
Compound microscopes, 9
Compounds, 23–27
  carbohydrates, **24**
  and cell transport, 29
  DNA, **26**
  enzymes, **25**
  lipids, **25**
  nucleic acids, **26**
  proteins, **25**
  and water, 27
  See also DNA; Proteins
Consumers of energy, 46, 55
Crick, Francis, 109
Cystic fibrosis, 141
Cytokinesis, 60–61, **6**

Cytoplasm, 15–19
in protein synthesis, 115–117

D

Darwin, Charles, 166
hypothesis, 166–175
Daughter cells, 58
Did You Know?, 24, 62, 93, 111, 145, 168
Diffusion, 30
facilitated, 32
Digital Learning
Apply It!, 9, 45, 55, 77, 85, 87, 97, 135, 143, 183
Art in Motion, 29, 32, 55, 96, 97, 109, 142, 151, 182, 183
Do the Math!, 25, 59, 121, 173
Interactive Art, 13, 16, 20, 21, 47, 48, 51, 52, 59, 60, 81, 82, 89, 90, 112, 113, 115, 116, 141, 142, 153, 154, 167, 169, 177, 178
My Reading Web, 2, 3, 42, 43, 72, 73, 106, 107, 132, 133, 164, 165
My Science Coach, 5, 7, 11, 19, 21, 23, 25, 27, 33, 46, 49, 53, 55, 57, 63, 65, 75, 76, 79, 83, 85, 88, 91, 93, 95, 97, 111, 113, 117, 120, 121, 123, 125, 136, 137, 139, 142, 143, 145, 151, 155, 171, 175, 179, 181, 183, 185
Planet Diary, 4, 5, 12, 13, 22, 23, 28, 29, 44, 45, 50, 51, 56, 57, 74, 75, 80, 81, 86, 87, 92, 93, 108, 109, 114, 115, 118, 119, 134, 135, 140, 141, 146, 147, 152, 153, 166, 167, 176, 177, 180, 181
Real-World Inquiry, 172, 173
Untamed Science, xxii, 1, 40, 41, 70, 71, 104, 105, 130, 131, 162, 163
Virtual Lab, 9, 47, 77, 78, 119, 120, 137
Vocab Flash Cards, 3, 43, 73, 107, 133, 165
Discrimination, genetic, 154
Diversity of species, 167
DNA, 26
copying, 58, 112–113
DNA fingerprinting, 152–153, 161
as evidence of evolution, 179
in protein synthesis, 115–117
structure of, 108–113
for tracking ancestry and origin, 39, 114, 128

DNA replication, 112–113
Do the Math! *See* Application of skills
Dominant alleles, 77, 103, 135, 139
Double-helix, 26
Down Syndrome, 142

E

Electron microscopes, 11, 38
Elements, 22
Endocytosis, 33
Endoplasmic reticulum (ER), 15, 16–17
Energy
and cell transport, 30–33
from cellular respiration, 50–53
chain of, 46
from fermentation, 54–55
from food, 22, 24–26
from photosynthesis, 46–49
producers and consumers, 46, 55
storing and releasing, 51
Environmental factors, impact of
on genes, 90
on phenotypes, 89
See also Acquired traits
Enzymes, 25
Ethics, 154
Evolution, 170
Darwin's hypothesis, 166–175
evidence of, 167, 176–179, 189
gradualism theory, 182
and natural selection, 172–175, 180, 188
punctuated equilibrium theory, 183
rate of, 180–183
Exocytosis, 33
Extremophiles, 50

F

F₁ and F₂ (filial) offspring, 76
Facilitated diffusion, 32
Fats, 25
Fermentation, 54–55
Fertilization, 75
and sex chromosomes, 137
Food energy, 22, 24–26, 45
and cell function, 5
and cellular respiration, 50–53
and fermentation, 54–55
for plants, 44, 46–49

Fossils, 167, 176, 177, 189
Franklin, Rosalind, 108

G

Gene therapy, 150–151
Genes, 77
sex-linked, **138**–139, 142
Genetic disorders, 140, **141**–145
counseling and treatment, 145
diagnosing, 143–144
Genetic Information Nondiscrimination Act (GINA), 154
Genetics, 75
advances in technology, 146–155, 160–161
cloning, 149
genetic code, 109–113
genetic disorders, 140–145
genetic engineering, 149–151
human, 134–145
impact of environment, 89–91
Mendel's experiments, 74–79
and mutation, 118–122, 129, 141
patterns of inheritance, 86–88, 134–136
phenotypes and genotypes, 84–85
and probability, 80–85
and protein synthesis, 111, 114–117
role of chromosomes, 92–97
and selective breeding, 146–148
using information from, 39, 114, 128, 152–153, 160–161
See also Evolution
Genome, 153
Genotype, 84
Glucose, 24
and cellular respiration, 50–53
in photosynthesis, 48–49
Golgi apparatus, 16–17, **18**
Gradualism, 182

H

Hemophilia, 142
Heredity, 74
See also Genetics; Inheritance
Heterotroph, 46
Heterozygous organisms, 84
Homologous structures, 178
Homozygous organisms, 84
Hooke, Robert, 6

INDEX

Human Genome Project, 153
Hybrid, **78**
Hybridization, **148**

I

Inbreeding, **148**
Incomplete dominance, **87**
Inheritance
heredity, **74**
human, 134–145
patterns of, 86–91, 134–136
polygenic, **88**
See also Genetics
Inquiry Skills. *See* Science Inquiry Skills; Science Literacy Skills
Interactivities. *See* Application of skills
Interphase, **58**, 60–61
Isolation of species, 180–181

K

Karyotype, **144**

L

Lab Zone
Inquiry Warm-Up, 4, 12, 22, 28, 44, 50, 56, 74, 80, 86, 92, 108, 114, 118, 134, 140, 146, 152, 166, 176, 180
Lab Investigation, 11, 53, 85, 111, 139, 175
Quick Lab, 5, 7, 19, 21, 23, 27, 33, 46, 49, 55, 57, 63, 76, 79, 83, 88, 91, 95, 97, 113, 117, 120, 123, 136, 142, 145, 151, 155, 171, 179, 181, 183
Lactic acid, 54, 68
Leeuwenhoek, Anton van, 4, 6
Lenses (microscopes), 8–9
Lipids, **25**
and cell transport, 29
Lysosomes, 16–17, **19**

M

Magnification of microscopes, 8–9
Magnifying glasses, 8
Math. *See* Application of skills
Measuring microscopic objects, 10
Meiosis, **96**–97

Mendel, Gregor, 74
experiments, 74–79
Messenger RNA, **115**
Microscopes, 4, **6**–12
compound, 9
electron, 11, 38
fluorescent, 12
magnification of, 8–9
optical, 38
resolution of, 10
Mitochondria, **15**
and cellular respiration, 52
Mitosis, **59**–61
Molecules, 23
and smell, 28
Movement in and out of cells
active transport, **32**
diffusion, **30**, 31
of large particles, 33
osmosis, **31**
passive transport, **30**–32
through cell membrane, 29
Multicellular organisms, **20**–21
Multiple alleles, **88**
Mutation, **119**
and cancer, 121–122, 129
and genetic disorders, 141
helpful and harmful, 118, 120
My Planet Diary
Biography, 74, 108
Blog, 134
Careers, 92
Discovery, 86, 114, 140, 176
Field Trip, 80
Fun Facts, 28, 50, 146, 180
Misconception, 22, 44, 118
Science Stats, 56
Technology, 12, 152
Voices from History, 4, 166

N

Natural selection, **172**–175
and environmental changes, 176, 180, 188
and genetic changes, 176
Nitrogen bases, **109**–111
Nucleic acids, **26**
Nucleolus, 14
Nucleus, **14**, 16–17
in protein synthesis, 115–117

O

Oils, 25
Organ, **21**
Organ system, **21**

Organelles, **14**
Organisms
autotrophic and heterotrophic, **46**
function of cells in, 4–5, 20–21
heterozygous and homozygous, **84**
and mutation, 120
purebred, **75**
structure of cells in, 13–19
unicellular and multicellular, 20–21
Osmosis, **31**
Overproduction, 172
Oxygen, role of
in cell function, 5
in cell transport, 30, 32
in cellular respiration, 50–53
in photosynthesis, 47–49

P

Passive transport, **30**–32
Pedigree, 143
Phenotype, **84**
Photosynthesis, **46**–49
Pigment, 47
Plants
cytokinesis in, 62
function of cells in, 4–5, 20–21
and photosynthesis, 46–49
structure of cells in, 13–19
Pollination, 75
Polygenic inheritance, **88**
Privacy, genetic, 155
Probability, 80, **81**–83
Process Skills. *See* Science Inquiry Skills; Science Literacy Skills
Producers of energy, 46, 55
Proteins, **25**
and cell transport, 29, 32
cellular production of, 14–18
as evidence of evolution, 179
protein synthesis, 111, 114–117
Punctuated equilibrium, **183**
Punnett square, **82**–83
Purebred organisms, **75**

R

Reading Skills
reading/thinking support
graphic organizers, 17, 21, 25, 27, 48, 52, 53, 56, 66, 77, 84, 147, 173

strategies
  apply concepts, 7, 21, 25, 46, 65, 83, 87, 99, 120, 125, 126, 139, 151, 158, 185, 186
  define, 11, 18, 76, 155, 175, 179
  describe, 16, 21, 27, 59, 88, 91, 95, 113, 171, 177
  estimate, 10, 11, 35
  explain, 11, 46, 49, 65, 99, 110, 111, 120, 136, 142, 151
  identify, 13, 33, 46, 48, 52, 57, 78, 111, 139, 151, 181, 183
  interpret data, 56, 63, 88, 149, 157, 174
  interpret diagrams, 23, 35, 49, 53, 60, 65, 76, 95, 96, 111, 112, 115, 119, 125, 126, 137, 143, 157, 169, 178
  interpret photos, 10, 45, 121, 144
  interpret tables, 19, 52, 60, 82, 84, 99, 135, 179
  list, 58, 63, 88, 123, 145, 171, 182
  make generalizations, 19, 47, 66, 157, 170
  make judgments, 149, 185
  mark text, 8, 20, 90, 110, 122, 138
  name, 32, 49, 53
  read graphs, 26, 63, 85
  review, 6, 14, 27, 33, 55, 83, 91, 113, 117, 120, 139
target reading skills
  ask questions, 62, 147
  compare and contrast, 11, 25, 33, 35, 36, 54, 59, 62, 76, 90, 99, 100, 157, 182, 185
  identify supporting evidence, 79
  identify the main idea, 20, 83, 110, 178
  outline, 142
  relate cause and effect, 7, 27, 30, 53, 66, 78, 79, 85, 95, 100, 122, 138, 157, 173, 175
  relate text and visuals, 14, 94, 150
  sequence, 7, 35, 46, 48, 63, 66, 109
  summarize, 52, 65, 78, 90, 95, 100, 117, 154, 155, 172
Recessive alleles, 77, 103, 135, 139
Replication, DNA, 58, 112–113
Resolution of microscopes, 10
Respiration, cellular, 51–53

Ribosomes, 14–17
  role in protein synthesis, 115–117
RNA
  messenger and transfer, **115**
  in protein synthesis, 115–117

S

Scanning electron microscope (SEM), 38
Scanning tunneling microscope (STM), 38
Science Inquiry Skills
  basic process skills
    calculate, 9, 59, 81, 121, 136, 137, 139, 142, 174
    classify, 5, 24, 27, 35, 46, 84, 89
    communicate, 12, 22, 28, 44, 74, 80, 93, 114, 118, 138, 140, 146, 153, 166, 176, 179, 180
    estimate, 10, 35
    graph, 27, 149
    infer, xxii, 8, 19, 21, 31, 35, 36, 51, 75, 85, 104, 110, 126, 136, 142, 152, 168, 183, 185
    measure, 10
    observe, 11, 33, 70, 75, 148, 167, 177
    predict, 9, 30, 31, 33, 63, 65, 77, 79, 82, 86, 99, 136, 141
Science Literacy Skills
  integrated process skills
    control variables, 54
    design experiments, 93, 115
    develop hypotheses, 40, 55, 130, 162, 170, 171, 186
    draw conclusions, 20, 26, 77, 85, 123, 125, 136, 144, 148, 175, 185
    evaluate impact on society, 155
    form operational definitions, 125
    make models, 18, 29, 99, 143, 154, 183
    pose questions, 50
    relate evidence and explain, 95
  scientific literacy
    identify faulty reasoning, 100
Science Matters. *See* Application of skills
Scientific theory, 170
Selection, artificial, 171

Selection, natural, 172–175
  and environmental changes, 176, 180, 188
  and genetic changes, 176
Selective breeding, 146, **147**–148, 171
Selectively permeable cell membranes, 29
Sex cells, 93–97
Sex chromosomes, 93–95, **137**–139
Sex-linked genes, 138–139
  and genetic disorders, 142
Sickle-cell disease, 141
Smells, 28
Specialized cells, 20
Species, 167
  new, 180–181
Starch, 24
Sugar, 24
  and facilitated diffusion, 32
  and photosynthesis, 48–49

T

Temperature, cellular, 27
Tissue, 21
Traits, 74
  cloning, 149
  dominant and recessive, **77,** 103, 135, 139
  genetic engineering, 149–151
  human inheritance patterns, 134–136
  inherited and acquired, 86–91, 102
  and selective breeding, 146–148
  visible and genetic, 84
  See also Alleles; Genetics
Transfer RNA, 115
Transmission electron microscope (TEM), 38
Tumor, 122

U

Unicellular organisms, 20

V

Vacuoles, 16–17, **18**
  and cell transport, 33

INDEX

Page numbers for key terms are printed in **boldface** type.

Variation, 173

Vocabulary Skills
high-use academic words, 132, 148
identify multiple meanings, 164, 169
prefixes, 2, 8, 15
suffixes, 72, 84
word origins (Greek or Latin), 42, 47, 106, 119

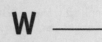

Waste elimination
and cell function, 5
and cellular respiration, 51
by Golgi apparatus and vacuoles, 18–19, 33

Water
and cell transport, 30
importance of, 27
and osmosis, 31

Watson, James, 109

X

X- and Y-chromosomes. *See* Sex chromosomes

ACKNOWLEDGMENTS

Staff Credits

The people who made up the *Interactive Science* team—representing composition services, core design digital and multimedia production services, digital product development, editorial, editorial services, manufacturing, and production—are listed below.

Jan Van Aarsen, Samah Abadir, Ernie Albanese, Zareh MacPherson Artinian, Bridget Binstock, Suzanne Biron, MJ Black, Nancy Bolsover, Stacy Boyd, Jim Brady, Katherine Bryant, Michael Burstein, Pradeep Byram, Jessica Chase, Jonathan Cheney, Arthur Ciccone, Allison Cook-Bellistri, Rebecca Cottingham, AnnMarie Coyne, Bob Craton, Chris Deliee, Paul Delsignore, Michael Di Maria, Diane Dougherty, Kristen Ellis, Theresa Eugenio, Amanda Ferguson, Jorgensen Fernandez, Kathryn Fobert, Julia Gecha, Mark Geyer, Steve Gobbell, Paula Gogan-Porter, Jeffrey Gong, Sandra Graff, Adam Groffman, Lynette Haggard, Christian Henry, Karen Holtzman, Susan Hutchinson, Sharon Inglis, Marian Jones, Sumy Joy, Sheila Kanitsch, Courtenay Kelley, Chris Kennedy, Toby Klang, Greg Lam, Russ Lappa, Margaret LaRaia, Ben Leveillee, Thea Limpus, Dotti Marshall, Kathy Martin, Robyn Matzke, John McClure, Mary Beth McDaniel, Krista McDonald, Tim McDonald, Rich McMahon, Cara McNally, Melinda Medina, Angelina Mendez, Maria Milczarek, Claudi Mimo, Mike Napieralski, Deborah Nicholls, Dave Nichols, William Oppenheimer, Jodi O'Rourke, Ameer Padshah, Lorie Park, Celio Pedrosa, Jonathan Penyack, Linda Zust Reddy, Jennifer Reichlin, Stephen Rider, Charlene Rimsa, Stephanie Rogers, Marcy Rose, Rashid Ross, Anne Rowsey, Logan Schmidt, Amanda Seldera, Laurel Smith, Nancy Smith, Ted Smykal, Emily Soltanoff, Cindy Strowman, Dee Sunday, Barry Tomack, Patricia Valencia, Ana Sofia Villaveces, Stephanie Wallace, Christine Whitney, Brad Wiatr, Heidi Wilson, Heather Wright, Rachel Youdelman

Photography

Cover, Front and Back

flower, Dr. Jeremy Burgess/Science Photo Library/Photo Researchers, Inc.; **stem,** Anna Subbotina/Shutterstock.

Front matter

Page vi, Solvin Zankl/Nature Picture Library; **vii,** Thinkstock/Corbis; **viii,** Blickwinkel/Alamy; **x,** HALEY/SIPA/Newscom; **xi,** Mark Conlin/Alamy; **xiii,** iStockphoto.com; **xv br,** JupiterImages/Getty Images; **xviii laptop,** iStockphoto.com; **xx bl,** Thomas Deerinck, NCMIR/Science Source; **xx br;** Adrian Bailey/Aurora Photos; **xxi** ZSSD/SuperStock.

Chapter 1

Pages xxii–1 spread, Solvin Zankl/Nature Picture Library; **3 t,** Perennou Nuridsany/Photo Researchers, Inc.; **3 m2,** Michael Rolands/iStockphoto.com; **3 b,** Michael Abbey/Photo Researchers, Inc.; **4,** Biophoto Associates/Photo Researchers, Inc.; **5 skateboarder,** Nils-Johan Norenlind/age Fotostock; **5 cell,** Steve Gschmeissner/Photo Researchers, Inc.; **6 l,** Dr. Cecil H. Fox/Photo Researchers, Inc.; **6 m,** Dr. Jeremy Burgess/Photo Researchers, Inc.; **6 tr,** Science and Society/SuperStock; **6 br,** Dorling Kindersley; **7 tl inset,** M. I. Walker/Photo Researchers, Inc.; **7 tr inset,** Perennou Nuridsany/Photo Researchers, Inc.; **7 b inset,** John Walsh/Photo Researchers, Inc.; **7 bkgrnd,** David Spears/Clouds Hill Imaging Ltd./Corbis; **8 tl,** Paul Taylor/Riser/Getty Images, Inc.; **8 tr,** TheRocky41/Shutterstock; **8 bl,** Wes Thompson/Corbis; **8 br,** Millard H. Sharp/Photo Researchers, Inc.; **8 magnifying glass,** Dorling Kindersley; **10–11 t,** A. Syred/Photo Researchers, Inc.; **12,** Dr. Torsten Wittmann/Photo Researchers, Inc.; **14 tl,** Alfred Paskieka/Photo Researchers, Inc.; **14 br,** Bill Longcore/Photo Researchers, Inc.; **15,** CNRI/Photo Researchers, Inc.; **18,** Photo Researchers, Inc.; **19,** Biophoto Associates/Science Photo Library; **20 tr,** TheRocky41/Shutterstock; **20 br,** Thomas Deerinck, NCMIR/Science Source; **20 tl,** Professors P. Motta and S. Correr/Science Photo Library/Photo Researchers, Inc.; **20 bl,** Biophoto Associates/Photo Researchers Inc.; **22,** Tierbild Okapia/Photo Researchers, Inc.; **23,** Digital Vision/Getty Images, Inc.; **24 r,** Michael Rolands/iStockphoto.com; **24 l,** Dorling Kindersley; **25,** Tstarr/Shutterstock; **28,** Michael Lamotte/Cole Group/Getty Images; **31 t,** Perennou Nuridsany/Photo Researchers, Inc.; **31 b,** Perennou Nuridsany/Photo Researchers, Inc.; **33 all,** Michael Abbey/Photo Researchers, Inc.; **34,** Science and Society Picture Library; **36,** Dorling Kindersley.

Interchapter Feature

Page 38 bkgrnd and t inset, Kim Taylor and Jane Burton/Dorling Kindersley; **38 b,** David M. Phillips/Photo Researchers, Inc.; **39 mr,** Martin Shields/Photo Researchers, Inc.

Chapter 2

Pages 40–41 spread, Thinkstock/Corbis; **43 t,** age Fotostock/SuperStock; **43 m1,** Vincenzo Lombardo/Getty Images; **43 b,** Kent Wood/Getty Images; **43 m2,** Ed Reschke/Peter Arnold, Inc.; **44,** David Cook/Blue Shift Studios/Alamy; **45 r inset,** age Fotostock/SuperStock; **45 l inset,** Adrian Bailey/Aurora Photos; **45 bkgrnd,** Robbert Koene/Getty Images; **47 bkgrnd,** Rich Iwasaki/Getty Images; **49,** Yuji Sakai/Getty Images; **50,** Doug Scott/age fotostock/Alamy; **54,** Vincenzo Lombardo/Getty Images; **55,** Noah Clayton/Getty Images; **56,** George Grall/National Geographic Image Collection; **56 bkgrnd,** George Grall/National Geographic Image Collection; **57 r,** Eric Bean/Getty Images; **57 r inset,** Michael Poliza/Getty Images; **57 l,** SDM IMAGES/Alamy; **60 and 61 all,** Ed Reschke/Peter Arnold, Inc; **62 t,** Dr. Gopal Murti/Photo Researchers, Inc.; **62 b,** Kent Wood/Getty Images; **64,** Ed Reschke/Peter Arnold, Inc.

Interchapter Feature

Page 68 ml, Andres Rodriguez/Alamy; **69 bkgrnd,** Thomas Deerinck, NCMIR/Photo Researchers, Inc.

Chapter 3

Pages 70–71, ZSSD/SuperStock; **73 t,** Timothy Large/iStockphoto.com; **73 bl,** Frank Krahmer/Getty Images; **73 bm,** Burke/Triolo/JupiterUnlimited; **73 br,** Burke/Triolo/JupiterUnlimited; **74 t,** Bettmann/Corbis; **74 b,** Maximilian Stock Ltd./Getty Images; **76,** Andrea Jones/Alamy; **79 l,** Herman Eisenbeiss/Photo Researchers, Inc.; **79 r,** WildPictures/Alamy; **79 bkgrnd,** Monika Gniot/Shutterstock; **80 l inset,** J. Pat Carter/AP Images; **80 bkgrnd,** National Oceanic and Atmospheric Administration (NOAA); **81,** Brand X/JupiterImages; **82–83 spread,** Monika Gniot/Shutterstock;

84, Alexandra Grablewski/JupiterImages; 85 l, Timothy Large/iStockphoto.com; 85 r, Jomann/Dreamstime.com; 85 bkgrnd, Agg/Dreamstime.com; 86 inset, Joel Sartore/Getty Images; 86 bkgrnd, Erik Rumbaugh/iStockphoto.com; 87 black hen, Mike Dunning/Dorling Kindersley; 87 red flower, Burke/Triolo/JupiterUnlimited; 87 white flower, Burke/Triolo/JupiterUnlimited; 87 pink flower, Frank Krahmer/Getty Images; 87 white rooster, CreativeAct-Animals Series/Alamy; 87 mixed rooster, Dorling Kindersley; 88 r, Jay Brousseau/Getty Images; 88 l, Geoff Dann/Dorling Kindersley; 88 m, Benjamin LEFEBVRE/Fotolia; 89 tl, Radius Images/Photolibrary New York; 89 bkgrnd, Randy Faris/Corbis; 89 tm, Stuart McClymont/Getty Images; 89 tr, Blickwinkel/Alamy; 89 bl, Michael Melford/Getty Images; 89 br, Tetra Images/Alamy; 89 pushpins, Luis Carlos Torres/iStockphoto.com; 90 black hen, Mike Dunning/Dorling Kindersley; 90 white flower, Burke/Triolo/JupiterUnlimited; 90 r, Radius Images/Photolibrary New York; 90 white rooster, CreativeAct-Animals Series/Alamy; 90 mixed rooster, Dorling Kindersley; 90 red flower, Burke/Triolo/JupiterUnlimited; 90 pink flower, Frank Krahmer/Getty Images; 90–91 flowers, Tomas Bercic/iStockphoto.com; 90–91 sky, Serg64/Shutterstock, Inc.; 91 tr, Wally Eberhart/Getty Images; 91 bl, Joel Sartore/Getty Images; 91 tl, Stuart McClymont/Getty Images; 92 r, Patrick Landmann/Science Source; 92 l, James King-Holmes/Science Source; 93 grasshopper, proxyminder/iStockphoto.com; 93 skunk, Eric Isselée/iStockphoto.com; 93 shrimp, Jane Burton/Dorling Kindersley; 93 mosquito, Frank Greenaway/Dorling Kindersley; 93 corn, Cathleen Clapper/iStockphoto.com; 93 t, Robbin Moran; 98, Blickwinkel/Alamy.

Interchapter Feature
Page 102 bkgrnd, We Shoot/Alamy; 103 br, Dorling Kindersley.

Chapter 4
Pages 104–105 spread, David Doubilet/National Geographic/Getty Images; 107 m2, Christian Charisius/Reuters; 107 b, Scott Camazine/Science Source; 108 l, Science Source/Photo Researchers, Inc.; 108 r, Omikron/Photo Researchers, Inc.; 108–109 t, Gerald C. Kelley/Photo Researchers, Inc.; 110 tl, Andrew Syred/Photo Researchers, Inc.; 110 diamonds, Mark Evans/iStockphoto.com; 113, Dr. Gopal Murti/Science Photo Library/Photo Researchers, Inc.; 115, JupiterImages; 114 l, Dorling Kindersley; 114 r, Bedrock Studios/Dorling Kindersley; 118 bkgrnd, Peter Cade/Getty Images, Inc.; 118 inset, Russell Glenister/image100/Corbis; 120 br, Christian Charisius/Reuters; 120 tl, Brian Lasenby/Shutterstock; 121 t, Scott Camazine/Science Source; 121 b, Dorling Kindersley.

Interchapter Feature
Page 128 inset, Denis Poroy/AP Images; 128 bkgrnd, D. Robert Franz/ImageState/Alamy; 129 tl, Dave King/Dorling Kindersley; 129 b, adam korzeniewski/Alamy; 129 inset, Jamie Marshall/Dorling Kindersley.

Chapter 5
Pages 130–131 spread, HALEY/SIPA/Newscom; 133 m1, Oliver Meckes & Nicole Ottawa/Photo Researchers, Inc.; 133 t both, Addenbrookes Hospital/Photo Researchers, Inc.;

133 m2, www.splashnews.com/Newscom; 133 b, Choi Byung-kil/Yonhap/AP Images; 135, Timothey Kosachev/iStockphoto.com; 136, China Daily Information Corp-CDIC/Reuters; 137 x chromosomes, Addenbrookes Hospital/Photo Researchers, Inc.; 137 x and y chromosomes, Addenbrookes Hospital/SPL/Photo Researchers, Inc.; 138 r, JupiterImages/Brand X/Alamy; 138 l, Prisma/SuperStock; 140 l, Paul Cotney/iStockphoto.com; 140 r, Lisa Svara/iStockphoto.com; 140 m, John Long/iStockphoto.com; 141, Oliver Meckes & Nicole Ottawa/Photo Researchers, Inc.; 143, Nancy Hamilton/Photo Researchers, Inc.; 144 r, Leonard Lessin/Science Source; 144 l, Leonard Lessin/Science Source; 145 t, iStockphoto.com; 145 b, Tomas Ovalle/The Fresno Bee/AP Images; 146 inset, HO/Reuters/Corbis; 146–147 bkgrnd, Anke van Wyk/Shutterstock; 149, www.splashnews.com/Newscom; 151, Choi Byung-kil/Yonhap/AP Images; 152, PeJo/Shu/Shutterstock; 153, Laura Doss/Photolibrary New York; 153 double helix, Andrey Prokhorov/iStockphoto.com; 154, Kenneth C. Zirkel/iStockphoto.com; 154 bkgrnd, David Fairfield/Getty Images; 156 b, Tomas Ovalle/The Fresno Bee/AP Images; 156 t, JupiterImages/Brand X/Alamy; 158, Leonard Lessin/Science Source.

Interchapter Feature
Page 160 bkgrnd, Sam Ogden/Photo Researchers, Inc.; 161 bkgrnd, Ed Reschke/Getty Images; 161 inset, Stocksearch/Alamy.

Chapter 6
Pages 162–163 spread, Mark Conlin/Alamy; 166 bl inset, Dorling Kindersley; 166 bkgrnd, Andreas Gross/Westend 61/Alamy; 166 t, The Gallery Collection/Corbis; 167 bl inset, Nigel Reed/QED Images/Alamy; 167 br, Wardene Weisser/Bruce Coleman Inc./Alamy; 167 t, Oyvind Martinsen/Alamy; 167 m, Enzo & Paolo Ragazzini/Corbis; 168 t, Steve Bloom Images/Alamy; 168 br, Joe McDonald/Corbis; 168 bl, Rosemary Calvert/Getty Images; 170 bkgrnd, Magdalena Duczkowska/iStockphoto.com; 170 m inset, Steve Shott/Dorling Kindersley; 170 l inset, GK Hart/Vikki Hart/Getty Images; 170 r inset, Dorling Kindersley; 171 m, PetStock Boys/Alamy; 171 r, Keturah De Klerk/Getty Images; 171 l, Georgette Douwma/Nature Picture Library; 174, Mark Conlin/Getty Images; 175 bkgrnd, Bloomberg/Getty Images; 176 bcr, illustration, nsf/Alamy; 176 br, fossil, Corbin17/Alamy; 176 l, Gordon Wiltsie/National Geographic Stock; 178 m, Ed Robinson/Design Pics/Corbis; 178 l, Winfried Wisniewski/Zefa/Corbis; 178 r, SuperStock; 180 tr, Copyright © 2007 Gerald McCormack/Cook Islands Biodiversity Database, Version 2007.2. Cook Islands Natural Heritage Trust, Rarotonga. Online at http://cookislands.bishopmuseum.org; 180 maggots, xpixel/Shutterstock; 181 l inset, Thomas & Pat Leeson/Photo Researchers, Inc.; 181 r inset, Thomas & Pat Leeson/Photo Researchers, Inc.; 181 bkgrnd, kojihirano/Fotolia; 186, S. Borisov/Shutterstock; 184 bl, Thomas & Pat Leeson/Photo Researchers, Inc.; 184 br, Thomas & Pat Leeson/Photo Researchers, Inc.; 184 m, Model by Tyler Keillor/Courtesy of University of Chicago; 184 t, Joe McDonald/Corbis.

Interchapter Feature
Page 188 inset, Joshua Roper/Alamy.

this is your book

you can write in it

this space is yours—great for drawing diagrams and making notes

this is your book

you can write in it

212

this is your book

you can write in it

this is your book

you can write in it

this is your book

you can write in it